CREATING
THE
CONSTITUTION

Also available from the Copley Series,
Sources of the American Tradition

AMERICAN VISIONS AND REVISIONS
1607–1865
Edited by David Grimsted

THE UNION IN CRISIS
1850–1877
Edited by Robert W. Johannsen

SOURCES OF THE AMERICAN TRADITION

CREATING THE CONSTITUTION

EDITED BY
JOHN P. KAMINSKI & RICHARD LEFFLER

Copley Publishing Group
Acton, Massachusetts 01720

Copyright © 1999 by Copley Publishing Group.
All rights reserved
Printed in the United States of America

ISBN 1-58390-001-2

Library of Congress Catalog Card Number: 98-073898

No part of this book may be reproduced in any manner without written permission from the publisher.

Copley Publishing Group
138 Great Road
Acton, MA 01720
800.562.2147 • Fax: 978.263.9190
E-mail: publish@copleycustom.com

Contents

Introduction	ix
Editorial Method	xv
A Ratification Chronology	xvi

Chapter 1—Anticipating the Convention

Introduction	1
The Calling of the Constitutional Convention	2
A Spirit of Faction and Rebellion	5
George Washington—Father of His Country	8
A Crisis or a Little Rebellion	11
Advice to the Convention: Break Up the Union	14
Should There Be Reform or Radical Change?	18
James Madison and the Origins of the Constitution	21
Can the Convention Solve America's Problems?	25
The Unpopular Political Philosophy of John Adams	28

Chapter 2—The Constitutional Convention

Introduction	31
Connecticut Debates Electing Delegates to the Constitutional Convention	42
A Revolution in Favor of Government: The Virginia Plan	45
The Revolution Pursued: A National Government Proposed	49
Shall This New Government Be Democratic?	53
How Long Should Representatives and Senators Serve?	57
A Last-Ditch Attempt to Avoid a National Government	61
Alexander Hamilton Sketches a Plan of Government	64
The Continuing Newspaper Debate	68
The Convention Seeks the Assistance of God	71

Celebrating the Fourth of July 1787	74
Continuing Debate Over Representation	78
The Great Compromise Averts Disruption of the Convention	81
The Presidency Debated	85
Property Qualifications and Democracy	88
Should Only Land Holders Be Allowed to Vote?	91
News Reports of Convention Proceedings: 18th-Century Leaks	94
Slavery and the Constitution, Part I	98
Slavery and the Constitution, Part II	101
How Should the Constitution Be Ratified?	105
Objections Create a Moment of Peculiar Solemnity	109
Benjamin Franklin Appeals for Unanimity in Signing the Constitution	112

Chapter 3—The Public Debate Begins

Introduction	116
The Newspaper Campaign in Favor of the Constitution Begins	118
A Little 18th-Century Misinformation	121
The Beginning of the Onslaught	124
Federalists Appeal to Self-Interest	127
"A New Combatant" Joins the Fray	130
The Federalist Essay Number 1	133
An Antifederalist Election-Day Appeal	136
The Attack on Personalities Begins	139
An Antifederalist Charge: This Is a Government for the Rich	142
James Madison Turns Republican Theory Upside Down	145
Antifederalists Charge: The Revolution Is Betrayed	148
The Constitution Creates a Democratic Form of Government	151
The First Official Dissent to the Constitution	154
Absent Diplomats: John Adams and Thomas Jefferson	157
Antifederalist Riot in Carlisle, Pa.	160
Political Pressure Applied to Sam Adams	164
The Constitution Creates a Republican Form of Government	167
The Constitution and the Foreign Slave Trade: An Insult to God	170

Chapter 4—The People Decide

Introduction	173
The Old Patriots of '75 Debate the Constitution	175
Massachusetts Ratifies the Constitution	179
George Washington Defends the Constitution	182
A Federalist Satire	185
John Hancock Defends the Massachusetts Convention	188
Mercy Warren Sees Danger in the Constitution	191
A Defense of the Electoral College	194
Property and Liberty Both Secured by the Constitution	197
The Constitution Is What the Court Says It Is	200
The Publication of the Book Version of *The Federalist*	203
Was There a Conspiracy to Stop Antifederalist Newspapers?	206
Absolute Power Corrupts Absolutely	210
The Senate Criticized	213
Point and Counterpoint	216
Washington Reflects on the Present and Future	219
American Rights Must Be Spelled Out	222
The Political Name Calling Gets Rough	225
Interstate Efforts to Influence the Course of Ratification	228
No Bill of Rights Is Needed Says *The Federalist*	232
The Virginia Convention Begins	235
An Antifederalist Effort to Stave Off Civil War	238
Slavery Debated in the Virginia Convention	241
One Final Word From Mr. Madison	244

Index   **247**

Introduction

When Supreme Court Justice Thurgood Marshall said, some time ago, that the Constitution was flawed and that he saw little wisdom or foresight in the Framers, it shocked a lot of people.

His remarks made news because most people today revere the Constitution. They would agree with Thomas Jefferson, who called the members of the Constitutional Convention "demigods." The great British statesman William Gladstone would probably get widespread agreement with his statement that the Constitution "is the most wonderful work ever struck off at a given time by the brain and purpose of man."

But Justice Marshall's criticism is mild compared to some of the things said about the Framers and their product in the debate that raged over the ratification of the Constitution in 1787–88. For instance, a pamphleteer in New York wrote of the Convention: "Some of the characters which compose it I revere; others I consider as of small consequence, and a number are suspected of being great public defaulters, and to have been guilty of notorious peculation and fraud, with regard to our public property in the hour of our distress."

The Convention, of course, had met behind closed doors. Little was known of its proceedings. This became the subject of severe criticism during the debate over the adoption of the Constitution. Samuel Bryan of Pennsylvania, one of the most prolific and virulent critics of the Constitution, writing as "Centinel," charged that "the evil genius of darkness presided at its birth, it came forth under the veil of mystery, its true features being carefully concealed, and every deceptive art has been and is practising to have this spurious brat received as the genuine offspring of heaven-born liberty."

The opponents of the Constitution, called Antifederalists, believed that the current government under the Articles of Confederation needed fixing. The Confederation government had no power to tax. Its major source of money was to request the states to supply a yearly "requisition." Many of the states were badly in arrears. As a result, the Confederation government did not have enough money even to finance the interest on the debts owed to the foreign nations that had helped pay for the Revolution. The government was also unable to pay the interest on the money that Americans had loaned to it during the Revolution. And there was no national currency. The "Continental" had long since become worthless.

The Confederation was also unable to regulate commerce, either between the states or with foreign nations. Some of the states adopted import duties that discriminated against other states. Great Britain, the major trading partner with America before the Revolution, was unwilling to enter into a commercial treaty with the United States. In fact, the British adopted trade regulations that discriminated against American shipping, which had a devastating effect on American merchants and shipping. Many people believed that if the government had the power to regulate trade, the British would be more willing to enter into a commercial treaty. In the mid-1780s, the United States suffered from a major economic depression; it was commonly believed that the cause of this depression was the inability of the government to regulate trade among the states and with foreign nations. Antifederalists agreed that the Confederation government should have such power.

But they were shocked that the Constitution went so far beyond simply giving the Confederation Congress these additional powers. The Constitution was not a revision of the Articles of Confederation but a totally new government with vastly more power, so much power that they feared for the liberty of the country and the future viability of the states.

Antifederalists believed that the Constitution would give the federal government enough power to destroy the states, which were then considered the bulwarks of liberty. They feared that the House of Representatives, the only branch of government directly elected by the people, was too small (only 65 members sat in the first House) to represent all the people and too weak to resist the power of the Senate and the President.

Antifederalists worried that the Senate would become a tool of the rich and the well-educated few (their shorthand way of referring to this elite was to call them the aristocracy) and that the President would, alternately, become either a king or be controlled by the aristocratic Senate. They were afraid that the Supreme Court and the inferior federal courts would defend the interests of the federal government at the expense of the states, would make justice available only to the wealthy, and would overwhelm the state courts, which Antifederalists believed were better able to defend the interests of the ordinary people.

Of all the shortcomings that Antifederalists saw in the Constitution, probably the most stunning was that the Constitution did not contain a bill of rights. Seven of the state constitutions contained a bill of rights; in the other states, protections for civil liberty were written into the body of their constitutions or enacted as legislation. Antifederalists asked why there was no protection in the proposed Constitution for freedom of the press and religion, the right to petition for redress of grievances, or critical procedural rights in criminal cases, such as the right against self-incrimination, the right to legal counsel, and the right to cross-examine witnesses and confront one's accusers. Some saw the absence of a bill of rights as a proof that the Framers intended to establish a despotism.

Antifederalists demanded that changes be made in the Constitution and especially that a bill of rights be added that would secure liberty. They warned against adopting this new government without amendments because, as Richard Henry Lee of Virginia wrote, it had "been found from Universal experience that the most express declarations and reservations are necessary to protect the just rights and liberty of mankind from the silent, powerful, and ever active conspiracy of those who govern."

Federalists, those who supported the Constitution, responded that none of these fears was justified and that no changes could be made in the Constitution until it was ratified and put into effect. They argued that the choice was: either accept this Constitution as it was, with the possibility of amendments after it goes into effect, or reject it and risk anarchy or civil war.

Federalists sought to assure the country that the concerns raised about the Constitution were unjustified. They argued that the federal government would not destroy the states because most power still remained with the states; the powers of the federal government were limited to those that were delegated to it by the Constitution. They argued that the checks and balances among the House of Representatives, the Senate, the President, and the courts guaranteed that no one person or small group could ever control the government. Federalists claimed that of the three branches, the judiciary would be the "least dangerous." They denied that a bill of rights was needed because of the strict limits placed on federal power. In fact, they argued that a bill of rights might be dangerous in two ways. First, a listing of rights could never be complete, and if a right were not mentioned the implication might be that it was left unprotected. Second, if the bill of rights mentioned freedom of the press, for instance, someone might argue that this implied that there was a power in the Constitution for the federal government to legislate in some way concerning the press—Congress might not prohibit freedom of the press, but it might pass "proper" regulations concerning the press.

The Constitution specified that ratification had to be accomplished by conventions elected by the people in each state. Once nine states ratified, the Constitution was to go into effect among the ratifying states.

On December 7, 1787, Delaware's Convention became the first to ratify the Constitution, by a vote of 30–0. This was quickly followed by Pennsylvania on December 12 (46–23), New Jersey on December 18 (38–0), Georgia on December 31 (26–0), and Connecticut on January 9, 1788, (128–40). None of these state conventions proposed amendments. The minority in the Pennsylvania Convention presented amendments, but Federalists refused even to allow them to be entered on the journal.

Federalists in the Massachusetts Convention, however, ran into trouble. They could not ratify the Constitution without a compromise: the Convention would adopt the Constitution, but it would also instruct the state's representatives and senators in the first Congress under the Constitution to advocate a list of amendments. Similar demands for amendments were then made by the conventions of New Hampshire, South Carolina, Virginia, New York, and North Carolina. Antifederalists in Maryland's Convention would have proposed amendments, but the Federalist majority refused to allow amendments to come to the floor.

Finally, on June 21, 1788, New Hampshire became the ninth state to ratify the Constitution. Virginia and New York followed on June 25 and July 26, respectively. In addition to calling for amendments, New York's Convention called for a second constitutional convention to propose amendments. On August 2, North Carolina refused to ratify the Constitution until amendments were adopted. North Carolina did not ratify until November 1789 and Rhode Island delayed its ratification until May 1790.

But if Antifederalists were unable to prevent the ratification of the Constitution, they were successful in another important way. It was their insistent demand, throughout the long debate over ratification, that a bill of rights be added to the Constitution that would secure the rights of the people from the tyranny of a too-powerful federal government. Federalists denied that the government was too powerful and that tyranny was a real danger, but, finally, they were forced by necessity to agree that after the Constitution was operative amendments to it would be considered. Without this promise, it is unlikely that the Constitution could have been ratified in Massachusetts, Virginia, or New York.

Ultimately, the Antifederalist demand for a bill of rights was fulfilled. On June 8, 1789, James Madison proposed a bill of rights to an unreceptive House of Representatives. Many representatives—both Federalists and Antifederalists—felt that the consideration of amendments was premature; other issues needed the immediate attention of Congress, such as the establishment of the executive departments, the creation of the federal judiciary, and the enactment of tariffs to provide the new government with revenue. Madison, however, remained steadfast, arguing that amendments were necessary to satisfy the fears of Antifederalists. As the basis for his proposal, Madison used the amendments that had been proposed by the several state conventions. After considerable debate and alteration, on September 25 Congress adopted a proposal for amendments to the Constitution, including the ten amendments now known as the Bill of Rights. These amendments were adopted by the required number of states when Virginia ratified them on December 15, 1791. In March

1792 Secretary of State Thomas Jefferson declared the amendments to be in effect.

What is extraordinary about the ratification of the Constitution is not that the Constitution was perfect and the people were unanimous in support of it. In fact, the people were badly divided over the wisdom of adopting the Constitution and Federalists and Antifederalists alike realized that the Constitution was imperfect. Many people were shocked and frightened because the Constitution did not have a bill of rights and feared that the liberty that had been fought for in the Revolution, at tremendous cost in blood and money, might be lost. Others objected to the compromises embodied in the document, particularly those in which concessions were made to the South concerning slavery. Federalists readily admitted that the Constitution had flaws, but they also maintained that, as the product of accommodation among thirteen different states, it was the best constitution that could be obtained at that time, and that amendments could be obtained when deficiencies became apparent.

Despite the grave reservations raised by Antifederalists, the states ratified the Constitution. Antifederalists, concerned though they were that freedom might be endangered, acceded to the will of the majority. They did not resist or resort to violence. They participated in the system created by the Constitution and the new government, and many of their fears were eliminated when Congress proposed the Bill of Rights.

The Constitution has served us well for 200 years. Part of the reason for its success goes back to the beginning: Americans have been willing to trust each other's devotion to liberty, to compromise when necessary, and to abide by the rule of law.

Editorial Method

Eighteenth-century documents are somewhat different from their modern equivalents. Spelling was different, often capriciously so. Many nouns were capitalized. Commas were used more frequently. Abbreviations were used commonly and the ampersand (&) was used instead of the word "and." In newspapers, many different kinds of type were used, including italics, small capitals, and large capitals. Newspaper essayists often used pseudonyms, such as "Brutus," "Centinel," or "A Citizen of New York." We have retained these pen names. Where the real name of the author is known, it is identified in the headnotes and in parentheses in the headings.

Despite these peculiarities, eighteenth-century documents are usually not hard for modern readers to understand. Consequently, the documents in this book are printed as they were written, for the most part. Occasionally, however, we have made changes in the form of the document. We have not always printed entire documents, and when we have omitted material this is usually indicated with ellipses (. . .). We have added paragraph breaks in long blocks of text and we have spelled out abbreviations. Explanatory material has been placed in square brackets [ ]. Full names have been provided for speakers in the legislatures and conventions. With these exceptions, words have never been changed and are rendered exactly as they were written.

The material in this volume appeared originally in weekly installments in the *Milwaukee Sentinel* from February 1987 through June 1988 as part of the celebration of the bicentennial of the U.S. Constitution. Many of the documents appeared simultaneously in the *Capital Times* of Madison, Wisconsin. It is remarkable, indeed, that these newspapers saw the value of reprinting eighteenth-century documents, many of which have not appeared in newspapers for 200 years. It is somewhat humbling as well to consider that many of these wonderfully subtle and sophisticated documents were prepared for publication in the newspapers two centuries ago with the intention of persuading the general public to support or oppose the Constitution.

The editors of this series wish to thank two modern-day newspaper editors for the service they rendered their readers: Bob Wills of the *Milwaukee Sentinel* and Dave Zweifel of the *Capital Times*.

A Ratification Chronology

1786

August–January 1787	Shays' Rebellion in Massachusetts
11–14 September	Annapolis Convention calls for a constitutional convention
20 September	Congress receives Annapolis Convention report
23 November–10 February 1787	Virginia, New Jersey, Pennsylvania, North Carolina, New Hampshire, Delaware, and Georgia appoint delegates to the convention in Philadelphia

1787

21 February	Congress calls for a convention to meet in Philadelphia on the second Monday in May to revise Articles of Confederation
3 March–17 May	Massachusetts, New York, South Carolina, Maryland, and Connecticut elect delegates to the convention in Philadelphia
14 March, 5 May, 16 June	Rhode Island refuses to elect delegates to the to the convention in Philadelphia
25 May	A quorum is present in the Constitutional Convention
29 May	Edmund Randolph introduces the Virginia Plan, which is debated in the Convention
15 June	William Paterson introduces the New Jersey Plan as an alternative to the Virginia Plan

19 June	Convention rejects the New Jersey Plan and votes to proceed using the Virginia Plan
13 July	Congress adopts Northwest Ordinance
6 August	Committee of Detail submits draft constitution to the Convention
12 September	Committee of Style submits report to the Convention
17 September	Convention delegates sign Constitution and Convention adjourns
20 September	Constitution is read in Congress
26–28 September	Congress debates Constitution and sends it to the states for their consideration
6 October	James Wilson becomes first member of Constitutional Convention publicly to defend Constitution
27 October	First essay of *The Federalist* published in New York City
20 November–15 December	Pennsylvania Convention; ratifies 46–23 on 12 December
3–7 December	Delaware Convention; ratifies 30–0 on 7 December
11–20 December	New Jersey Convention; ratifies 38–0 on 18 December
25 December–5 January 1788	Georgia Convention; ratifies 26–0 on 31 December

1788

3–9 January	Connecticut Convention; ratifies 128–40 on 9 January
9 January–7 February	Massachusetts Convention; ratifies 187–168 on 6 February and proposes amendments
12–22 February	New Hampshire Convention meets and adjourns without voting on Constitution

24 March	Rhode Island referendum on Constitution boycotted by some Federalists; Constitution rejected 2,711–239
21–29 April	Maryland Convention; ratifies 63–11 on 26 April
12–24 May	South Carolina Convention; ratifies 149–73 on 23 May and proposes amendments
2–27 June	Virginia Convention; ratifies 89–79 on 25 June and proposes amendments
17 June–26 July	New York Convention; ratifies 30–27 on 26 July, proposes amendments, and calls for second constitutional convention
18–21 June	New Hampshire Convention (second session) ratifies 57–47 on 21 June becoming ninth state to ratify, satisfying requirement for ratification of Constitution, and proposes amendments
2 July	New Hampshire ratification read in Congress. Committee appointed to prepare an act for putting Constitution into effect
21 July–4 August	North Carolina Convention; refuses to ratify Constitution without amendments on 2 August
13 September	Congress adopts act setting dates for election of President of U.S. and meeting of first Congress under Constitution

1789

1 April	A quorum is present in U.S. House of Representatives
6 April	A quorum is present in U.S. Senate
30 April	George Washington is inaugurated as President of the United States

8 June	James Madison proposes a bill of rights in House of Representatives
25 September	Congress proposes amendments to the Constitution for states' consideration
2 October	President Washington sends amendments to the states for their approval
16–23 November	Second North Carolina Convention ratifies Constitution 194–77 on 21 November

1790

1–6 March	Rhode Island Convention meets and adjourns without voting on Constitution
24–29 May	Rhode Island Convention (second session) ratifies Constitution 34–32 on 29 May and proposes amendments

1791

15 December	First ten amendments to Constitution ratified by the eleventh state, Virginia, satisfying the requirement for ratification of amendments to Constitution

1792

1 March	Secretary of State Thomas Jefferson notifies states that first ten amendments to the Constitution have been ratified

CHAPTER 1
Anticipating the Convention

INTRODUCTION

Early in 1787, many people in the United States despaired for the future of the country. The Revolution had been won at great cost, and a new government under the Articles of Confederation had been created. But there was a common belief that the government was failing. The debt incurred during the war could not be repaid, the nation was in depression, a farmers' rebellion was occurring in western Massachusetts and there were disturbances elsewhere as well, and there was fear that the Union itself would break apart.

One reason for optimism was that in February the Confederation Congress had voted to call a Constitutional Convention to propose revisions in the Articles of Confederation. Many of the states had already appointed delegates to the Convention, including Virginia. But the greatest of all Virginians, George Washington, was not sure the Convention would succeed or if he should attend as a delegate. Well aware of the nation's respect, almost veneration, for Washington, James Madison and others urged the former commander in chief to attend.

At the same time, Madison was contemplating what kinds of reforms should be made in the government, and he was developing a proposal for radical changes. Washington and the rest of the Virginia delegation agreed with Madison that a drastic change in the government was necessary. Many of Madison's ideas were introduced at the Constitutional Convention in the form of the "Virginia Plan," which served as the basis for debate in the Convention and helped shape the Constitution as we know it today.

The Calling of the Constitutional Convention

The first document below was originally printed in the Boston Independent Chronicle *on 15 February 1787 and within three months was reprinted in nineteen newspapers throughout the United States. The second document, the congressional resolution calling the Constitutional Convention, is transcribed from the original handwritten resolution sent by Congress to Virginia. News of Congress' action was printed more than forty times throughout the country. The last item is an excerpt of a letter from James Madison, a member of Congress, to fellow Virginian Edmund Pendleton, in which Madison wrote about the problems facing the country.*

Boston Independent Chronicle, 15 February 1787

How long, asks a correspondent, are we to continue in our present inglorious acquiescence in the shameful resistance that some of the States persist in, against federal and national measures? How long is Massachusetts to suffer the paltry politics, weak jealousy, or local interests of New-York and Pennsylvania, to distract our own government, and keep us holden to those wretched measures which has so long made America the pity or contempt of Europe? How long are we to distress our own numerous citizens with the weight of Continental taxes, and support our delegation in an assembly, which has no powers to maintain the reputation, or advance the real interest of our Commonwealth? This State has made reiterated and strenuous exertions to restore that firmness, confidence, and greatness, which distinguished united America from 1774 to 1782, but to little purpose: It is therefore now time to form a new and stronger union. The five States of New-England, closely confederated, can have nothing to fear. Let then our General Assembly immediately recall their Delegates from the shadowy Meeting which still bears the name of Congress, as being a useless and expensive establishment. Send proposals for instituting a new Congress, as the Representative of the nation of New-England, and leave the rest of the Continent to pursue their own imbecile and disjointed plans, until they have experimentally learnt the folly, danger and disgrace of them, and acquired magnanimity and wisdom sufficient to join a confederation that may rescue them from destruction.

RESOLUTION OF CONGRESS CALLING THE CONSTITUTIONAL CONVENTION, 21 FEBRUARY 1787

Whereas there is provision in the Articles of Confederation and perpetual Union for making alterations therein by the assent of a Congress of the United States and of the Legislatures of the several States; And Whereas experience hath evinced that there are defects in the present Confederation, as a mean to remedy which several of the States and particularly the State of New York by express instructions to their Delegates in Congress have suggested a Convention for the purposes expressed in the following resolution and such Convention appearing to be the most probable mean of establishing in these States a firm National Government—

Resolved That in the opinion of Congress it is expedient that on the second Monday in May next a Convention of Delegates who shall have been appointed by the several States be held at Philadelphia for the sole and express purpose of revising the Articles of Confederation and reporting to Congress and the several Legislatures such alterations and provisions therein as shall when agreed to in Congress and confirmed by the States render the federal Constitution adequate to the exigencies of Government and the preservation of the Union—

JAMES MADISON TO EDMUND PENDLETON, NEW YORK, 24 FEBRUARY 1787

... Upon the whole therefore it seems probable that a meeting will take place, and that it will be a pretty full one. What the issue of it will be is among the other arcana of futurity and nearly as inscrutable as any of them. In general I find men of reflection much less sanguine as to a new than despondent as to the present System. Indeed the present System neither has nor deserves advocates; and if some very strong props are not applied will quickly tumble to the ground. No money is paid into the public Treasury; no respect is paid to the federal authority. Not a single State complies with the requisitions, several pass them over in silence, and some positively reject them. The payments ever since the peace have been decreasing, and of late fall short even of the pittance necessary for the Civil list of the Confederacy. It is not possible that a Government can long last under these circumstances. If the approaching Convention should not agree on some remedy, I am persuaded that some very different arrangement will ensue. The late turbulent scenes in Massts. & infamous ones in Rhode Island, have done inexpressible injury to the republican character in that part of the U. States; and a propensity towards Monarchy is said to have been produced by it in some leading minds. The bulk of the people will probably prefer the lesser evil of a partition of the Union into three more practicable and energetic Governments. The latter idea I find after long confinement to individual speculations & private circles, is beginning to shew itself in the Newspapers. But tho' it is a lesser evil, it is so great a one that I hope the danger of it will rouse all the real friends to the Revolution to exert themselves in favor of such an organization of the Confederacy, as will perpetuate the Union, and redeem the honor of the Republican name.

A Spirit of Faction and Rebellion

Stephen Higginson was a Boston merchant and one of the wealthiest men in America. His letter below to Nathan Dane, a Massachusetts delegate to Congress, typifies the ambivalence people felt about the proposed Constitutional Convention scheduled to meet in Philadelphia in May 1787. After all, neither the Articles of Confederation nor the state constitutions provided for such a convention. But many people shared Higginson's opinion that there was no alternative. They feared that the Convention was the last peaceful opportunity to strengthen the powers of Congress.

In his second paragraph, Higginson alludes to the successful suppression of the agrarian uprising known as Shays' Rebellion, a poorly-organized effort of indebted farmers trying to stave off foreclosures. Although the uprising was crushed, Higginson still believed that the rebels were dangerous, that they were levellers, who lacked virtue and had "too high a taste for luxury and dissipation, to sit down contented in their proper line." Higginson also feared that this spirit of rebellion might spread to other states. This view of the Rebellion was fairly common and gave impetus to the movement for a convention to strengthen the federal government.

STEPHEN HIGGINSON TO NATHAN DANE
BOSTON, 3 MARCH 1787

... Though this measure [the Constitutional Convention] may not appear to be perfectly regular and conventions are not known any more in the form of the federal Government, than in that of this state; yet, I confess I am full in the Idea of its expediency, from a conviction, that there is no other mode that can give us any chance of obtaining a Government, capable of managing the affairs of the Union. It is to be sure far from being certain, whether such a Government can be established by means of the intended convention, or whether any advantage to the Union, will result from it. But as it is clear, in my mind; that we can not long exist under our present system; and that unless we soon acquire more force to the Union by some means or other, Insurgents will arise and eventually take the reins from us; I am for trying any measure that promises even a possibility of success. We must either brace up the powers of the Union to a degree capable of supporting and encouraging the affairs of the nation with dignity and energy, and this by an act of deliberation and choice or we shall inevitably be thrown into general confusion and convulsions, which will result in one or more Governments, established with the loss of much blood, violent and despotic in its nature, and the effect of necessity and chance. In this situation, when no other mode is suggested which affords even a gleam of hope, I am clearly of opinion that to decline a proposition of this kind, though the effect may be very uncertain, would be imprudent—for I cannot see that, in any event, the result of the Convention can be against us. If no system can there be advised to save us from confusion and distress, and we must take our chance for what may arise out of a general disorder, the sooner we are brought to a decision upon this point the better; it is surely uncomfortable to remain longer in our present situation, and the sooner and more rapidly disorder overtakes us, the shorter will its duration be and of less extent will probably be the political distress which will result. While we have any hope of warding off the evil by means of a convention, we shall not patiently submit to a temporary anarchy, nor propose to claim any advantages from a state of convulsion; but having tried the experiment and found that our National Government must arise out of necessity alone, and be the effect of confusion, we shall then give way to dire necessity, and with vigilance turn every event to a good purpose.

... The rebellion appears to be in a good degree crushed, the force of the rebels is dispersed. But the seeds yet remain in the soil, the spirit of faction and rebellion is far from being subdued; nor can it be rooted out without the cooperation of the other N. E. States—while our rebels can find a shelter in those States, they will not only retain this disposition themselves, but they will communicate it to the Citizens of those States, whose minds are as prone to rebellion as ours, and from the same causes. The evil appears to me to arize naturally and necessarily out of our case. The people of the interior parts of these States have by far too much political knowledge and too strong a relish for unrestrained freedom, to be governed by our feeble system, and too little acquaintance with real sound policy or rational freedom and too little virtue to govern themselves. They have become too well acquainted with their own weight in the political scale, under such governments as ours and have too high a taste for luxury and dissipation, to sit down contented in their proper line, when they see others possessed of much more property than themselves. With these feelings and sentiments, they will not be quiet while such distinctions exist as to rank and property; and sensible of their own force, they will not rest easy till they possess the reins of Government, and have divided property with their betters, or they shall be compelled by force to submit to their proper stations and mode of living.

Which of these events are the most likely to happen, and how, is in my mind very uncertain. The end of this rebellion both as to the time and manner of it equally so of course.

GEORGE WASHINGTON—
FATHER OF HIS COUNTRY

George Washington was the most revered person in America in 1787. In the darkest days of the Revolution he had been given enormous power which he had not abused. He was acclaimed for the glorious victory over the British that had secured independence. After the war, at the height of power, he had retired to Mount Vernon to the life of a gentleman farmer "under the shadow of my own vine and my own fig tree." He was the paradigm of the citizen-soldier in republican America.

By 1787 Washington believed that a crisis was at hand. He wished to see the proposed Philadelphia Convention strengthen the central government. If it failed, he expected that there would be widespread support for a peaceful, though perhaps extra-constitutional change.

The Virginia legislature elected Washington as one of its seven delegates to the Convention on December 4, 1786. Yet Washington was reluctant to attend the Convention, and on December 21 he wrote to Governor Edmund Randolph that he would not attend. Washington hesitated because he did not wish to waste his prestige on a failing venture, and he had already turned down an invitation to attend the general meeting of the Society of the Cincinnati, which was meeting in Philadelphia at the same time as the Convention. This society was much criticized. It was open only to former Continental Army officers and to their first-born sons. It smacked of aristocracy. Washington was sensitive to this criticism, and though he was president-general of the society, he declined to attend the meeting.

Because of these doubts, Washington asked a number of his friends for advice. In the letters below Washington asked Confederation Secretary at War Henry Knox for his opinion and Knox responded. On March 28 Washington finally wrote Governor Randolph that he would attend the Convention.

GEORGE WASHINGTON TO HENRY KNOX
MOUNT VERNON, 8 MARCH 1787

... A Convention I wish to see tried—after which, if the present government is not efficient, conviction of the propriety of a change will dissiminate through every rank, and class of people and may be brought about in peace—till which, however necessary it may appear in the eyes of the more discerning, my opinion is, that it can not be effected without great contention, and much confusion.—It is among the evils, and perhaps is not the smallest, of democratical governments, that the people must *feel*, before they will *see*.—When this happens, they are roused to action—hence it is that this form of government is so slow.—I am indirectly, and delicately pressed to attend this convention.—Several reasons are opposed to it in my mind, and not the least my having declined attending the General Meeting of the Cincinnati, which is to be holden in Philadelphia at the same time, on account of the disrespect it might *seem* to offer to that Society, to be there on another occasion.—A thought however has lately run through my mind, which is attended with embarrassment.—It is, whether my non-attendance in this Convention will not be considered as a dereliction to republicanism—nay more—Whether other motives may not (however injuriously) be ascribed to me for not exerting myself on this occasion in support of it.—Under these circumstances let me pray you, my dear Sir; to inform me confidentially, what the public expectation is on this head.—That is, whether I will, or ought to be there?—You are much in the way of obtaining this knowledge, and I can depend upon your friendship—candour—and judgment in the communication of it, as far as it shall appear to you—My final determination (if what I have already given to the Executive of this State is not considered in that light) cannot be delayed beyond the time necessary for your reply.

Henry Knox to George Washington
New York, 19 March 1787

As you have thought proper my dear Sir, to request my opinion respecting your attendance at the convention, I shall give it with the utmost sincerity and frankness.

I imagine that your own satisfaction or chagrin and that of your friends will depend entirely on the result of the convention—For I take it for granted that however reluctantly you may acquiesce, that you will be constrained to accept of the president's Chair. Hence the proceedings of the convention will more immediately be appropriated to you than to any other person—

Were the convention to propose only amendments and patch work to the present defective confederation, Your reputation would in a degree suffer—But were an energetic, and judicious system to be proposed under Your signature, it would be a circumstance highly honorable to your fame, in the judgement of the present and future ages; and doubly entitle you to the glorious republican epithet—The Father of Your Country.

But the men generally chosen, being of the first information, great reliance may be placed on the wisdom and vigor of their Councils and judgement, and therefore the balance of my opinion preponderates greatly in favor of your attendance.

I am persuaded that your name has had already great influence to induce the States to come into the measure—That your attendance will be grateful, and your absence chagrining—That your presence would confer on the assembly a national complexion, and that it would more than any other circumstance induce a compliance to the propositions of the convention.

Virginia Independent Chronicle, 11 April 1787

It is with peculiar satisfaction we inform the public, that our illustrious fellow citizen, GEORGE WASHINGTON, Esq; has consented to serve on the ensuing Federal Convention to be held in Philadelphia the second Monday in May next; and that His Excellency EDMUND RANDOLPH, Esq; purposes leaving this city early in that month, on the same business.—Should a delegation attend from each, or a majority of the states,—chosen with that circumspection and wisdom, which governed the Legislature of *this Commonwealth*,—what happy consequences may not all the true friends to Federal Government promise themselves, from the united Zeal, Policy, and Ability, of so *August an Assembly*.

A Crisis or a Little Rebellion

The Massachusetts newspaper article below expresses concerns that were shared by many people in the aftermath of Shays' Rebellion in the fall and winter of 1786–87. The uprising was a poorly organized attempt by farmers to stave off farm foreclosures by stopping the operations of the courts. These "rebels" carried to an extreme the feeling of many others who were affected by the economic conditions after the Revolution.

A depression and a shortage of money made it impossible for large numbers of farmers to pay their debts or their taxes. They called for the issuance of paper money and for laws that would allow them to delay repaying their debts or to pay their debts with commodities or property. They called for cutting the expenses of government and for lower taxes. They blamed government officeholders, courts, and lawyers for their predicament. In Massachusetts they held county conventions that demanded relief and changes in the state constitution.

Finally, in August and September 1786, violence broke out and courts in five counties were closed. The militia routed the insurgents in February 1787. This was only the most serious of several outbreaks of agrarian violence. Other incidents occurred in New Hampshire, Connecticut, Pennsylvania, Maryland, Virginia, and South Carolina. Accounts of these outbreaks exaggerated the demands of the insurgents and created the fear "that a beginning of anarchy with all its calamitys has approached, and [we] have no means to stop the dreadful work," as Virginia congressman Henry Lee wrote George Washington.

Not everyone shared these fears. After all, despite the outbreaks, the nation was largely peaceful. Thomas Jefferson, ambassador to France, did not view these violent episodes as the beginning of anarchy. In January 1787 he wrote James Madison that "a little rebellion now and then is a good thing, and as necessary in the political world as storms in the physical." In November he wrote to John Adams's son-in-law, William Stephens Smith, that "The tree of liberty must be refreshed from time to time with the blood of patriots and tyrants. It is its natural manure." The New Haven Gazette *item below is an excerpt from Jefferson's reply to a letter from Ezra Stiles, president of Yale College. Stiles had written of "some Tumults and popular Insurrections" in America. This newspaper version of Jefferson's reply was reprinted twelve times in New Hampshire, Massachusetts, New York, and Pennsylvania.*

Charlestown (Massachusetts) American Recorder
16 March 1787

The combustibles are collected—the mine is prepared—the smallest spark may again produce an explosion!

This is a crisis in our affairs, which requires all the wisdom and energy of government; for every man of sense must be convinced, that our disturbances have arisen, more from a want of power, than the abuse of it—from the relaxation, and almost annihilation of our federal government—from the feeble, unsystematic, temporising, inconstant character of our own state—from the derangement of our finances—the oppressive absurdity of our mode of taxation—and from the astonishing enthusiasm and perversion of principles among the people. It is not extraordinary that commotions have been excited. It is strange, that under the circumstances which we have been discussing, that they did not appear sooner, and terminate more fatally. For let it be remarked, that a feeble government produces more factions than an oppressive one. The want of power first makes individuals pretended legislators, and then, active rebels. Where parents want authority, children are wanting in duty. It is not possible to advance further in the same path. Here the ways divide, the one will conduct us to anarchy, and next to foreign or domestic tyranny: the other, by the wise and vigorous exertion of lawful authority, will lead to permanent power, and general prosperity. I am no advocate for despotism; but I believe the probability to be much less of its being introduced by the corruption of our rulers, than by the delusion of the people. Experience has demonstrated, that new maxims of administration are indispensible. It is not, however, by six penny retrenchments of salaries—nor by levying war against any profession of men—nor by giving substance and existence to the frothy essences and fantastic forms of speculation—nor is it by paper money, or an abolition of debts—nor by implicit submission to the insolence of ignorant conventions—nor by the temporary expedients of little minds, that authority can be rendered stable, and the people prosperous. A well digested, liberal, permanent system of policy is required. And, when adopted, must be supported, in spite of faction, against every thing but amendment. And when amendment should be given, let not the confederation be forgot.

While the bands of union are so loose, we are no more entitled to the character of a nation than the hordes of vagabond traitors. Reason has ever condemned our paltry prejudices upon this important subject. Now that experience has come in aid of reason, let us renounce them. For what is there now to prevent our subjugation by a foreign power, but their contempt of the acquisition? It is time to render the federal head supreme in the United States. It is also time to render the general court [the legislature] supreme in Massachusetts. Conventions have too long, and indeed, too unequally divided power. Until this is effected, we cannot depend upon the success of any plans of reformation. When this is done, we ought to attempt the revival of public and private credit. With what decency can we pretend, that republics are supported by virtue, if we presume upon the foulest of all motives—our own advantage, to release the obligation of contracts?

NEW HAVEN GAZETTE, 19 APRIL 1787

Extract of a letter from a distinguished personage in France to his friend in this city, dated Paris, Dec. 24, 1786.

"The commotions which have taken place in America, as far as they are yet known to me, offer nothing threatening. They are a proof that the people have liberty enough, and I could not wish them less than they have. If the happiness of the mass of the people can be secured at the expence of a little tempest now and then, or even of a little blood, it will be a precious purchase. *Malo libertatem periculosam quam quietam servitutem* [I prefer liberty at risk to peaceful servitude]. Let common sense and common honesty have fair play, and they will soon set things to rights. . . ."

Advice to the Convention: Break Up the Union

*S*ectionalism and the fear of disunion existed in the months leading up to the Philadelphia Convention. In August 1786 Virginia congressman James Monroe reported that a meeting had taken place in New York to discuss dividing the Union at the Hudson River. In October, Dr. Benjamin Rush of Philadelphia wrote that "Some of our enlightened men who begin to despair of a more complete union of the States in Congress have secretly proposed an Eastern, Middle, and Southern Confederacy, to be united by an alliance offensive and defensive." In the aftermath of Shays' Rebellion many feared a monarchy or separate confederacies if the federal government were not strengthened. John Marshall reported that Patrick Henry had been heard to say that he preferred a breakup of the Confederation rather than to allow Congress to enter into a commercial treaty with Spain that was favorable to the North but harmful to Southern interests.

One of the most important achievements of the Constitution is that it solved two major problems that gave credence to the argument in favor of separate confederacies. First, a single government for the whole Union seemed to contradict the commonly accepted doctrine that a republic could not exist over a large territory. Second, it was not clear that the states would give up their status as sovereign powers; if they did not, how could two governments—the federal and the state governments—be sovereign at the same time?

Poetry and song were commonly used in political debate in the 18th century. In the poem below, "Nestor" invokes verse to impress on the Convention the importance of the Union.

Reason
New York Daily Advertiser, 24 March 1787

A THOUGHT for the DELEGATES TO THE CONVENTION to be held at Philadelphia.

Instead of attempting to amend the present articles of confederation with a view to retain them as the form of government, or instead of attempting one general government for the whole community of the United States, would it not be preferable to distribute the States into three Republics, who should enter into a perpetual League or Alliance for mutual defence. This league or alliance must as in all cases of compact between Independent Nations, depend on National Faith.—Self preservation however would almost inevitably produce an observance, as each state would have much to apprehend from the subjugation of either of the others.—Reflections on the subject in the abstract, would have suggested to us, and our own experience has fully convinced us, that there can be only one sovereignty in a government; the notion therefore of a government by confederation between several Independent States, and each state still retaining its sovereignty, must be abandoned, and with it every attempt to amend the present articles of confederation.—No possible amendment will prevent a disunion, and being wholly separated we shall be easily broken.—There are objections to the scheme of one general government.—The national concerns of a people so numerous, with a Territory so extensive will be proportionably difficult and important.—This will require proportionate powers in the administration, especially in the chief executive; greater perhaps than will consist with the principles of a democratic form. For these reasons the plan of three republics as a substitute, is proposed for public consideration. The question is of great magnitude; it is only briefly hinted here, but deserves to be attentively and candidly considered by all who have a solicitude for the liberties, and consequently for the happiness of their country. Our fate, as far as it can depend on human means, is committed to the convention; as they decide, so will our lot be. It must be the wish of the delegates, and it certainly is both our duty and interest to aid them in the arduous business intrusted to them. One way to this is by a public communication of sentiments. I have thrown in my mite, let others do the same; thus the *truth* may be discovered.

New-York, March 19, 1787.

Lycurgus
New York Daily Advertiser, 2 April 1787

Mr. Childs, In your Paper of the 24th instant, I observe a piece signed REASON, proposing a dissolution of the Confederation and a division of the United States into three republics.

The question is of the utmost magnitude, and though it may at first view appear impracticable, yet on investigation, it will appear to be founded on the best established principles of human polity. It is easy to see that the confederation cannot long subsist in its present form: Containing such an immense territory, extending through such a variety of climates, and over people whose manners, customs, and religion are different, and whose interests are often opposed to that of each other. The members that compose it, must perpetually differ in opinion, and little cordiality can long subsist among people who have such different views and interests to pursue.

All political writers of eminence agree, that a republic should not comprehend a large territory; experience bears testimony to the truth of this observation; Partial evils may always be remedied, but it is impossible to provide against *those*, that incessantly arise from radical imperfections.

In vain do we make general laws, and expect obedience to them, if they are not adapted to the habits and manners of the people, and calculated to the climate.

In order to obviate the above objections, I would suggest the propriety of adding a fourth republic. The first to contain the states of New-Hampshire, Massachusetts, Rhode-Island and Connecticut, to which Vermont might be added. The second to contain New-York, New-Jersey, Pennsylvania, Delaware and Maryland. The third, Virginia, the two Carolinas, and Georgia. And the fourth to contain, the state of Franklin [Tennessee], Kentuckey, and the lands lying on the Ohio.

This is a division that seems to be pointed out by climate, whose effect no positive law ever can surpass.

The religion, manners, customs, exports, imports, and general interest of each, being then the same, no opposition arising from differences in these (as at present) would any longer divide their councils, unanimity would render us secure at home, and respected abroad, and promote agriculture, manufactures, and commerce.

I cannot, however, agree with *Reason,* in opinion, that each state must part with its sovereignty, on the contrary I think it essentially necessary that they should in every respect retain the same sovereignty and internal jurisdiction, they do at present, otherwise the republics would fall to pieces by internal imperfection.

These are humbly submitted as the outlines of a plan, which an abler pen may hereafter reduce into a permanent system, from which may result peace, liberty, and security to our country.

New-York, March 30, 1787.

Nestor
Massachusetts Centinel, 13 June 1787

The careful sire of old—who found Death coming
—call'd his sons around.
They heard with rev'rence what he spake—
"Here!—try this bunch of sticks to break."
They took the bundle, every swain
Endeavoured—but the task was vain.
"Observe" the dying father cry'd
And took the sticks himself—and try'd,
When separated, lo how quick
He breaks asunder every stick!
"Learn my dear boys by this example,
So strong, so pertinent—so ample,
That union saves you all from ruin
But *to divide* is your undoing.
For if you take them *one by one*,
See with what ease the task is done!
Singly—how quickly broke in twain,
How *firm* the aggregate THIRTEEN.
Is not the tale, Columbians clear?
What application needs there here?
This motto to your hearts apply
Ye Senators, "UNITE or DIE."

SHOULD THERE BE REFORM OR RADICAL CHANGE?

Nathan Dane, of Beverly, Massachusetts, was a graduate of Harvard and a lawyer. He served in the Massachusetts legislature in the 1780s. From 1785 to 1788 he was a delegate to Congress, where he played a major role in drafting the Northwest Ordinance of 1787. Dane County, Wisconsin, is named in his honor.

Dane was wary of the idea of a constitutional convention because he feared that such a convention might make wholesale changes in the form of government. Nevertheless, it was Dane's motion that Congress adopted on Feb. 21, 1787 when it called for the meeting of the Convention.

Though Dane opposed wholesale changes in the Articles of Confederation, he favored strengthening the federal government. Dane, like most Americans, realized that the Confederation government was too weak. Dane hoped that the Convention might succeed, but he had his doubts. He did not share Thomas Jefferson's opinion that the Convention was an assembly of "demigods."

When Dane saw the Constitution he opposed it. As he had feared, the Convention had not merely reformed the Articles of Confederation, it had totally replaced them. But like many other Antifederalists, once the required nine states had ratified the Constitution, he ended his opposition and sought amendments in the manner specified by the Constitution.

If Dane did not want wholesale change, George Washington did. He, James Madison, and other nationalists believed that the Articles were hopeless. They wanted a totally new government. In the letter below, Washington calls for radical proposals even if they should not be adopted. But if they were not adopted, and all other attempts at reform failed, what did he then have in mind? This is a question that will forever remain unanswered.

NATHAN DANE TO GEORGE CABOT
NEW YORK, 30 MARCH 1787

I believe the people of the united States in general to be as virtuous and as much attached to order and Good Government as any people whatever—but there are in every class some profuse, turbulent embarrassed and vile characters who will keep our Governments in perpetual commotions and danger till they shall be more Strengthened and confirmed. These characters in Massachusetts, Rhode Island, Pennsylvania, Maryland, the Western Country, etc. etc., who under a daring leader might shake the foundations of our present governments, would under a firm efficient head or federal Government be only monuments of their own unimportance. But I can say nothing new to you relative to public affairs. Things have I think for several months preserved their natural Course. All measures in the several States of importance—all measures relative to the proposed Convention or that have taken place I have seen published in our Boston papers. The States have all determined to send members to it except Rhode Island & Connecticut—the latter will probably send. This Convention by thinking men every where is considered as a bold and untried measure & nothing can be more variant than opinions respecting the result of it. In some it produces sanguine expectations in others it most evidently produces an extreme depression of Spirits. They seem to feel themselves launched into the ocean embarked on a hazardous and untried voyage and bound to an unknown Shore. No man that I have heard converse on the subject seems to have formed any definite ideas of what alterations the Convention will propose—and much will certainly depend on the abilities prudence and characters of the men who shall meet in the Convention. There are many good men chosen to it and many very unsound and uncertain politicians. It is doubtful whether Gen. Washington will attend and Gov. [Patrick] Henry of Virginia has resigned—but on the whole I think there is a good appointment of men if they all attend. The danger is in my mind that the best & most Judicious men will not attend. It is a work of immense magnitude to mend so complicated a machine of Government as our's is—and to infuse into it sufficient energy. It is in my mind a work adequate to the abilities of the most industrious and able politicians at least during thirty or forty years to come. I wish among others most ardently to see our governments rendered equal & free firm & efficient in the Course of a few years but I cannot in moments of sober reflection form an idea that we shall. Nay fortune must be propitious too. Our object is a wise government in which freedom & protection Strength and energy are united or a government in which there shall be a kind of balance of power of the different classes of men, in which the laws shall be made by the people's representatives & executed independant of the popular opinions, in which persons and property shall be punctually protected and secured to it at moderate expence. How many nations have Struggled for ages and failed in obtaining these great objects? Our nation excepted can we name another on earth that ever has according to our ideas fully obtained them?

GEORGE WASHINGTON TO JAMES MADISON
MOUNT VERNON, 31 MARCH 1787

... It gives me pleasure to hear that there is a probability of a full Representation of the States in Convention, but if the delegates come to it under fetters, the salutary ends proposed will in my opinion be greatly embarrassed & retarded, if not altogether defeated. I am anxious to know how this matter really is, as my wish is, that the Convention may adopt no temporising expedient, but probe the defects of the Constitution to the bottom, and provide radical cures, whether they are agreed to or not. A conduct like this, will stamp wisdom and dignity on the proceedings, and be looked to as a luminary, which sooner or later will shed its influence.

James Madison and the Origins of the Constitution

On March 27, 1787, Virginia Governor Edmund Randolph wrote James Madison a brief letter telling him that he had been thinking about the upcoming Constitutional Convention. Randolph believed that the basic form of the Articles of Confederation should be retained and that alterations "should be grafted on." He thought the Convention should propose the "best" possible revisions and not limit itself to changes that the states might be expected to accept.

Madison had already given a lot of thought to the problems of the Confederation, and he had some ideas about what the Convention should propose. Madison's response of April 8, brilliantly stated the essence of the plan that Governor Randolph would present to the Convention on May 29. Clearly, Madison was the principle author of this "Virginia Plan," which served as the basis for the debate in the Convention.

Madison proposed several critical ideas. (1) The good parts of the Articles should be retained, but only as parts of a wholly new form of government. (2) The federal government should be supreme in national affairs and act directly on the people, not through the states. State and local governments should have authority only in their internal affairs. (3) The basis of representation in Congress should be changed. Under the Articles of Confederation the states each had one vote. Now, Madison wanted representation to be proportional to population. The vote of Delaware should not have the same influence as the vote of Virginia. (4) The federal government should have veto power over state laws. (5) There should be a two-house Congress. (6) There should be national judicial and executive branches. (7) There should be a national council of revision which could revise or veto all bills passed by Congress. (8) The federal government should protect the states from foreign and domestic violence. (9) The new plan should be ratified by the people, not by the state legislatures.

Madison knew these ideas were extreme (and some, in fact, were rejected by the Convention), but as he wrote to Washington on April 16, "Temporising applications will dishonor the Councils which propose them" and might worsen the situation. "Radical attempts, although unsuccessful, will at least justify the authors of them."

James Madison to Edmund Randolph
New York, 8 April 1787

... I think with you that it will be well to retain as much as possible of the old Confederation, tho' I doubt whether it may not be best to work the valuable articles into the new System, instead of engrafting the latter on the former. I am also perfectly of your opinion that in framing a system, no material sacrifices ought to be made to local or temporary prejudices. ...

I hold it for a fundamental point that an individual independence of the States, is utterly irreconcileable with the idea of an aggregate sovereignty. I think at the same time that a consolidation of the States into one simple republic is not less unattainable than it would be inexpedient. Let it be tried then whether any middle ground can be taken which will at once support a due supremacy of the national authority, and leave in force the local authorities so far as they can be subordinately useful.

The first step to be taken is I think a change in the principle of representation. According to the present form of the Union, an equality of suffrage [of the states], if not just towards the larger members of it, is at least safe to them, as the liberty they exercise of rejecting or executing the acts of Congress, is uncontroulable by the nominal sovereignty of Congress. Under a system which would operate [directly on the people] without the intervention of the States, the case would be materially altered. A vote from Delaware would have the same effect as one from Massachusetts or Virginia.

Let the national Government be armed with a positive & compleat authority in all cases where uniform measures are necessary. As in trade etc. etc. Let it also retain the powers which it now possesses.

Let it have a negative in all cases whatsoever on the Legislative Acts of the States as the King of Great Britain heretofore had. This I conceive to be essential and the least possible abridgement of the State Sovereignties. Without such a defensive power, every positive power that can be given on paper will be unavailing. It will also give internal stability to the States. There has been no moment since the peace at which the federal assent would have been given to paper money etc. etc.

Let this national supremacy be extended also to the Judiciary department. If the judges in the last resort depend on the States & are bound by their oaths to them and not to the Union, the intention of the law and the interests of the nation may be defeated by the obsequiousness of the Tribunals to the policy or prejudices of the States. It seems at least essential that an appeal should lie to some national tribunals in all cases which concern foreigners, or inhabitants of other States. The admiralty jurisdiction may be fully submitted to the national government....

A Government formed of such extensive powers ought to be well organized. The Legislative department may be divided into two branches: One of them to be chosen every ___ years by the Legislatures or the people at large; the other to consist of a more select number, holding their appointments for a longer term and going out in rotation. Perhaps the negative on the State laws may be most conveniently lodged in this branch. A Council of Revision may be superadded, including the great ministerial officers.

A National Executive will also be necessary. I have scarcely ventured to form my own opinion yet either of the manner in which it ought to be constituted or of the authorities with which it ought [to be] cloathed.

An article ought to be inserted expressly guarantying the tranquility of the States against internal as well as external dangers.

To give the new system its proper energy it will be desirable to have it ratified by the authority of the people, and not merely by that of the Legislatures.

I am afraid you will think this project, if not extravagant, absolutely unattainable and unworthy of being attempted. Conceiving it my self to go no further than is essential, the objections drawn from this source are to be laid aside. I flatter myself however that they may be less formidable on trial than in comtemplation. The change in the principle of representation will be relished by a majority of the States, and those too of most influence. The Northern States will be reconciled to it by the *actual* superiority of their populousness: the Southern by their *expected* superiority in this point. This principle established, the repugnance of the large States to part with power will in a great degree subside, and the smaller States must ultimately yield to the predominant Will. It is also already seen by many & must by degrees be seen by all that unless the Union be organized efficiently & on Republican Principles, innovations of a much more objectionable form may be obtruded, or in the most favorable event, the partition of the Empire into rival & hostile confederacies, will ensue.

CAN THE CONVENTION SOLVE AMERICA'S PROBLEMS?

The two letters below were written by Virginians who eventually opposed the adoption of the Constitution.

John Dawson was a member of the Virginia legislature. Dawson's letter described the agricultural depression of the mid-1780s, when farms were being sold off for debt and non-payment of taxes and when commodity prices (in this case the terrible commodity of human beings) had collapsed. Dawson clearly believed that if relief were not provided, the consequence would be violence. He saw the Constitutional Convention as a possible solution.

William Grayson was a member of Congress and was to become a member of the first U.S. Senate under the Constitution. Although his letter to William Short, aide to American ambassador to France Thomas Jefferson, addressed some of the same concerns as Dawson, he was less sympathetic to the plight of debtors and was principally concerned with the failure of Congress to raise sufficient revenue to pay for the civil list or to pay the interest on the national debt. Congress had financed the Revolutionary War by borrowing huge sums of money from Americans and from France and Holland. In the past the states simply did not comply with Congress' requests for money; but now some states openly passed resolutions refusing to pay their requisitions. The attempt to give Congress power to levy tariffs had recently been defeated by New York—the rejection by one state was enough to defeat a proposed amendment to the Articles of Confederation.

Grayson had little confidence that the Convention would offer or that the states would accept any meaningful solutions. As bad as things were, they were not bad enough for the states to accept profound changes. He had evidently spoken to fellow congressman James Madison about some of the ideas Madison was going to propose to the Convention (see last week's article), and he obviously thought there was no chance these ideas would be accepted.

JOHN DAWSON TO JAMES MADISON
FREDERICKSBURG, VA., 15 APRIL 1787

... I assure you that matters here wear a very disagreable aspect. The people of Caroline [County], have, I am informed, entered into an association and are determined to purchase no property sold [for debt] by execution. The extreme scarcity of hard money [gold or silver] is the reason urged, and indeed there is too much weight in it. Three days since I attended a Sheriffs sale in this county when very likely negroes, such as before the war, would have brought eighty pounds, were sold for thirty. In most of the counties petitions to the next assembly will be handed about for the payment of debts either in property, or by installments, and should both be refused, and the scarcity of money continue, I know not what may be the consequence, as I am informed that in some of the low counties they talk boldly of following the example of the insurgents in Massachusetts [Shays' Rebellion] and preventing the courts proceeding to business.

Much depends on the convention in May—the attention of almost every person is fixed on that body—and should the issue not be successful, which I am very sorry to find you suspect, I fear there will be an end to the General confederacy. You have I presume heard that General Washington has consented to attend—

WILLIAM GRAYSON TO WILLIAM SHORT
NEW YORK, 16 APRIL 1787

... I am sorry to inform you that American affairs in general wear the worst aspect you can possibly conceive. The people discontented. The public treasury without money, and the States either refusing or not complying with the requisitions of Congress—[New] Jersey last year rejected the requisition: & Connecticut this:—Only Virginia, N. York, & Pensylvania pay any thing towards the support of Government. Through their means the Dutch Interest & Civil list of the U. States have been paid since I have been in Congress: the rest of the Union appear to be in an insensible languor as to money supplies. The much talked of 5 percent Impost has been rejected by N. York. ...

Congress annually vote requisitions for the foreign & domestic interest which are totally disreguarded: It appears to me there is a considerable party in every State against the payment of the domestic debt:—& though this matter has shewed itself openly only in Massachusetts [in Shays' Rebellion] yet I am satisfyed a vigorous taxation would produce the same effect in many of the other States: Connecticut would have been in the situation of Massachusetts if she had passed the requisition—I don't pretend to say that the domestic debt is the only cause of discontent: I believe a dislike to the payment of private debt to be equally prevalent: Rhode Island has issued paper money to satisfy her people which has depreciated amazingly: North & South Carolina & N. York & Jersey did this some time since & Maryland is now about doing it:—Upon the whole it seems to be the current opinion that however excellent democratical governments may be in some respects, the payment of money & the preservation of the public faith is not among their good qualifications:

Congress have lately recommended a meeting of deputies to revise the foederal constitution [the Articles of Confederation]: they are to assemble the 2nd Monday in May next at Philadelphia—It is said General Washington (if he attends) will be President; if not Doctor [Benjamin] Franklin;—There are as great expectations here from the result of their deliberations as I presume there are in France from the [Assembly of] Notables:—I believe the whole will terminate in nothing; either the Assembly will not agree, or if they do agree, the States will not ratify. Our distresses are not sufficiently great to produce decisive alterations:—Besides the more slack the government the better the people like it: of course they will not give up any power which will prevent them from being compelled to make satisfaction to their Creditors:—They may perhaps go as far as granting the regulation of commerce to Congress, under such conditions, limitations, & restrictions as in all probability will render the exercise of the power impracticable.

Some of the gentlemen of the Convention are here & I have conversed freely with them as to the reform;—they are for going a great way: some of them are for placing Congress in loco of the King of Great Britain—besides their present powers:—for giving them a perpetual duty on imports & exports: Figure to yourself how the States will relish the idea of a negative on their laws etc. etc. etc.

The Unpopular Political Philosophy of John Adams

John Adams was one of the most prominent leaders of the American Revolution. In 1787 Adams was 52 years old and was serving as U.S. Minister to Great Britain in London. Although far removed from direct participation in American politics, Adams was kept informed of events by a number of correspondents.

Much of Adams's political thought was incorporated in his three-volume Defence of the Constitutions of Government of the United States of America. *The first volume of this monumental work was published in London in January 1787 and excerpts were immediately printed in newspapers throughout the United States.*

Adams worried about the animosities that existed between the democratic and aristocratic elements in society. If left unchecked, these two opposing forces would involve the country in social strife and eventually civil war. To avoid this conflict, Adams supported the establishment of a federal government in which a strong executive maintained a balance between the democratic element represented in one house of the legislature and an aristocratic element represented in the other branch.

Adams knew that he was taking a risk by expressing these political opinions. He wrote Thomas Jefferson that publishing the Defence *was "a hazardous enterprise, and it will be an unpopular work in America for a long time. . . . But as I have made it, early in life and all along, a rule to conceal nothing from the people which appeared to me material for their happiness and prosperity, however unpopular it might be at the time, or with particular parties, I am determined not now to begin to flatter popular prejudices and party passions, however they may be countenanced by great authorities."*

His prediction was prophetic. Although many Americans praised the Defence, *others believed that Adams's diplomatic tour in Great Britain had corrupted his revolutionary principles, and his career was damaged by charges that he favored an aristocracy or a monarchy.*

Massachusetts Gazette, 20 April 1787

His Excellency John Adams, Esquire, Minister Plenipotentiary from the United States at the Court of Great Britain, has lately published a very valuable book, entitled, "A Defence of the Constitutions of Government of the United States of America." In the preface is the following paragraph—well worthy the attention of every American at this important crisis of our publick affairs.—

"The people in America have now the best opportunity, and the greatest trust, in their hands, that Providence ever committed to so small a number since the transgression of the first pair: if they betray their trust, their guilt will merit even greater punishment than other nations have suffered, and the indignation of Heaven. If there is one *certain truth* to be collected from the history of all ages, it is this: that the people's rights and liberties, and the democratical mixture in a constitution, can never be preserved without a strong executive, or, in other words, without separating the executive power from the legislative. If the executive power, or any considerable part of it, is left in the hands either of an aristocratical or a democratical assembly, it will corrupt the legislature as necessarily as rust corrupts iron, or as arsenic poisons the human body; and when the legislature is corrupted, the people are undone."

Sidney

Philadelphia Independent Gazetteer, 6 June 1787

... In this excellent work, the principles of republican governments are fully unfolded, and the most undeniable proofs adduced, that a people cannot long be free or happy under a government that consists of a single legislature. His arguments in favor of two or three legislative branches and a powerful executive, drawn from history, from reason, and even from the works of nature, are unanswerable, and will probably serve, joined with the melancholy experience we have had of the folly, instability, and tyranny of single legislatures, to banish those dangerous experiments in government out of our country.

It is to be hoped every freeman in the United States will furnish himself with a copy of this invaluable book. It is more essentially the duty of every person concerned in any way in the government of our country to read and study it.

Indeed, I should be glad to see every man who is elected to serve in our assemblies, councils, senates, congress or convention, subscribe a declaration (added to those which are required in most of the states) that he not only believes in the old and new testaments, and that he will faithfully discharge the duties of his station, but that he has read "Adams's Defence of the American Constitutions," or as it might more properly be called Adams's Defence of a mixed, or compound Legislature in all republican governments.

"D," BALTIMORE MARYLAND GAZETTE, 3 JULY 1787

A correspondent observes that having carefully perused Mr. *John Adams's* late "Vindication of the Constitutions of Government of the United States of America," he was greatly disappointed; for instead of a vindication, or defence, he found this performance of a different complexion, and evidently militating against the present established systems. Mr. Adams, says our correspondent, seems to bring us back again to the English government; as he repeatedly insists on the necessity of *three independent Branches in the Legislature,* and is particularly fond of a *strong Executive.* Surely the air of Europe has not infected our Plenipotentiary? *This language* is by no means consistent with republicanism, and there are other passages in this writer which point direct to monarchy, or what is the same, *"a first Magistrate* possessed exclusively of the Executive power."—This book will not gain so many proselytes in America, as Common Sense in the beginning of the year 1776.

SENEX
VIRGINIA INDEPENDENT CHRONICLE, 15 AUGUST 1787

To the *Citizens of the United States of America.* I have read, with a great deal of attention, Mr. Adams's *pretended* Defence of the American Constitutions.—It is, as far as I can judge, one of the most deep wrought systems of political deception, that ever was penned by the ingenuity of man. It is a capital picture I must readily confess; but without adverting to the specimens of an Angelo or a Raphael, I will venture to affirm, that it exhibits the truest mixture of light and shade, that ever entered the imagination of a painter. Americans, beware!—for if you imbibe a particle of his political poison, you are undone for ever. . . .

CHAPTER 2
The Constitutional Convention

Introduction

Beginning in November 1786, all of the state legislatures, except Rhode Island, elected delegates to the Constitutional Convention. Many of the greatest political figures in the country were delegates; some of the delegates were less well known and not as talented.

Scheduled to meet on May 14, 1787, a majority of the state delegations did not arrive in Philadelphia until May 25. In the meantime, the Virginia delegation caucused daily and devised the "Virginia Plan," based on ideas developed by James Madison. Once the Convention elected officers (George Washington was chosen to be president) and had adopted rules, the Governor of Virginia, Edmund Randolph, introduced the Virginia Plan, which advocated a radical change in the form of government, abandoning the Articles of Confederation and proposing an entirely new, far more powerful form of government.

This new government would consist of three branches: a legislative, an executive, and a judicial. The legislature was to consist of two houses, the first elected by the people and the second elected by the first house. This legislature, or Congress, was to have the power to legislate in all matters in which the states were incompetent, it could veto state laws that violated the Constitution, and it could call forth the force of the Union to enforce its will. It would have the power to tax and to regulate commerce. The executive would execute the laws, and the executive and judiciary together could veto laws passed by Congress. State officeholders would be obligated to swear obedience to the Constitution. Finally, these proposals were to be adopted or rejected not by the state legislatures (as provided by the Articles of Confederation), but by specially elected conventions chosen by the people in each state.

These revolutionary proposals served as the basis of debate from May 30 to June 15, when an alternative proposal, the "New Jersey

Plan," was introduced. This plan would have retained most of the Articles of Confederation. Congress would still represent the states, not the people directly, but it would have the power to regulate commerce and to collect requisitions itself if the states did not. Congress would appoint an executive and there would be a supreme court. Federal laws and treaties were to be "supreme," and force could be used to compel obedience.

Congress debated both the Virginia and the New Jersey plans on June 16, 18, and 19, and finally decided to proceed using the Virginia Plan as the basis of debate. This was a decisive moment in the constitutional history of the United States.

It remained for the Convention to flesh out this government and to resolve many thorny issues. The Convention still had to decide how to divide authority between the federal government and the state governments, the branches of the federal government, the large and the small states, and the Northern States and the Southern States. Were the states to be equally represented in Congress, or was apportionment to be based on population? How much power, and of what kind, was to be given to the executive branch? Who was to be allowed to vote for this new government: should only the wealthy and well educated have the vote, or should all citizens? Should Congress have the power to prohibit the importation of slaves from Africa? Should the Constitution be submitted for adoption to the legislatures of the states, or should it be submitted to the consideration of the people directly? These are a few of the difficult issues the Convention had to resolve.

Finally, on September 15, 1787, James Madison moved that the Constitution be adopted by the Convention. The Convention agreed and ordered the Constitution to be engrossed (that is, written on parchment) for signature by the delegates. On Monday, September 17, all but three of the delegates present signed the Constitution. The three non-signers, Elbridge Gerry of Massachusetts, and George Mason and Edmund Randolph of Virginia refused to sign because they feared that the new government was too powerful and that the absence of a bill of rights created the danger of a tyranny. All of the other delegates present signed their names to it. The Constitution was then revealed to the public and published in newspapers and as broadsides throughout the United States.

Character Sketches of the Delegates to the Constitutional Convention

The delegates to the Constitutional Convention that was to meet in Philadelphia in May 1787 were elected by the states from November 1786 to June 1787. Reaction to the delegates varied considerably. Thomas Jefferson was in Paris as U.S. Minister to France. When he heard of the appointments, he wrote John Adams "it really is an assembly of demi-gods." However, Nathan Dane said (above), "There are many good men chosen to it [the Convention] and many very unsound and uncertain politicians."

Another writer commented: "I do not wish to detract from their merits, but I will venture to affirm, that twenty assemblies of equal number might be collected, equally respectable both in point of ability, integrity, and patriotism. Some of the characters which compose it I revere; others I consider as of small consequence, and a number are suspected of being great public defaulters, and to have been guilty of notorious peculation and fraud, with regard to public property in the hour of our distress."

Many years after the Convention, James Madison reflected on the delegates. "But whatever may be the judgment pronounced on the competency of the architects of the Constitution, or whatever may be the destiny of the edifice prepared by them, I feel it a duty to express my profound and solemn conviction, derived from my intimate opportunity of observing and appreciating the views of the convention, collectively and individually, that there never was an assembly of men, charged with a great and arduous trust, who were more pure in their motives, or more exclusively or anxiously devoted to the object committed to them."

The following are short character sketches of the most prominent of the Convention delegates written by William Pierce, himself a delegate from Georgia, and by the Comte de Moustier, France's Minister to the U.S., who was stationed in New York City. Moustier's sketches have been set in italic type.

New Hampshire

John Langdon is a Man of considerable fortune, possesses a liberal mind, and a good plain understanding.—about 40 years old.

One of the most interesting and most amiable men in the United States. Mr. Langdon made a great fortune in commerce and is the Robert Morris of his state. He likes to spend money and has attached many citizens to him because of his generosities.

Nicholas Gilman is modest, genteel, and sensible. There is nothing brilliant or striking in his character, but there is something respectable and worthy in the Man.—about 30 years of age.

A pretentious young man; hardly liked by his colleagues; he is called in derision, THE CONGRESS.

Massachusetts

Rufus King is a Man much distinguished for his eloquence and great parliamentary talents. He was educated in Massachusetts, and is said to have good classical as well as legal knowledge. He has served for three years in the Congress of the United States with great and deserved applause, and is at this time high in the confidence and approbation of his Country-men. This Gentleman is about thirty three years of age, about five feet ten Inches high, well formed, an handsome face, with a strong expressive Eye, and a sweet high toned voice. In his public speaking there is something peculiarly strong and rich in his expression, clear, and convincing in his arguments, rapid and irresistible at times in his eloquence but he is not always equal. His action is natural, swimming, and graceful, but there is a rudeness of manner sometimes accompanying it. But take him *tout en semble,* he may with propriety be ranked among the Luminaries of the present Age.

Elbridge Gerry's character is marked for integrity and perseverance. He is a hesitating and laborious speaker;—possesses a great degree of confidence and goes extensively into all subjects that he speaks on, without respect to elegance or flower of diction. He is connected and sometimes clear in his arguments, conceives well, and cherishes as his first virtue, a love for his Country. Mr. Gerry is very much of a Gentleman in his principles and manners;—he has been engaged in the mercantile line and is a Man of property. He is about 37 years of age.

Elbridge Gerry is a small man, very intriguing and without much finesse. He has been the most active member of Congress for the longest time.

He has acquired a great knowledge of public affairs, which he makes the best use of to appear worthy in the opinion of his fellow-citizens.

Connecticut

William Samuel Johnson is a character much celebrated for his legal knowledge; he is said to be one of the first classics in America, and certainly possesses a very strong and enlightened understanding.

As an Orator in my opinion, there is nothing in him that warrants the high reputation which he has for public speaking. There is something in the tone of his voice not pleasing to the Ear,—but he is eloquent and clear,—always abounding with information and instruction.... Dr. Johnson is about sixty years of age, possesses the manners of a Gentleman, and engages the Hearts of Men by the sweetness of his temper, and that affectionate style of address with which he accosts his acquaintance.

Roger Sherman exhibits the oddest shaped character I ever remember to have met with. He is awkward, unmeaning, and unaccountably strange in his manner. But in his train of thinking there is something regular, deep and comprehensive; yet the oddity of his address, the vulgarisms that accompany his public speaking, and that strange New England cant which runs through his public as well as his private speaking make everything that is connected with him grotesque and laughable;—and yet he deserves infinite praise,—no Man has a better Heart or a clearer Head. If he cannot embellish he can furnish thoughts that are wise and useful. He is an able politician, and extremely artful in accomplishing any particular object;—it is remarked that he seldom fails. I am told he sits on the Bench in Connecticut, and is very correct in the discharge of his Judicial functions. In the early part of his life he was a Shoe-maker;—but despising the lowness of his condition, he turned Almanack maker, and so progressed upwards to a Judge. He has been several years a Member of Congress, and discharged the duties of his Office with honor and credit to himself, and advantage to the State he represented. He is about 60.

Oliver Ellsworth is a Judge of the Supreme Court in Connecticut;—he is a Gentleman of a clear, deep, and copious understanding; eloquent, and connected in public debate; and always attentive to his duty. He is very happy in a reply, and choice in selecting such parts of his adversary's arguments as he finds make the strongest impressions,—in order to take off the force of them, so as to admit the power of his own. Mr. Elsworth is about 37 years of age, a Man much respected for his integrity, and venerated for his abilities.

In general the men of this state have a national character that is rarely found in the other parts of this continent. They are nearing republican simplicity; they are completely at ease without opulence. Rural economy and domestic industry have grown for a long time in Connecticut; the people are happy there.

New York

Alexander Hamilton is deservedly celebrated for his talents. He is a practicioner of the Law, and reputed to be a finished Scholar. To a clear and strong judgment he unites the ornaments of fancy, and whilst he is able, convincing, and engaging in his eloquence the Heart and Head sympathize in approving him. Yet there is something too feeble in his voice to be equal to the strains of oratory;—it is my opinion that he is rather a convincing Speaker, than a blazing Orator. Colonel Hamilton requires time to think,—he enquires into every part of his subject with the searchings of phylosophy, and when he comes forward he comes highly charged with interesting matter, there is no skimming over the surface of a subject with him, he must sink to the bottom to see what foundation it rests on.—His language is not always equal, sometimes didactic like Bolingbroke's at others light and tripping like Stern's. His eloquence is not so defusive as to trifle with the senses, but he rambles just enough to strike and keep up the attention. He is about 33 years old, of small stature, and lean. His manners are tinctured with stiffness, and sometimes with a degree of vanity that is highly disagreeable.

New Jersey

William Paterson is one of those kind of Men whose powers break in upon you, and create wonder and astonishment. He is a Man of great modesty, with looks that bespeak talents of no great extent,— but he is a Classic, a Lawyer, and an Orator;—and of a disposition so favorable to his advancement that every one seemed ready to exalt him with their praises. He is very happy in the choice of time and manner of engaging in a debate, and never speaks but when he understands his subject well. This Gentleman is about 34 years of age, of a very low stature.

Pennsylvania

Benjamin Franklin is well known to be the greatest phylosopher of the present age;—all the operations of nature he seems to understand,—the very heavens obey him, and the Clouds yield up their Lightning to be imprisoned in his rod. But what claim he has to the politician, posterity must determine. It is certain that he does not shine much in public Council,—he is no Speaker, nor does he seem to let politics engage his attention. He is, however, a most extraordinary Man, and tells a story in a style more engaging than anything I ever heard. Let his Biographer finish his character. He is 82 years old, and possesses an activity of mind equal to a youth of 25 years of age.

Present president of this state, too well known to need the praise which we give him. He feels more than all other Americans that to be truly patriotic one must be a friend of France. Unfortunately, this philosopher, who has braved the lightning of the heavens and of the English Parliament, will not much longer struggle against the infirmities of age. We regret that immortality only pertains to his name and his writings.

James Wilson ranks among the foremost in legal and political knowledge. He has joined to a fine genius all that can set him off and show him to advantage. He is well acquainted with Man, and understands all the passions that influence him. Government seems to have been his peculiar Study, all the political institutions of the World he knows in detail, and can trace the causes and effects of every revolution from the earliest stages of the Greecian commonwealth down to the present time. No man is more clear, copious, and comprehensive than Mr. Wilson, yet he is no great Orator. He draws the attention not by the charm of his eloquence, but by the force of his reasoning. He is about 45 years old.

Distinguished lawyer. . . . A haughty man, intrepid aristocrat, active, eloquent, profound, dissembler. . . . His active involvement in public affairs has deranged his fortune and has not permitted him to set his affairs straight.

Gouverneur Morris is one of those Genius's in whom every species of talents combine to render him conspicuous and flourishing in public debate:—He winds through all the mazes of rhetoric, and throws around him such a glare that he charms, captivates, and leads away the senses of all who hear him. With an infinite stretch of fancy he brings to view things when he is engaged in deep argumentation, that render all the labor of reasoning easy and pleasing. But with all these powers he is fickle and inconstant,—never pursuing one train of thinking,—nor ever regular. He has gone through a very extensive course of reading, and is acquainted with all the sciences. No Man has more wit,—nor can any one engage the attention more than Mr. Morris. He was bred to the Law, but I am told he disliked the profession, and turned merchant. He is engaged in some great mercantile matters with his namesake Mr. Robert Morris [a wealthy Philadelphia merchant and another Pennsylvania delegate]. This Gentleman is about 38 years old, he has been unfortunate in losing one of his Legs, and getting all the flesh taken off his right arm by a scald, when a youth.

Citizen of the State of New York, but always connected with Robert Morris and having represented Pennsylvania several times. Celebrated lawyer, one of the best organized minds on the continent, but without manners, and, if one believes his enemies, without principles; extremely interesting in conversation having studied finances with special care. He works constantly with Robert Morris. He is feared more than admired, but few regard him with esteem.

Delaware

John Dickinson has been famed through all America, for his Farmers Letters; he is a Scholar, and said to be a Man of very extensive information. When I saw him in the Convention I was induced to pay the greatest attention to him whenever he spoke. I had often heard that he was a great Orator, but I found him an indifferent Speaker. With an affected air of wisdom he labors to produce a trifle,—his language is irregular and incorrect,—his flourishes (for he sometimes attempts them), are like expiring flames, they just shew themselves and go out;—no traces of them are left on the mind to chear or animate it. He is, however, a good writer and will ever be considered one of the most important characters in the United States. He is about 55 years old, and was bred a Quaker.

The Constitutional Convention

Author of the Letters of a Pennsylvania Farmer. Very rich man, was of the anti-English party at the beginning of the Revolution, without, however, favoring independence which he actually voted against publicly. He is old, feeble, and without influence.

Maryland

Luther Martin was educated for the Bar, and is Attorney general for the State of Maryland. This Gentleman possesses a good deal of information, but he has a very bad delivery, and so extremely prolix, that he never speaks without tiring the patience of all who hear him. He is about 34 years of age.

Virginia

George Washington is well known as the Commander in chief of the late American Army. Having conducted these states to independence and peace, he now appears to assist in framing a Government to make the People happy. Like Gustavus Vasa, he may be said to be the deliverer of his Country;—like Peter the great he appears as the politician and the States-man; and like Cincinnatus he returned to his farm perfectly contented with being only a plain Citizen, after enjoying the highest honor of the Confederacy,—and now only seeks for the approbation of his Country-men by being virtuous and useful. The General was conducted to the Chair as President of the Convention by the unanimous voice of its Members. He is in the 52d. year of his age.

George Mason is a Gentleman of remarkable strong powers, and possesses a clear and copious understanding. He is able and convincing in debate, steady and firm in his principles, and undoubtedly one of the best politicians in America. Mr. Mason is about 60 years old, with a fine strong constitution.

James Madison is a character who has long been in public life; and what is very remarkable every Person seems to acknowledge his greatness. He blends together the profound politician, with the Scholar. In the management of every great question he evidently took the lead in the Convention, and tho' he cannot be called an Orator, he is a most agreeable, eloquent, and convincing Speaker. From a spirit of industry and application which he possesses in a most eminent degree, he always comes forward the best informed Man of any point in debate. The affairs of the United States, he perhaps, has the most correct knowledge of, of any Man in the Union. He has been twice a Member of Congress, and was always thought one of the ablest Members that ever sat in that Council. Mr. Maddison is about 37 years of age, a Gentleman of great modesty,—with a remarkable sweet temper. He is easy and unreserved among his acquaintance, and has a most agreeable style of conversation.

Educated, wise, moderate, docile, studious; can be more profound than Mr. Hamilton, but less brilliant; intimate friend of Mr. Jefferson and sincerely attached to France. He has been in Congress since a youth and he seems to be especially dedicated to public affairs. He could one day be governor of his state, if his modesty would allow him to accept this position. In the past he has refused the office of president of Congress. This is a man who must be studied for a long time to form a just opinion of him.

Edmund Randolph is Governor of Virginia,—a young Gentleman in whom unite all the accomplishments of the Scholar, and the Statesman. He came forward with the postulata, or first principles, on which the Convention acted [the Virginia Plan], and he supported them with a force of eloquence and reasoning that did him great honor. He has a most harmonious voice, a fine person and striking manners. Mr. Randolph is about 32 years of age.

North Carolina

Hugh Williamson is a Gentleman of education and talents. He enters freely in public debate from his close attention to most subjects, but he is no Orator. There is a great degree of good humour and pleasantry in his character; and in his manners there is a strong trait of the Gentleman. He is about 48 years of age.

Physician and former professor of astronomy—bizarre to an excess, loves to harangue but speaks with sense. It is difficult to know his character well; it is even possible that he might not have any, but his lengthy service has given him much influence in Congress.

South Carolina

John Rutledge is one of those characters who was highly mounted at the commencement of the late revolution;—his reputation in the first Congress gave him a distinguished rank among the American Worthies. He was bred to the Law, and now acts as one of the Chancellors of South Carolina. This Gentleman is much famed in his own State as an Orator, but in my opinion he is too rapid in his public speaking to be denominated an agreeable Orator. He is undoubtedly a man of abilities, and a Gentleman of distinction and fortune. Mr. Rutledge was once Governor of South Carolina. He is about 48 years of age.

Governor during the war, member of Congress, of the Convention and in general employed on all great occasions. The most eloquent but the proudest and most imperious man in the United States. He uses his great influence and his knowledge as a lawyer to his advantage by avoiding his debts which greatly exceed his fortune.

Charles Cotesworth Pinckney is a Gentleman of Family and fortune in his own State. He has received the advantage of a liberal education, and possesses a very extensive degree of legal knowledge. When warm in a debate he sometimes speaks well,—but he is generally considered an indifferent Orator. Mr. Pinckney was an Officer of high rank in the American army, and served with great reputation through the War. He is now about 40 years of age.

Charles Pinckney is a young Gentleman of the most promising talents. He is, altho' only 24 years of age, in possession of a very great variety of knowledge. Government, Law, History and Phylosophy are his favorite studies, but he is intimately acquainted with every species of polite learning, and has a spirit of application and industry beyond most Men. He speaks with great neatness and perspicuity, and treats every subject as fully, without running into prolixity, as it requires. He has been a Member of Congress, and served in that Body with ability and eclat.

Georgia

My own character I shall not attempt to draw, but leave those who may choose to speculate on it, to consider it in any light that their fancy or imagination may depict. I am conscious of having discharged my duty as a Soldier through the course of the late revolution with honor and propriety; and my services in Congress and the Convention were bestowed with the best intention towards the interest of Georgia, and towards the general welfare of the Confederacy. I possess ambition, and it was that, and the flattering opinion which some of my Friends had of me, that gave me a seat in the wisest Council in the World, and furnished me with an opportunity of giving these short Sketches of the Characters who composed it.

CONNECTICUT DEBATES ELECTING DELEGATES TO THE CONSTITUTIONAL CONVENTION

When the Connecticut legislature assembled on May 10, 1787, most of the other states had already voted to send delegates to the Constitutional Convention that was scheduled to meet in Philadelphia on May 14. A vigorous debate took place in the Connecticut assembly on May 12 over the wisdom of sending delegates to the national convention. This debate was published in the Hartford Connecticut Courant on May 21, 1787, and is the only debate over the election of delegates to the Convention recorded in the newspapers of any state.

Connecticut had ample reason to favor a stronger central government. As a small, agricultural state, most of the foreign goods Connecticut residents consumed were first imported into either New York City or Boston, where state duties were imposed, and then re-imported into Connecticut.

Connecticut supported the national tariff proposed by Congress, the Impost of 1783, which would benefit all the states. But New York's refusal to ratify the Impost defeated it. Frustrated with its economic plight, the Connecticut legislature in October 1786 told Congress that the state had no money to pay its share of the federal requisition.

The Constitutional Convention offered another chance to reform the Confederation. Still, there was the fear that a stronger central government would diminish the state and endanger liberty.

PROCEEDINGS OF THE CONNECTICUT GENERAL ASSEMBLY SATURDAY, MAY 12, 1787

General Jedidiah Huntington: Mr. Speaker, The measure under consideration is recommended by Congress, and has been either anticipated or acceded to by most of the states; I would therefore from respect to Congress and affection to our sister states, have this state concur with them. I should stop here, Mr. Speaker, if I had not reason to think that there are some gentlemen who are of opinion that the confederation is sufficient for its purposes, and some who believe we should be better without any—I beg therefore, to be indulged in some observations on the subject.

The [Articles of] confederation was framed whilst this country was smarting under the hand of arbitrary power: it seems to have been the leading object of the framers of it to erect an authority over this country without committing absolutely any power to it; the compact between the several states has not any penalty annexed to it for the breach of its conditions, nor is it provided with any power of coercing a compliance; the observance of it depends entirely on the meer good will and pleasure of each state; whenever therefore any state refuses a compliance with a requisition made agreeably to the confederation, all obligation on the part of the other states is dissolved.

If this reasoning is just we have not any confederation—at any rate it is an inefficient one. The importance of a general government, a superintending power, that shall extend to all parts of our extensive territory, to secure peace and the administration of justice between one state and another, and between these states and foreign nations, must be obvious to the least reflection. All rational calculations must very much fail us, if the diversity of sentiments, manners, and local circumstances, the unequal distribution of public debt, and the jealousies of trade, do not create animosities and contentions of the most serious nature—where and when they will terminate Omniscience only knows. Shall we trust the event to accident, and leave a government to arise out of the distractions of the people? Or, shall we in a cool and dispassionate hour, consult with our sister states on the expediency of making alterations in the confederation. . . .

Abraham Granger declared himself to be opposed to sending delegates to the Convention; he conceived it would be disagreeable to his constituents; he thought the liberties of the people would be endangered by it—that the constitution of this state was already sufficient for every purpose, added to the articles of confederation, in which sufficient power was already delegated to Congress, and concluded by saying, that he imagined these things would have a tendency to produce a regal government in this country.

Hosea Humphry, on the same side with Mr. Granger, observed, that he thought it would be best to oppose the measure in the first instance—that if Connecticut should send, and the Convention should recommend to the states any alteration in the articles of confederation, and a majority of the states should comply with such recommendation and adopt the measures proposed by it, the majority would compel the minority to comply also, however opposed the latter might be to any change in the federal government; and he concluded by saying that he approved of the wisdom and policy of Rhode-Island, in refusing to send delegates to the Convention, and that the conduct of that state, in this particular, was worthy of imitation....

Jeremiah Wadsworth: ... It is alarming indeed when there is not any force in the foederal government, and when there are not wanting men who boldly declare that it would be better to go back to Great-Britain. It is said, Sir, there is not wanting at least one member of assembly who wishes we had been conquered by the British at any period of the war. Mr. [Daniel] Perkins objects to having any power to enforce the acts of the foederal government. If there is to be no power of coercion, there is to be no government; if his objections are serious they go to the destroying all government; for without power to enforce obedience there can be none....

No state has more reason to wish for an alteration of the articles of confederation than Connecticut. Fertile and well cultivated, we have large exports from the produce of our land, and we consume much foreign produce—the profits of importation go entirely to our neighbour states [New York and Massachusetts]; there is collected by them at least one hundred thousand dollars impost which we pay.... Capt. Granger fears arbitrary power and the destruction of the poor, and says we shall all become asses—This state may well be compared to the strong ass, couching down not only under two but twenty burthens, and they will finally crush us out of existence....

James Davenport: The determination of the present question may be important; it is certainly a serious time as it respects government; much has been said on the subject, but I cannot refrain from offering my sentiments upon it. The gentlemen opposed to sending delegates to the convention, say that the articles of confederation need not revision—that they are fully adequate to the purposes for which they were intended; this amounts to a declaration that we want no continental government, for what power has congress now? they have it is true the power of demanding money, but have they the power of collecting it? The conduct of this house in treating with neglect, if not with contempt, their requisitions, determines that they have not.

A Revolution in Favor of Government: The Virginia Plan, 29 May 1787

The Constitutional Convention was scheduled to meet in Philadelphia on May 14. It was a time of crisis. George Washington wrote Thomas Jefferson that "the situation of the general government, if it can be called a government, is shaken to its foundation, and liable to be overturned by every blast. In a word, it is at an end; and, unless a remedy is soon applied, anarchy and confusion will inevitably ensue." *People who shared Washington's view (and not all did), looked anxiously to the Convention.* George Mason, a Virginia delegate, wrote to his son that "The expectations and hopes of all the Union centre in this Convention. God grant that we may be able to concert effectual means of preserving our country from the evils which threaten us." *James Madison wrote Jefferson that* "The whole Community is big with expectation. And there can be no doubt but that the result will in some way or other have a powerful effect on our destiny."

But when May 14 arrived, only two states were represented, not enough to begin. By May 17, however, the entire Virginia delegation was present in Philadelphia, and the delegates met in caucus every day for two or three hours. In these caucuses the delegation agreed upon a set of resolutions based on James Madison's ideas. These resolutions, which have come to be called the Virginia Plan, marked a revolution in favor of government.

Finally, on Friday, May 25, seven states were represented in Convention—a quorum—and the Convention could proceed. The first order of business was unanimously to elect George Washington president of the Convention. A secretary was elected and a committee was appointed to prepare rules. The Convention then adjourned to Monday.

On May 28 and 29, the Convention adopted rules, including three critical ones: (1) each state delegation was to have one vote; (2) the proceedings of the Convention were to be secret, "in order to secure unbiassed discussion within doors, and to prevent misconceptions & misconstructions without," *according to Madison; and (3) the Convention could reconsider any matter.*

Once the rules were adopted, Governor Edmund Randolph of Virginia "opened the main business" *with the powerful and dramatic speech outlined below. He then presented to the Convention the Virginia Plan, fifteen resolutions that changed the nature of American government forever.*

The first resolution proposed "that the articles of Confederation ought to be so corrected & enlarged as to accomplish the objects proposed by their institution; namely, 'common defence, security of liberty and general welfare.'" The resolutions that followed not only revised the Articles of Confederation, but annihilated them and created an entirely new form of government.

The resolutions created a two-house Congress apportioned according to either population or the contributions of taxes. This Congress was to have veto power over any state law violating the federal Constitution. Congress had power "to call forth the force of the Union against any member of the Union failing to fulfill its duty." The legislature was to choose a national executive to execute the laws and exercise executive power. A national court system was established. The executive and some number from the judiciary were together to have veto power over acts of Congress. Every state was guaranteed a republican, or representative, government. State officers—legislative, executive, and judicial—were to be bound by oath to support the Constitution.

On May 30, the debate over the Virginia Plan began, and in essence, continued until the Constitution was completed on September 17, 1787. Various delegates took notes of the debates. Madison's notes are the best known and most complete. But notes were also taken by Alexander Hamilton, Rufus King, James McHenry, William Paterson, William Pierce, Robert Yates, and others.

CONVENTION DEBATES, 29 MAY 1787

(From James Madison's Notes)

Edmund Randolph of Virginia opened the main business in a long speech in which he pointed out the various defects of the federal system, the necessity of transforming it into a national efficient Government, and the extreme danger of delaying this great work, concluding with sundry propositions as the outlines of a proper form.

He expressed his regret, that it should fall to him, rather than those, who were of longer standing in life and political experience, to open the great subject of their mission. But, as the convention had originated from Virginia, and his colleagues supposed, that some proposition was expected from them, they had imposed this task on him.

He then commented on the difficulty of the crisis, and the necessity of preventing the fulfillment of the prophecies of the American downfall. He observed that in revising the foederal system we ought to inquire 1. into the properties, which such a government ought to possess, 2. the defects of the confederation, 3. the danger of our situation & 4. the remedy.

I. The character of such a government ought to secure 1. against foreign invasion: 2. against dissentions between members of the Union, or seditions in particular states: 3. to procure to the several States various blessings, of which an isolated situation was incapable: 4. to be able to defend itself against incroachment [by the states]: & 5. to be paramount to the state constitutions.

II. In speaking of the defects of the [articles of] confederation he professed a high respect for its authors, and considered them as having done all that patriots could do, in the then infancy of the science, of constitutions, & of confederacies,—when the inefficiency of requisitions was unknown—no commercial discord had arisen among any states—no rebellion had appeared as in Massachusetts—foreign debts had not become urgent—the havoc of paper money had not been foreseen—treaties had not been violated—and perhaps nothing better could be obtained from the jealousy of the states with regard to their sovereignty.

He then proceeded to enumerate the defects: 1. that the confederation produced no security against foreign invasion; congress not being permitted to prevent a war nor to support it by their own authority—Of this he cited many examples; most of which tended to shew, that they could not cause infractions of treaties or of the law of nations, to be punished: that particular states might by their conduct provoke war without controul; and that neither militia nor draughts, being fit for defence on such occasions, enlistments only could be successful, and these could not be executed without money.

2. that the foederal government could not check the quarrels between states, nor a rebellion in any [state], not having constitutional power Nor means to interpose according to the exigency:

3. that there were many advantages, which the U.S. might acquire, which were not attainable under the confederation—such as a productive impost—counteraction of the commercial regulations of other nations—pushing of commerce ad libitum—etc. etc.

4. that the foederal government could not defend itself against the incroachments from the states:

5. that it was not even paramount to the state constitutions, ratified as it was in many of the states [by the state legislatures, instead of by the people].

III. He next reviewed the danger of our situation [and] appealed to the sense of the best friends of the U.S.—the prospect of anarchy from the laxity of government every where; and to other considerations.

IV. He then proceeded to the remedy; the basis of which he said, must be the republican principle.

He concluded with an exhortation, not to suffer the present opportunity of establishing general peace, harmony, happiness and liberty in the U.S. to pass away unimproved.

(From James McHenry's Notes)

Having pointed out its defects, let us not be affraid to view with a steady eye the perils with which we are surrounded. Look at the public countenance from New Hampshire to Georgia. Are we not on the eve of war, which is only prevented by the hopes from this convention.

Our chief danger arises from the democratic parts of our [state] constitutions. It is a maxim which I hold incontrovertible, that the powers of government exercised by the people swallows up the other branches. None of the constitutions have provided sufficient checks against the democracy. The feeble Senate of Virginia is a phantom. Maryland has a more powerful senate, but the late distractions in that State, have discovered that it is not powerful enough. The check established in the constitution of New York and Massachusetts is yet a stronger barrier against democracy, but they all seem insufficient.

(From Robert Yates's Notes)

He closed these remarks with a set of resolutions, fifteen in number, which he proposed to the convention for their adoption, and as leading principles whereon to form a new government—He candidly confessed that they were not intended for a federal government—he meant a strong *consolidated* union, in which the idea of states should be nearly annihilated.

THE REVOLUTION PURSUED: A NATIONAL GOVERNMENT PROPOSED 30 MAY 1787

On Monday, May 29, 1787, Edmund Randolph had presented the Virginia Plan to the Constitutional Convention. The first resolution read as if the Virginia Plan were simply amendments to the Articles of Confederation. This was probably done in deference to the call of the Convention, which had spoken only of revising the Articles to make them adequate to the needs of the Union. In fact, though, the Virginia Plan annihilated the Articles of Confederation and served as the basis for a new Constitution.

On the first day of debate on the Virginia Plan, May 30, Gouverneur Morris of Pennsylvania pointed out that Randolph's first resolution was inadequate. Randolph then withdrew the first resolution and proposed three more in its place, truly stating the ambition of the Virginia Plan: the rejection of the Articles of Confederation and the creation of a national government. Some delegates objected that such a sweeping reform was beyond the authority of the Convention, and therefore the first two new resolutions were deferred, and debate proceeded on the third, "Resolved, That a national government ought to be established, consisting of a supreme judicial, legislative, and executive."

CONVENTION DEBATES, 30 MAY 1787

(From Robert Yates's Notes)

Convention met pursuant to adjournment.

The convention, pursuant to order, resolved itself into a committee of the whole—Mr. Gorham (a member from Massachusetts) appointed chairman.

Edmund Randolph of Virginia then moved his first resolve, to wit: "Resolved, that the articles of the confederation ought to be so corrected and enlarged, as to accomplish the objects proposed by their institution, namely, common defence, security of liberty, and general welfare."

Gouverneur Morris of Pennsylvania observed, that it was an unnecessary resolution, as the subsequent resolutions would not agree with it. It was then withdrawn by the proposer [Randolph], and in lieu thereof the following were proposed, to wit:

1. *Resolved,* That a union of the states, merely federal [a confederation], will not accomplish the objects proposed by the articles of the confederation, namely, common defence, security of liberty, and general welfare.

2. *Resolved,* That no treaty or treaties among any of the states as sovereign, will accomplish or secure their common defence, liberty or welfare.

3. *Resolved,* That a national government ought to be established, consisting of a supreme judicial, legislative and executive.

In considering the question on the first resolve, various modifications were proposed, when Mr. [Charles Cotesworth] Pinckney observed, at last, that if the convention agreed to it, it appeared to him that their business was at an end; for as the powers of the house in general were to revise the present confederation, and to alter or amend it as the case might require; to determine its insufficiency or incapability of amendment or improvement, must end in the dissolution of the powers [of the Convention].

This remark had its weight, and in consequence of it, the 1st and 2d resolve was dropt, and the question agitated on the third.

This last resolve had also its difficulties; the term *supreme* required explanation—It was asked whether it was intended to annihilate state governments? It was answered, only so far as the powers intended to be granted to the new government should clash with the states, when the latter was to yield.

(From James McHenry's Notes)

Edmund Randolph explains the intention of the 3d Resolution. Repeats the substance of his yesterdays observations. It is only meant to give the national government a power to defend and protect itself. To take therefore from the respective legislatures or States, no more sovereignty than is competent to this end....

Elbridge Gerry of Massachusetts: Does not rise to speak to the *merits* of the question before the Committee but to the *mode.*

A distinction has been made between a *federal* and *national* government. We ought not to determine that there is this distinction for if we do, it is questionable not only whether this convention can propose a government totally different or whether Congress itself would have a right to pass such a resolution as that before the house. The commission from Massachusetts empowers the deputies to proceed agreeably to the recommendation of Congress. This [is] the foundation of the convention. If we have a right to pass this resolution, we have a right to annihilate the confederation.

Proposes—In the opinion of this convention, provision should be made for the establishment of a foederal legislative, judiciary, and executive.

Gouverneur Morris: Not yet ripe for a decision, because men seem to have affixed different explanations to the terms before the house. 1. We are not now under a foederal government. 2. There is no such thing. A foederal government is that which has a right to compel every part to do its duty. The foederal government has no such compelling capacities, whether considered in their legislative, judicial or Executive qualities.

The States in their appointments, Congress in their recommendations, point directly to the establishment of a *supreme* government capable of "the common defence, security of liberty and general welfare."

Cannot conceive of a government in which there can exist two supremes [state and federal]. A federal agreement which each party may violate at pleasure cannot answer the purpose. One government better calculated to prevent wars or render them less expensive or bloody than many.

We had better take a supreme government now, than a despot twenty years hence—for come he must.

(From James Madison's Notes)

Gouverneur Morris explained the distinction between a *federal* and *national, supreme,* Government; the former being a mere compact resting on the good faith of the parties; the latter having a compleat and *compulsive* operation. He contended that in all communities there must be one supreme power, and one only.

On the question as moved by Mr. [Pierce] Butler on the third proposition it was resolved in Committee of the Whole that a national Government ought to be established consisting of a supreme Legislative, Executive, & Judiciary.

(From Robert Yates's Notes)

For the resolution—Massachusetts, Pennsylvania, Delaware, Virginia, North-Carolina, South-Carolina.

Against it—Connecticut, New-York divided, [New] Jersey and the other states unrepresented.

SHALL THIS NEW GOVERNMENT BE DEMOCRATIC?

On May 31 the Convention continued its consideration of the Virginia Plan, when it agreed "without debate or dissent" to the third resolution, "that the national Legislature ought to consist of two branches."

The Convention then took up the fourth resolution, "that the members of the first branch of the National Legislature ought to be elected by the people of the several States." This led to a profound discussion over how much democracy there should be in the new government. There was considerable disagreement, because of the recent experience of the state governments.

Ironically, the advocates for democracy included the patrician slaveholders George Mason and James Madison of Virginia and the aristocratic attorney James Wilson of Pennsylvania; the opponents were Elbridge Gerry of Massachusetts and Roger Sherman of Connecticut, from supposedly democratic New England. The Convention decided in favor of direct election of the House of Representatives by the people.

The Convention then turned to the second house of Congress. Who should elect the Senate—the people, the House of Representatives, or the state legislatures? Again, the question was how much influence should the people have? On May 31 the Convention could not agree and the question was postponed, but ultimately it was decided to leave the election of the Senate to the state legislatures. The Convention, therefore, tempered the democracy of the House of Representatives with the Senate.

CONVENTION DEBATES, MAY 31, 1787

(From James Madison's Notes)

Roger Sherman of Connecticut opposed the election [of the House of Representatives] by the people, insisting that it ought to be by the State Legislatures. The people he said, immediately should have as little to do as may be about the Government. They want [i.e., lack] information and are constantly liable to be misled.

Elbridge Gerry of Massachusetts. The evils we experience flow from the excess of democracy. The people do not want [i.e., lack] virtue; but are the dupes of pretended patriots. In Massachusetts it has been fully confirmed by experience that they are daily misled into the most baneful measures and opinions by the false reports circulated by designing men, and which no one on the spot can refute.... He had he said been too republican heretofore: he was still however republican, but had been taught by experience the danger of the levelling spirit.

George Mason of Virginia argued strongly for an election of the larger branch by the people. It was to be the grand depository of the democratic principle of the Government. It was, so to speak, to be our House of Commons—It ought to know & sympathise with every part of the community; and ought therefore to be taken not only from different parts of the whole republic, but also from different districts of the larger members of it, which had in several instances particularly in Virginia, different interests and views arising from difference of produce, of habits etc. He admitted that we had been too democratic but was afraid we should incautiously run into the opposite extreme. We ought to attend to the rights of every class of the people. He had often wondered at the indifference of the superior classes of society to this dictate of humanity & policy, considering that however affluent their circumstances, or elevated their situations, might be, the course of a few years, not only might but certainly would, distribute their posterity throughout the lowest classes of Society. Every selfish motive therefore, every family attachment, ought to recommend such a system of policy as would provide no less carefully for the rights—and happiness of the lowest than of the highest of orders of Citizens.

James Wilson of Pennsylvania contended strenuously for drawing the most numerous branch of the Legislature immediately from the people. He was for raising the federal pyramid to a considerable altitude, and for that reason wished to give it as broad a basis as possible. No government could long subsist without the confidence of the people. In a republican Government this confidence was peculiarly essential. He also thought it wrong to increase the weight of the State Legislatures by making them the electors of the national Legislature. All interference between the general and local Governments should be obviated as much as possible. On examination it would be found that the opposition of States to federal measures had proceeded much more from the Officers of the States, than from the people at large.

James Madison of Virginia considered the popular election of one branch of the national Legislature as essential to every plan of free Government. He observed that in some of the States one branch of the Legislature was composed of men already removed from the people by an intervening body of electors. . . . He was an advocate for the policy of refining the popular appointments by successive filtrations, but thought it might be pushed too far. He wished the expedient to be resorted to only in the appointment of the second branch of the Legislature, and in the Executive & judiciary branches of the Government. He thought too that the great fabric to be raised would be more stable and durable if it should rest on the solid foundation of the people themselves, than if it should stand merely on the pillars of the Legislatures.

Elbridge Gerry did not like the election by the people. The maxims taken from the British constitution were often fallacious when applied to our situation which was extremely different. Experience he said had shewn that the State Legislatures drawn immediately from the people did not always possess their confidence. He had no objection however to an election by the people if it were so qualified that men of honor & character might not be unwilling to be joined in the appointments. He seemed to think the people might nominate a certain number out of which the State legislatures should be bound to choose.

Pierce Butler of South Carolina thought an election by the people an impracticable mode.

On the question for an election of the first branch of the national Legislature by the people, Massachusetts ay, Connecticut divided, New York ay, New Jersey no, Pennsylvania ay, Delaware divided, Virginia ay, North Carolina ay, South Carolina ay. [Ayes—6; noes—2; divided—2.]

The Committee proceeded to Resolution 5, "that the second (or senatorial) branch of the National Legislature ought to be chosen by the first branch out of persons nominated by the State Legislatures."

Richard Dobbs Spaight of North Carolina contended that the 2d. branch ought to be chosen by the State Legislatures and moved an amendment to that effect.

Pierce Butler . . . called on Mr. Randolph the mover of the propositions, to explain the extent of his ideas, and particularly the number of members he meant to assign to this second branch.

Edmund Randolph of Virginia: . . . If he was to give an opinion as to the number of the second branch, he should say that it ought to be much smaller than that of the first; so small as to be exempt from the passionate proceedings to which numerous [i.e., large] assemblies are liable. He observed that the general object was to provide a cure for the evils under which the U.S. laboured; that in tracing these evils to their origin every man had found it in the turbulence and follies of democracy: that some check therefore was to be sought for against this tendency of our Governments: and that a good Senate seemed most likely to answer the purpose.

How Long Should Representatives and Senators Serve?

On May 31, the Constitutional Convention had agreed to create a two-house Congress, but it had not decided the terms of office.

Most state constitutions called for the annual election of representatives and senators. In Connecticut and Rhode Island, representatives were elected every six months; in South Carolina, every two years. In Maryland, senators were elected every five years.

The agreement over length of term was closely associated with the controversy over the degree of democracy in the new government.

Advocates for annual elections referred to English precedents, arguing that liberties were endangered when the British Septennial Act of 1717 replaced the Triennial Act of 1694. Those who favored less popular influence in the government wanted longer terms to insulate the representatives from their constituents.

Another issue raised in the debate on June 12 was the role of the convention. Should it recommend what was popular, or should it recommend what was right?

Should the convention follow the dictates of the perceived public opinion, or should it recommend the best form of government possible and attempt to change public opinion to accept the new constitution?

Convention Debates, 12 June 1787

(From James Madison's Notes)

On the House of Representatives

Roger Sherman and Oliver Ellsworth of Connecticut moved to fill the blank left in the 4th Resolution for the periods of electing the members of the first branch with the words "every year." Mr. Sherman observing that he did it in order to bring on some question.

John Rutledge of South Carolina proposed "every two years."

Daniel of St. Thomas Jenifer of Maryland proposed "every three years" observing that the too great frequency of elections rendered the people indifferent to them, and made the best men unwilling to engage in so precarious a service.

James Madison of Virginia seconded the motion for three years. Instability is one of the great vices of our republics, to be remedied. Three years will be necessary, in a Government so extensive, for members to form any knowledge of the various interests of the States to which they do not belong, and of which they can know but little from the situation and affairs of their own. One year will be almost consumed in preparing for and traveling to & from the seat of national business.

Elbridge Gerry of Massachusetts. The people of New England will never give up the point of annual elections. They know of the transition made in England from triennial to Septennial elections, and will consider such an innovation here as the prelude to a like usurpation. He considered annual Elections as the only defence of the people against tyranny. He was as much against a triennial House as against a hereditary Executive.

James Madison observed that if the opinions of the people were to be our guide, it would be difficult to say what course we ought to take. No member of the Convention could say what the opinions of his Constituents were at this time; much less could he say what they would think if possessed of the information & lights possessed by the members here; & still less what would be their way of thinking 6 or 12 months hence. We ought to consider what was right & necessary in itself for the attainment of a proper Government. A plan adjusted to this idea will recommend itself—The respectability of this convention will give weight to their recommendation of it. Experience will be constantly urging the adoption of it, and all the most enlightened & respectable citizens will be its advocates. Should we fall short of the necessary & proper point, this influential class of citizens will be turned against the plan, and little support in opposition to them can be gained to it from the unreflecting multitude.

Elbridge Gerry repeated his opinion that it was necessary to consider what the people would approve. This had been the policy of all Legislators. If the reasoning of Mr. Madison were just, and we supposed a limited Monarchy the best form in itself, we ought to recommend it, tho' the genius of the people was decidedly adverse to it, and having no hereditary distinctions among us, we were destitute of the essential materials for such an innovation.

On the question for triennial election of the 1st branch [Ayes—7; noes—4].

On the Senate

Richard Dobbs Spaight of North Carolina moved to fill the blank for the duration of the appointments to the 2d branch of the National Legislature with the words "7 years."

Roger Sherman thought 7 years too long. He grounded his opposition he said on the principle that if they did their duty well, they would be reelected. And if they acted amiss, an earlier opportunity should be allowed for getting rid of them. He preferred 5 years which would be between the terms of 1st branch & of the executive.

William Pierce of Georgia proposed 3 years. 7 years would raise an alarm. Great mischiefs had arisen in England from their septennial act which was reprobated by most of their patriotic Statesmen.

Edmund Randolph of Virginia was for the term of 7 years. The Democratic licentiousness of the State Legislatures proved the necessity of a firm Senate. The object of this 2d. branch is to controul the democratic branch of the National Legislature. If it be not a firm body, the other branch being more numerous, and coming immediately from the people, will overwhelm it. The Senate of Maryland constituted on like principles had been scarcely able to stem the popular torrent. No mischief can be apprehended, as the concurrence of the other branch, and in some measure, of the Executive, will in all cases be necessary. A firmness & independence may be the more necessary also in this branch, as it ought to guard the Constitution against encroachments of the Executive who will be apt to form combinations with the demagogues of the popular branch.

James Madison considered 7 years as a term by no means too long. What we wished was to give to the Government that stability which was every where called for, and which the enemies of the Republican form alleged to be inconsistent with its nature. He was not afraid of giving too much stability by the term of seven years. His fear was that the popular branch would still be too great an overmatch for it. It was to be much lamented that we had so little direct experience to guide us. . . . In the States where the Senates were chosen in the same manner as the other branches of the Legislature, and held their seats for 4 years, the institution was found to be no check whatever against the instabilities of the other branches. He conceived it to be of great importance that a stable & firm Government organized in the republican form should be held out to the people. If this be not done, and the people be left to judge of this species of Government by the operations of the defective systems under which they now live, it is much to be feared the time is not distant when, in universal disgust, they will renounce the blessing which they have purchased at so dear a rate, and be ready for any change that may be proposed to them.

On the question for "seven years," as the term for the 2d branch [Ayes—8; noes—1; divided—2].

A LAST-DITCH ATTEMPT TO AVOID A NATIONAL GOVERNMENT

On June 15, William Paterson of New Jersey presented to the Convention an alternative to the powerfully nationalist Virginia Plan. He proposed that the Articles of Confederation be "revised, corrected & enlarged."

Congress was to remain one house, and each state was to have one vote. But Congress was given the power to levy import duties or stamp taxes, to regulate commerce, and to collect requisitions itself if the states refused. Congress was to appoint an executive who would be removable if a majority of the states requested it. The executive was to appoint a supreme court, the members serving for life.

The plan provided that federal laws and treaties were to be the "supreme law of the respective States" and if any state refused to obey, force could be used to "compel an obedience."

After a one-day delay, so that Paterson and his allies "would be better prepared to explain & support" their proposal, the Convention debated both plans on June 16, 18, and 19. In addition to comparing the merits of the two plans, two other major issues were discussed: (1) did the Convention have the power to abandon the Articles of Confederation; and (2) should it propose something so radical, which might not be supported by the people.

Finally, on June 19 the Convention voted 7 to 3, with one state divided, in favor of the Virginia Plan. Only New York, New Jersey, and Delaware voted in favor of Paterson's Plan. Maryland was divided.

The Convention then continued debate on the amended Virginia Plan. The course of American government was set: a dramatically new Constitution would be proposed creating a powerful national government.

CONVENTION DEBATES, SATURDAY, 16 JUNE 1787

(From James Madison's Notes)

John Lansing of New York: . . . He grounded his preference of Mr. Paterson's plan, chiefly on two objections against that of Mr. Randolph (i.e., the Virginia Plan). 1. want of power in the Convention to discuss & propose it. 2. the improbability of its being adopted. He was decidedly of opinion that the power of the Convention was restrained to amendments of a federal nature, and having for their basis the Confederacy in being. The Act of Congress (calling the Convention), the tenor of the Acts of the States (authorizing delegates), the commissions produced by the several deputations all proved this. And this limitation of the power to an amendment of the Confederacy, marked the opinion of the States, that it was unnecessary & improper to go farther. He was sure that this was the case with his State. New York would never have concurred in sending deputies to the convention, if she had supposed the deliberations were to turn on a consolidation of the States, and a National Government. Was it probable that the States would adopt & ratify a scheme, which they had never authorized us to propose? and which so far exceeded what they regarded as sufficient? . . . The States will never feel a sufficient confidence in a general Government to give it a negative on their laws. The Scheme is itself totally novel. There is no parallel to it to be found. The authority of Congress is familiar to the people, and an augmentation of the powers of Congress will be readily approved by them.

William Paterson of New Jersey said as he had on a former occasion given his sentiments on the plan proposed by Mr. Randolph he would now avoiding repetition as much as possible give his reasons in favor of that proposed by himself. He preferred it because it accorded 1. with the powers of the Convention. 2. with the sentiments of the people. If the confederacy was radically wrong, let us return to our States, and obtain larger powers, not assume them of ourselves. I came here not to speak my own sentiments, but the sentiments of those who sent me. Our object is not such a Government as may be best in itself, but such a one as our Constituents have authorized us to prepare, and as they will approve. . . .

James Wilson of Pennsylvania: . . . With regard to the *power of the Convention*, he conceived himself authorized to *conclude nothing*, but to be at liberty to *propose any thing*. In this particular he felt himself perfectly indifferent to the two plans.

With *regard to the sentiments of the people,* he conceived it difficult to know precisely what they are. Those of the particular circle in which one moved, were commonly mistaken for the general voice. He could not persuade himself that the State Governments & sovereignties were so much the idols of the people, nor a National Government so obnoxious to them, as some supposed. Why should a National Government be unpopular? Has it less dignity? Will each Citizen enjoy under it less liberty or protection? Will a Citizen of *Delaware* be degraded by becoming a Citizen of the *United States?* Where do the people look at present for relief from the evils of which they complain? Is it from an internal reform of their Government? No. Sir, It is from the National Councils that relief is expected. For these reasons he did not fear, that the people would not follow us into a national Government and it will be a further recommendation of Mr. Randolph's plan that it is to be submitted to *them* (i.e., the people in conventions) and not to the *Legislatures,* for ratification. . . .

Charles Cotesworth Pinckney of South Carolina: The whole comes to this, as he conceived. Give New Jersey an equal vote, and she will dismiss her scruples, and concur in the National system. He thought the Convention authorized to go any length in recommending, which they found necessary to remedy the evils which produced this Convention.

Edmund Randolph of Virginia was not scrupulous on the point of power. When the salvation of the Republic was at stake, it would be treason to our trust, not to propose what we found necessary. He painted in strong colours, the imbecility of the existing confederacy, & the danger of delaying a substantial reform. . . . There are certainly reasons of a peculiar nature where the ordinary cautions must be dispensed with; and this is certainly one of them. He would not as far as depended on him leave any thing that seemed necessary, undone. The present moment is favorable, and is probably the last that will offer.

The true question is whether we shall adhere to the federal plan or introduce the national plan. The insufficiency of the former has been fully displayed by the trial already made. . . . A National Government alone, properly constituted, will answer the purpose; and he begged it to be considered that the present is the last moment for establishing one. After this select experiment (i.e., the Convention), the people will yield to despair.

ALEXANDER HAMILTON SKETCHES A PLAN OF GOVERNMENT

Alexander Hamilton had said little in the Constitutional Convention during the first weeks of debate. The New York delegation was balanced 2 to 1 against Hamilton's strongly nationalist ideas.

Finally, on June 18, 1787, during the debate over the Virginia and New Jersey Plans, Hamilton delivered a lengthy, impassioned speech in which he expressed dissatisfaction with both plans, particularly the latter.

Hamilton submitted his thoughts not in the form of a plan of government, but as a sketch, to illustrate the kinds of amendments he would propose to the Virginia Plan.

He proposed a two-house legislature. The Assembly would be elected by the people every three years; the Senate would be elected for life. The Senate and a national Governor, also with a lifetime term, would both be chosen by electors selected by the people. The Governor would have an absolute veto over acts passed by the legislature and would have the sole power to appoint the heads of the departments of Finance, War, and Foreign Affairs. Other federal officers would be nominated by the Governor and confirmed by the Senate. The Senate would have the sole power to declare war, while the Governor would direct the war once declared or begun. All military forces—the army and navy as well as "the Militia of all the States"—would "be under the sole and exclusive direction of the United States."

The judges of the supreme court were to hold their offices for life, and the legislature could appoint inferior courts. The governors of the states would be appointed by the national government and could veto state laws. All state laws violating the Constitution were declared void.

The Convention delegates admired Hamilton's brilliance and candor. But as Connecticut delegate William Samuel Johnson wrote, though the "gentleman from New York . . . has been praised by everybody, he has been supported by none."

Convention Debates, 18 June 1787

(From James Madison's Notes)

Alexander Hamilton: In his private opinion he had no scruple in declaring, supported as he was by the opinions of so many of the wise & good, that the British Government was the best in the world: and that he doubted much whether any thing short of it would do in America. He hoped Gentlemen of different opinions would bear with him in this, and begged them to recollect the change of opinion on this subject which had taken place and was still going on. It was once thought that the power of Congress was amply sufficient to secure the end of their institution. The error was now seen by every one. The members most tenacious of republicanism, he observed, were as loud as any in declaiming against the vices of democracy. This progress of the public mind led him to anticipate the time, when others as well as himself would join in the praise bestowed by Mr. Neckar [Jacques Necker, French Minister of Finance] on the British Constitution, namely, that it is the only Government in the world "which unites public strength with individual security."

In every community where industry is encouraged, there will be a division of it into the few & the many. Hence separate interests will arise. There will be debtors & Creditors etc. Give all power to the many, they will oppress the few. Give all power to the few they will oppress the many. Both therefore ought to have power, that each may defend itself against the other.... That we ought to go as far in order to attain stability and permanency, as republican principles will admit....

Having made these observations he would read to the Committee [of the Whole] a sketch of a plan which he should prefer to either of those under consideration. He was aware that it went beyond the ideas of most members. But will such a plan be adopted out of doors? In return he would ask will the people adopt the other plan? At present they will adopt neither. But he sees the Union dissolving or already dissolved—he sees evils operating in the States which must soon cure the people of their fondness for democracies—he sees that a great progress has been already made & is still going on in the public mind. He thinks therefore that the people will in time be unshackled from their prejudices; and whenever that happens, they will themselves not be satisfied at stopping where the plan of Mr. Randolph [the Virginia Plan] would place them, but be ready to go as far at least as he proposes. He did not mean to offer the paper he had sketched as a proposition to the Committee. It was meant only to give a more correct view of his ideas, and to suggest the amendments which he should probably propose to the plan of Mr. Randolph in the proper stages of its future discussion.

(From Robert Yates's Notes)

I am at a loss to know what must be done—I despair that a republican form of government can remove the difficulties. Whatever may be my opinion, I would hold it however unwise to change that form of government. I believe the British government forms the best model the world ever produced, and such has been its progress in the minds of the many, that this truth gradually gains ground. This government has for its object *public strength* and *individual security*. It is said with us to be unattainable. If it was once formed it would maintain itself. All communities divide themselves into the few and the many. The first are the rich and well born, the other the mass of the people. The voice of the people has been said to be the voice of God; and however generally this maxim has been quoted and believed, it is not true in fact. The people are turbulent and changing; they seldom judge or determine right. Give therefore to the first class a distinct permanent share in the government. They will check the unsteadiness of the second, and as they cannot receive any advantage by a change, they therefore will ever maintain good government. Can a democratic assembly, who annually revolve in the mass of the people, be supposed steadily to pursue the public good? Nothing but a permanent body can check the imprudence of democracy. Their turbulent and uncontrouling disposition requires checks. The senate of New-York, although chosen for four years, we have found to be inefficient. Will, on the Virginia plan, a continuance of seven years do it? It is admitted that you cannot have a good executive upon a democratic plan. See the excellency of the British executive [the King]—He is placed above temptation—He can have no distinct interests from the public welfare. Nothing short of such an executive can be efficient. . . .

I confess that this plan [his own] and that from Virginia are very remote from the idea of the people. Perhaps the Jersey plan is nearest their expectation. But the people are gradually ripening in their opinions of government—they begin to be tired of an excess of democracy—and what even is the Virginia plan, but *pork still, with a little change of the sauce.*

The Continuing Newspaper Debate

While the Constitutional Convention met in secret session throughout the summer of 1787, much speculation, both public and private, occurred over the outcome. Warnings were raised that there might be self-interested opposition to whatever the Convention might propose. Below are three newspaper items that expressed the belief that the fate of the country was in the hands of the Convention.

Although these three pieces were published in Philadelphia, they were all widely reprinted throughout the country by means of an informal news service in which printers exchanged their newspapers. For instance, the last item from the Independent Gazetteer *was reprinted 23 times in 10 states.*

Pennsylvania Gazette, 20 June 1787

It is agreed (says a Correspondent) on all hands, that our Convention are framing a wise and free government for us.—This government will be opposed *only* by our *Civil Officers* [i.e., state officeholders], who are afraid of new arrangements taking place, which shall jostle them out of office.—If these men are wise, they will be quiet, by which means they may succeed to their old offices—but if they are not, they may, probably, share the fate of the loyalists in the beginning of the late war. In the mean while, the Public are desired to beware of all essays and paragraphs that are opposed to a reform in our government, for they all must and will come from *Civil Officers,* or persons connected with them.

Civis to the Printers
Pennsylvania Packet, 25 June 1787

I observe . . . a correspondent says, "It is agreed on all hands, that our Convention are framing a wise and free government for us."—I wish with all my heart, that it may so turn out, to convince the world, that we are determined to support the dignity and consequence which we have assumed, and still maintain, among the nations of the earth— that of being an independent and separate empire of ourselves, without the assistance or interposition of any foreign power whatever; for to this shameful alternative we must undoubtedly be obliged to look, in case the result of this great and respectable assemblage of the Patriots of America should fail in answering the grand and necessary business for which they were called together. I am much in dread lest partial interests will be opposed to the general good—of this now tottering fabric—Liberty—Now is your time, O Saviours of your country! to repair, build up and compleat that noble edifice "where Freedom loves to dwell," and raise it from that ruinous heap of confusion, which now hangs over and threatens destruction to that once fair, once blest retreat. To exalt it to the clouds, so that angels may come down to view the solemnity, beauty and magnificence of Heaven-born Liberty—The eyes of thousands are now fixed on the Foederal Convention—expecting to see some great and laudable purposes adopted—calculated to remedy those evils which pervade almost every state in the union, and to put America on an equal footing with other free countries, who look on our rising greatness with a jealous eye, and are ever ready to snatch the opportunity of encreasing a general wreck, which must be the lot of all states and empires where government has not the power of protecting itself from the attacks of common enemies, or even check the malicious insinuations of treacherous and pretended friends to this country, who would rejoice at its downfall, and glory in the idea of our not being able to exist without a King.

It is the hope and desire of all good men, I believe, at this particular crisis in the affairs of America, that the distinguished characters both for integrity and ability, who compose the Convention, will strain every nerve to establish a permanent and well adapted system of republican government, or that which is most likely to promote the true interests and happiness of a people. With such a great and good patriot as Washington at their head, may we not expect the most salutary measures will be recommended to each state, to join unanimously in adopting the plans which our federal body shall think proper to agree to—even though it should affect the petty interests of one or two states in the union.—I say petty interests, because they are in fact so, when compared to the welfare of an extensive empire, which now is to be determined—whether or no we are to be ranked as slaves or free men, or left to struggle with darkness and obstinacy, in the paths of anarchy and confusion. God forbid it should be like the building of Babel; if the first attempt failed, the second may be crowned with success. "The wise counsels of a Franklin, and penetrating eye of your great Hero

[Washington], will give energy to every step you take in this business, and add vigour to the whole of your movements," said a writer in his address to that august Body. May guardian angels protect and endue them with wisdom to perfect the work they have undertaken, and raise to this country a name worthy to be written in letters of gold.

PHILADELPHIA INDEPENDENT GAZETTEER, 27 JUNE 1787

The present Federal Convention, says a correspondent, is happily composed of men who are qualified from education, experience and profession for the great business assigned to them.

The principles, the administration or executive duties of government will be pointed out by those gentlemen who have filled or who now fill the offices of first Magistrate in several of the states—while the commercial interests of America will be faithfully represented and ably explained by the mercantile part of the Convention. These gentlemen are assembled at a most fortunate period—in the midst of peace—with leisure to explore the perfections or defects of all the governments that ever existed—with passions uncontrouled by the resentments and prejudices kindled by the late war—and with a variety of experiments before them of the feebleness, tyranny, and licentiousness, of our American forms of government.

Under such circumstances, it will not be difficult for them to frame a Federal Constitution that will suit our country. The present Confederation may be compared to a *hut* or *tent*, accommodated to the emergencies of war—but it is now time to erect a castle of durable materials, with a tight roof and substantial bolts and bars to secure our persons and property from violence, and external injuries of all kinds. May this building rise like a pyramid upon the broad basis of the people! and may they have wisdom to see that if they delegate a little more power to their Rulers, the more liberty they will possess themselves, provided they take care to secure their *sovereignty* and *importance* by frequent elections, and rotation of offices.

The Convention Seeks the Assistance of God

On June 27, 1787, the Constitutional Convention took up the seventh and eighth resolutions of the revised Virginia Plan. These resolutions, which, according to John Rutledge of South Carolina, "involved the most fundamental points," dealt with the apportionment of representation in the House of Representatives and the Senate. Convention delegates from small states and delegates who favored a confederation rather than a national government opposed these resolutions because they abandoned the equal representation of the states under the Articles of Confederation. The resolutions proposed "some equitable ratio of representation" in proportion to population.

The deadlock over congressional representation threatened the Convention's very existence. Toward the end of the debate on June 28, delegates' nerves were frazzled. A general pessimism prevailed. At this critical juncture, Benjamin Franklin gave a conciliatory address that called upon the delegates to appeal to God for assistance. But, according to Franklin, "The Convention, except three or four persons, thought Prayers unnecessary." Although Franklin did not succeed in obtaining prayers at the Convention, he had, to a degree lessened the tension among delegates. It would not be the last time that the elder statesman tried to moderate differences among strong-willed delegates.

Convention Debates, 28 June 1787

(From James Madison's Notes)

Benjamin Franklin of Pennsylvania: Mr. President. The small progress we have made after 4 or five weeks close attendance & continual reasonings with each other—our different sentiments on almost every question, several of the last producing as many noes as ayes, is methinks a melancholy proof of the imperfection of the Human Understanding. We indeed seem to *feel* our own want of political wisdom, since we have been running about in search of it. We have gone back to ancient history for models of Government, and examined the different forms of those Republics which having been formed with the seeds of their own dissolution now no longer exist.

And we have viewed Modern States all round Europe, but find none of their Constitutions suitable to our circumstances.

In this situation of this Assembly, groping as it were in the dark to find political truth, and scarce able to distinguish it when presented to us, how has it happened, Sir, that we have not hitherto once thought of humbly applying to the Father of lights to illuminate our understandings? In the beginning of the Contest with Great Britain, when we were sensible of danger we had daily prayer in this room for the divine protection.—Our prayers, Sir, were heard, and they were graciously answered. All of us who were engaged in the struggle must have observed frequent instances of a Superintending providence in our favor. To that kind providence we owe this happy opportunity of consulting in peace on the means of establishing our future national felicity. And have we now forgotten that powerful friend? or do we imagine that we no longer need his assistance?

I have lived, Sir, a long time, and the longer I live, the more convincing proofs I see of this truth—*that GOD governs in the affairs of men*. And if a sparrow cannot fall to the ground without his notice, is it probable that an empire can rise without his aid? We have been assured, Sir, in the sacred writings, that "except the Lord build the House they labour in vain that build it." I firmly believe this; and I also believe that without his concurring aid we shall succeed in this political building no better than the Builders of Babel: We shall be divided by our little partial local interests; our projects will be confounded, and we ourselves shall become a reproach and bye word down to future ages. And what is worse, mankind may hereafter from this unfortunate instance, despair of establishing Governments by Human Wisdom and leave it to chance, war and conquest.

I therefore beg leave to move—that henceforth prayers imploring the assistance of Heaven, and its blessings on our deliberations, be held in this Assembly every morning before we proceed to business, and that one or more of the Clergy of this City be requested to officiate in that service—

Roger Sherman of Connecticut seconded the motion.

Alexander Hamilton of New York & several others expressed their apprehensions that however proper such a resolution might have been at the beginning of the convention, it might at this late day, 1. bring on it some disagreeable animadversions. & 2. lead the public to believe that the embarrassments and dissentions within the convention, had suggested this measure.

It was answered by **Doctor Franklin, Mr. Sherman & others,** that the past omission of a duty could not justify a further omission—that the rejection of such a proposition would expose the Convention to more unpleasant animadversions than the adoption of it: and that the alarm out of doors that might be excited for the state of things within would at least be as likely to do good as ill.

Hugh Williamson of North Carolina, observed that the true cause of the omission could not be mistaken. The Convention had no funds.

Edmund Randolph of Virginia proposed in order to give a favorable aspect to the measure, that a sermon be preached at the request of the convention on 4th of July, the anniversary of Independence,— & thenceforward prayers be used in the Convention every morning. Dr. Franklin seconded this motion. After several unsuccessful attempts for silently postponing the matter by adjourning, the adjournment was at length carried, without any vote on the motion.

Celebrating the Fourth of July 1787

July 4, 1776, was still fresh in the minds of the people in 1787. The celebration took on added significance because the Constitutional Convention was in session in Philadelphia, in the same room in which the Declaration of Independence had been adopted.

Speeches and banquet toasts all over America revealed a concern for the condition of the country. There was a genuine fear that all of the bloodshed and sacrifice of the Revolution would have been in vain unless the Articles of Confederation were revised. Orators, often young lawyers eager to advance their careers, expressed the hope that the Constitutional Convention would strengthen the central government and save the Revolution from failure.

Two examples of July 4th orations are given below. The first is by David Daggett, a 23-year-old New Haven lawyer, who later was a member of the Connecticut legislature, the U.S. Senate, and the Connecticut Supreme Court.

The second oration was delivered by James Campbell, a law student who was elected to serve as secretary of the Pennsylvania state ratifying convention in November 1787. Campbell's speech was delivered at the Reformed Calvinist Church in Philadelphia and was attended by delegates to the Constitutional Convention. Both speeches were printed as pamphlets and were reprinted in the Philadelphia American Museum, *a magazine with a national circulation.*

David Dagget Oration, New Haven, 4 July 1787

... The whole nation is now languishing under all those evils which have originated in consequence of systems of wretched policy—flagrant acts of injustice, and an impoverishing war.—The whole political frame is convulsed and threatened, from external attacks, and its own natural imbecility, with an immediate dissolution.

The eyes of all Europe are fixed upon us.—Their writers and orators, who extolled our success, and predicted our future greatness, now laugh at our folly—burlesque our policy, and contemn our dishonesty. They respect us for what we have been—admire us for what we might be, but despise us for what we are. . . .

The days of 1775, we cannot recall.—We cannot inspire our citizens with that disinterested love of their country, which caused them to encounter imprisonment,—exile,—slavery and death.—If we appeal to heaven—the cries of the widow and orphan, whom we have wickedly robbed, have already entered there, and called for vengeance! Will not then the righteous Lord, who loveth righteousness, "laugh at our calamity, and mock when our fear cometh?"— Shall then some insinuating courtier, or some formidable desperado, blast the hopes of this young empire? Shall they here erect a tyranny or a despotism more to be dreaded than death, in her most hideous forms?

Was it for this, *Columbus* to explore this new world, surmounted every obstacle,—braved death, in ten thousand different shapes, and finally expired in reproach and contempt? Was it for this, our venerable ancestors left their native country, and in defiance of millions of savages, and in hazard of every earthly pleasure, in a desert wilderness, layed the foundation of this empire? Was it for this, the brave sons of Mars, made that memorable opposition to our assailants, at Lexington? Was it for this, the immortal *Washington* quitted the enchanting scenes of domestic felicity and by a series of military achievements, equal to those of any hero of ancient or modern days, rescued us from that destruction with which we were threatened? Was it for this, that the brave, the heroic *Montgomery*, nobly fell a martyr to liberty, before the walls of Quebec? Was it for this, that illustrious *Body of Sages*, at Philadelphia, in defiance of British menaces, declared us *Independent*, and nobly fixed their names to the declaration? Was it for this, we exulted in the reduction of Burgoyne [at Saratoga] and Cornwallis [at Yorktown], those signal victories, which prostrated the exalted hopes of our haughty foes? Was it for this, we saw thousands of our youth, the hopes of their parents and their country, boldly embrace death? Was it for this, we saw whole villages sacked, beautiful towns laid in ashes, and almost whole states depopulated? Was it for this, we waded through seas of blood, to establish ourselves in that peace, and independence which promised us lasting honor and immortal felicity? Was all this done, I say, were we thus elevated to a summit of glory, which was the envy of all the empires of the world, only that we might exhibit a more complete scene of wretchedness and misery, and finally sink deeper in infamy and contempt? Forbid it heaven! Forbid it, oh my country! . . .

We must consent to a change of government.—Whether this change shall be partial or general, is not for me to say.—A more energetic, a more coercive power than at present is felt, must be vested in some public body.—This matter is submitted to a convention of the states, now sitting at Philadelphia. The unanimity of the states, in choosing delegates to this convention, is a forcible argument of the full conviction that the people feel of the weakness of the present system.—This measure has justly exalted the hopes of every patriot.—A measure from which we have nothing to fear, but every thing to hope.—At their head, sits the illustrious WASHINGTON, in description of whose finished and complete character, language fails.—There is *Franklin,* whose penetrating mind, looks through all the works of nature.—There are *Gerry, Sherman, Morris, Clymer, Wilson, Read* and *Wythe,* who made a declaration of that independence which we this day celebrate, and whose fame is coeval with our national importance.—Why need I particularize any?—Such a band of venerable personages, baffle all description! . . .

There is the collected wisdom of the community.—There is virtue enough to incline them, and knowledge enough to direct them to adopt a system calculated to make us a happy people.

JAMES CAMPBELL ORATION, PHILADELPHIA, 4 JULY 1787

. . . Nor have the martyrs of freedom bled in vain. No, my fellow-citizens, from their ashes, enriched by their blood, the tree of liberty shall yet grow and flourish among us: Methinks I already see the stately fabric of a free and vigorous government rising out of the wisdom of the *Foederal Convention;* I behold order and contentment pervading every part of the United States; our forests falling before the hand of labour; our fields doubling their encrease, from the effects of well-directed industry; our villages enlivened by useful manufactures, and our cities thriving under foreign and domestic commerce: I behold millions of freemen, covering the shores of our rivers and lakes with all the arts and enjoyments of civilized life, and on the Anniversary of this Day, 1887, shouting forth the praises of the *Heroes* and *Patriots,* who, in 1776, secured and extended to them all their *Happiness.*

PENNSYLVANIA HERALD, 14 JULY 1787

The auspicious Fourth of July, which crowned the toils of America with freedom and sovereignty has been commemorated in every district of the continent, with the fullest demonstrations of joy and gratitude. The fond recollection of past dangers, the veneration due to the memory of those heroes who have fallen in the defence of liberty and honor, and the respect that accompanies the characters of those patriots who have survived the glorious contest, naturally impress the mind with sentiments of gratitude and exultation.

But when we look forward to the happiness, the power, and the dignity, which the event of that great day ought to communicate to our posterity; it becomes us, in the pride of our honest triumphs, to provide the means for perpetuating the blessings we enjoy, and to expect with zeal and confidence, from the Foederal Convention, a system of government adequate to the security and preservation of those rights, which were promulged by the ever-memorable Declaration of Independency.

Continuing Debate Over Representation

The bitter deadlock in the Convention between the large and small states over the issue of representation in Congress continued from June 27 to July 16, despite several attempts at compromise. On July 2 the Convention tied five states to five on the proposition that each state have one vote in the Senate. To resolve the impasse, the Convention appointed a "grand" committee—one member from each state—and then adjourned until Thursday, July 5.

On July 5 the grand committee reported its proposed compromise. The House of Representatives, which it had already been decided would be apportioned according to population and thus would be controlled by the large states, have the sole power to originate bills for raising and appropriating money. Such money bills could not be altered or amended by the Senate. On the other hand, to protect the small states, each state would be given an equal vote in the Senate. The compromise required that both propositions "shall be generally adopted."

The debate reported below was in response to this compromise proposal.

Convention Debates, 5 July 1787

(From James Madison's Notes)

James Madison of Virginia: He conceived that the Convention was reduced to the alternative of either departing from justice in order to conciliate the smaller States, and the minority of the people of the United States, or of displeasing these by justly gratifying the larger States and the majority of the people. He could not himself hesitate as to the option he ought to make. The Convention with justice & the majority of the people on their side, had nothing to fear. With injustice and the minority on their side they had every thing to fear. It was in vain to purchase concord in the Convention on terms which would perpetuate discord among their Constituents. The Convention ought to pursue a plan which would bear the test of examination, which would be espoused & supported by the enlightened and impartial part of America, & which they could themselves vindicate & urge. It should be considered that although at first many may judge of the system recommended, by their opinion of the Convention, yet finally all will judge of the Convention by the system. The merits of the system alone can finally & effectually obtain the public suffrage. He was not apprehensive that the people of the small States would obstinately refuse to accede to a Government founded on just principles, and promising them substantial protection. He could not suspect that Delaware would brave the consequences of seeking her fortunes apart from the other States, rather than submit to such a Government. . . . Harmony in the Convention was no doubt much to be desired. Satisfaction to all the States, in the first instance still more so. But if the principal States comprehending a majority of the people of the United States should concur in a just & judicious plan, he had the firmest hopes that all the other States would by degrees accede to it.

Pierce Butler of South Carolina said he could not let down his idea of the people of America so far as to believe they would from mere respect to the Convention adopt a plan evidently unjust. He did not consider the privilege concerning money bils as of any consequence. He urged that the 2d. branch [the Senate] ought to represent the States according to their property.

Gouverneur Morris of Pennsylvania thought the form as well as the matter of the Report objectionable. . . . He conceived the whole aspect of it to be wrong. He came here as a Representative of America; he flattered himself he came here in some degree as a Representative of the whole human race; for the whole human race will be affected by the proceedings of this Convention. He wished gentlemen to extend their views beyond the present moment of time; beyond the narrow limits of place from which they derive their political origin. If he were to believe some things which he had heard, he should suppose that we were assembled to truck and bargain for our particular States. He cannot descend to think that any gentlemen are really actuated by these views. We must look forward to the effects of what we do. These alone ought to guide us. Much has been said of the sentiments of the people. They were unknown. They could not be known. All that we can infer is that if the plan we recommend be reasonable & right; all who have reasonable minds and sound intentions will embrace it, notwithstanding what had been said by some Gentlemen. Let us suppose that the larger States shall agree; and that the smaller refuse: and let us trace the consequences. The opponents of the system in the smaller States will no doubt make a party, and a noise for a time, but the ties of interest, of kindred & of common habits which connect them with the other States will be too strong to be easily broken. In New Jersey particularly he was sure a great many would follow the sentiments of Pennsylvania & New York. This Country must be united. If persuasion does not unite it, the sword will. He begged that this consideration might have its due weight. The scenes of horror attending civil commotion cannot be described, and the conclusion of them will be worse than the term of their continuance. The stronger party will then make traitors of the weaker; and the Gallows & Halter will finish the work of the sword. How far foreign powers would be ready to take part in the confusions he would not say. Threats that they will be invited have it seems been thrown out. He drew the melancholy picture of foreign intrusions as exhibited in the History of Germany, and urged it as a standing lesson to other nations. He trusted that the Gentlemen who may have hazarded such expressions, did not entertain them till they reached their own lips. . . .

Gunning Bedford of Delaware: He found that what he had said as to the small States being taken by the hand, had been misunderstood; and he rose to explain. He did not mean that the small States would court the aid & interposition of foreign powers. He meant that they would not consider the federal compact as dissolved until it should be so by the acts of the large States. In this case the consequence of the breach of faith on their part, and the readiness of the small States to fulfill their engagements, would be that foreign nations having demands on this Country would find it their interest to take the small states by the hand, in order to do themselves justice. This was what he meant. But no man can foresee to what extremities the small States may be driven by oppression. He observed also in apology that some allowance ought to be made for the habits of his profession [i.e., he was a lawyer] in which warmth was natural & sometimes necessary. But is there not an apology in what was said by Mr. Gouverneur Morris that the sword is to unite: by Mr. Gorham [of Massachusetts] that Delaware must be annexed to Pennsylvania and New Jersey divided between Pennsylvania and New York. To hear such language without emotion, would be to renounce the feelings of a man and the duty of a citizen—

The Great Compromise Averts Disruption of the Convention

*F*or three weeks the Constitutional Convention debated the issue of representation in the two branches of Congress. The Convention easily decided that the House of Representatives should be apportioned among the states on the basis of population. On July 2 the Convention tied on a vote to give each state an equal vote in the Senate. Three days later a committee recommended that the representation in the House remain unchanged, that the states have an equal vote in the Senate, and that the House have the sole power to originate money bills with no amendments allowed from the Senate. In one of the most important votes in the Convention, this compromise between the large and small states was accepted on July 16.

Several large-state delegates were upset over the compromise. Governor Edmund Randolph of Virginia moved for a temporary adjournment so that the large states could caucus. Such a caucus met just prior to the Convention session on the morning of July 17, at which the large states were unable to agree on an alternative plan for representation.

Convention Debates, Monday, 16 July 1787

(From James Madison's Notes)

Edmund Randolph of Virginia. The vote of this morning (involving an equality of suffrage in 2d branch) had embarrassed the business extremely. All the powers given in the Report from the Committee of the whole [the revised Virginia Plan, adopted on June 13], were founded on the supposition that a Proportional representation was to prevail in both branches of the Legislature—When he came here this morning his purpose was to have offered some propositions that might if possible have united a great majority of votes, and particularly might provide against the danger suspected on the part of the smaller States, by enumerating the cases in which it might lie, and allowing an equality of votes in such cases. But finding from the preceding vote that they persist in demanding an equal vote in all cases, that they have succeeded in obtaining it, and that New York if present would probably be on the same side, he could not but think we were unprepared to discuss this subject further. It will probably be in vain to come to any final decision with a bare majority on either side. For these reasons he wished the Convention might adjourn, that the large States might consider the steps proper to be taken in the present solemn crisis of the business, and that the small States might also deliberate on the means of conciliation.

William Paterson of New Jersey thought with Mr. Randolph that it was high time for the Convention to adjourn that the rule of secrecy ought to be rescinded, and that our Constituents should be consulted. No conciliation could be admissible on the part of the smaller States on any other ground than that of an equality of votes in the 2d. branch. If Mr. Randolph would reduce to form his motion for an adjournment sine die [without setting a date for reconvening], he would second it with all his heart.

Charles Cotesworth Pinckney of South Carolina wished to know of Mr. Randolph whether he meant an adjournment sine die, or only an adjournment for the day. If the former was meant, it differed much from his idea. He could not think of going to South Carolina, and returning again to this place. Besides it was chimerical to suppose that the States if consulted would ever accord separately, and beforehand.

Edmund Randolph had never entertained an idea of an adjournment sine die; & was sorry that his meaning had been so readily & strangely misinterpreted. He had in view merely an adjournment till tomorrow in order that some conciliatory experiment might if possible be devised, and that in case the smaller States should continue to hold back, the larger might then take such measures, he would not say what, as might be necessary.

William Paterson seconded the adjournment till tomorrow, as an opportunity seemed to be wished by the larger States to deliberate further on conciliatory expedients.

On the question for adjourning till tomorrow, the States were equally divided. . . . So it was lost.

Jacob Broom of Delaware thought it his duty to declare his opinion against an adjournment sine die, as had been urged by Mr. Paterson. Such a measure he thought would be fatal. Something must be done by the Convention though it should be by a bare majority.

Elbridge Gerry of Massachusetts observed that Massachusetts was opposed to an adjournment, because they saw no new ground of compromise. But as it seemed to be the opinion of so many States that a trial should be made, the State would now concur in the adjournment.

John Rutledge of South Carolina could see no need of an adjournment because he could see no chance of a compromise. The little States were fixt. They had repeatedly & solemnly declared themselves to be so. All that the large States then had to do, was to decide whether they would yield or not. For his part he conceived that although we could not do what we thought best, in itself, we ought to do something. Had we not better keep the Government up a little longer, hoping that another Convention will supply our omissions, than abandon every thing to hazard. Our Constituents will be very little satisfied with us if we take the latter course.

Edmund Randolph & Rufus King of Massachusetts renewed the motion to adjourn till tomorrow.

On the question Massachusetts ay, Connecticut no, New Jersey ay, Pennsylvania ay, Delaware no, Maryland ay, Virginia ay, North Carolina ay, South Carolina ay, Georgia divided. [Ayes—7; noes—2; divided—1.] Adjourned.

On the morning following before the hour of the Convention a number of the members from the larger States, by common agreement met for the purpose of consulting on the proper steps to be taken in consequence of the vote in favor of an equal Representation in the 2d. branch, and the apparent inflexibility of the smaller States on that point—Several members from the latter States also attended. The time was wasted in vague conversation on the subject, without any specific proposition or agreement. It appeared indeed that the opinions of the members who disliked the equality of votes differed so much as to the importance of that point, and as to the policy of risking a failure of any general act of the Convention by inflexibly opposing it. Several of them supposing that no good Government could or would be built on that foundation, and that as a division of the Convention into two opinions was unavoidable it would be better that the side comprising the principal States, and a majority of the people of America, should propose a scheme of Government to the States, than that a scheme should be proposed on the other side, would have concurred in a firm opposition to the smaller States, and in a separate recommendation, if eventually necessary. Others seemed inclined to yield to the smaller States, and to concur in such an Act, however imperfect & exceptional, as might be agreed on by the Convention as a body, though decided by a bare majority of States and by a minority of the people of the United States. It is probable that the result of this consultation satisfied the smaller States that they had nothing to apprehend from a Union of the larger, in any plan whatever against the equality of votes in the 2d. branch.

The Presidency Debated

The Convention had great difficulty forming the executive branch. By June 13 the Convention had agreed that the executive was to consist of a single person, who would be elected by Congress for seven years and be ineligible for a second term. The executive was given a delicate role: to protect the people from the "Legislative tyranny" of Congress, while not evolving into a monarchy.

The debate over the best method of electing such an executive and the term of office occupied much of the Convention's time.

On July 17 the Convention again considered the executive branch and reaffirmed that the president should be elected by Congress. The delegates, however, struck out the ineligibility for a second term. Two days later, the Convention voted to have electors choose the president, who could serve more than one six-year term. During the remaining two months of the Convention, the delegates continued to change their minds on these issues.

Convention Debates, 19 July 1787

(From James Madison's Notes)

Luther Martin of Maryland moved to reinstate the words "to be ineligible a 2d. time."

Gouverneur Morris of Pennsylvania: It is necessary to take into one view all that relates to the establishment of the Executive; on the due formation of which must depend the efficacy & utility of the Union among the present and future States. It has been a maxim in political Science that Republican Government is not adapted to a large extent of Country, because the energy of the Executive Magistracy can not reach the extreme parts of it. Our Country is an extensive one. We must either then renounce the blessings of the Union, or provide an Executive with sufficient vigor to pervade every part of it. This subject was of so much importance that he hoped to be indulged in an extensive view of it. One great object of the Executive is to controul the Legislature. The Legislature will continually seek to aggrandize & perpetuate themselves; and will seize those critical moments produced by war, invasion or convulsion for that purpose. It is necessary then that the Executive Magistrate should be the guardian of the people, even of the lower classes, against Legislative tyranny, against the Great & the wealthy who in the course of things will necessarily compose—the Legislative body. Wealth tends to corrupt the mind & to nourish its love of power, and to stimulate it to oppression. History proves this to be the spirit of the opulent.... The Executive therefore ought to be so constituted as to be the great protector of the Mass of the people.... If he is to be the Guardian of the people let him be appointed by the people.... These were the general ideas which occurred to him on the subject, and which led him to wish & move that the whole constitution of the Executive might undergo reconsideration....

Rufus King of Massachusetts did not like the ineligibility. He thought there was great force in the remark of Mr. [Roger] Sherman, that he who has proved himself to be most fit for an Office, ought not to be excluded by the constitution from holding it. He would therefore prefer any other reasonable plan that could be substituted. He was much disposed to think that in such cases the people at large would chuse wisely. There was indeed some difficulty arising from the improbability of a general concurrence of the people in favor of any one man. On the whole he was of opinion that an appointment by electors chosen by the people for the purpose, would be liable to fewest objections.

William Paterson's [of New Jersey] ideas nearly coincided he said with those of Mr. King. He proposed that the Executive should be appointed by Electors to be chosen by the States in a ratio that would allow one elector to the smallest and three to the largest States.

James Wilson of Pennsylvania: It seems to be the unanimous sense that the Executive should not be appointed by the Legislature, unless he be rendered in-eligible a 2d. time: he perceived with pleasure that the idea was gaining ground, of an election mediately or immediately by the people.

James Madison of Virginia: If it be a fundamental principle of free Govemment that the Legislative, Executive & Judiciary powers should be *separately* exercised; it is equally so that they be *independently* exercised. There is the same & perhaps greater reason why the Executive should be independent of the Legislature, than why the Judiciary should: A coalition of the two former powers would be more immediately & certainly dangerous to public liberty. It is essential then that the appointment of the Executive should either be drawn from some source, or held by some tenure, that will give him a free agency with regard to the Legislature. This could not be if he was to be appointable from time to time by the Legislature. . . . He was disposed for these reasons to refer the appointment to some other Source. The people at large was in his opinion the fittest in itself. It would be as likely as any that could be devised to produce an Executive Magistrate of distinguished Character. The people generally could only know & vote for some Citizen whose merits had rendered him an object of general attention & esteem. There was one difficulty however of a serious nature attending an immediate choice by the people. The right of suffrage was much more diffusive in the Northern than the Southern States; and the latter could have no influence in the election on the score of the Negroes. The substitution of electors obviated this difficulty and seemed on the whole to be liable to the fewest objections.

Elbridge Gerry of Massachusetts: If the Executive is to be elected by the Legislature he certainly ought not to be re-eligible. This would make him absolutely dependent. He was against a popular election. The people are uninformed, and would be misled by a few designing men. He urged the expediency of an appointment of the Executive by Electors to be chosen by the State Executives. . . . The popular mode of electing the chief Magistrate would certainly be the worst of all. . . .

On the question on Mr. Gouverneur Morris motion to reconsider generally the Constitution of the Executive—Mass. ay, Connecticut ay, New Jersey ay & all the others ay.

Oliver Ellsworth of Connecticut moved to strike out the appointment by the National Legislature, and insert "to be chosen by electors appointed by the Legislatures of the States. . . ."

The question as moved by Mr. Ellsworth being divided, on the 1st part shall the National Executive be appointed by Electors? [Ayes—6; noes—3; divided—1.]

On 2d. part shall the Electors be chosen by State Legislatures? [Ayes—8; noes—2.]

Luther Martin moved that the Executive be ineligible a 2d. time. . . .

On the question shall he be ineligible a 2d. time? [Ayes—2; noes—8.]

Property Qualifications and Democracy

The Convention adjourned for ten days on 26 July to allow a Committee of Detail to consider what the Convention had done so far and to prepare a draft Constitution. But on this last day before adjournment, the Convention debated whether or not to place restrictions on who could serve in Congress.

This debate led to a consideration of the nature of republican government, the division of society into interest groups, and the question of who should be represented in Congress.

Convention Debates, 26 July 1787

(From James Madison's Notes)

George Mason of Virginia moved "that the Committee of detail be instructed to receive a clause requiring certain qualifications of landed property & citizenship of the United States in members of the Legislature [Congress], and disqualifiying persons having unsettled Accounts with or being indebted to the U.S. from being members of the National Legislature"—He observed that persons of the latter descriptions had frequently got into the State Legislatures, in order to promote laws that might shelter their delinquencies; and that this evil had crept into Congress if Report was to be regarded.

Charles Pinckney of South Carolina seconded the motion. . . .

Gouverneur Morris of Pennsylvania: If qualifications are proper, he would prefer them in the electors rather than the elected. . . .

Rufus King of Massachusetts observed that there might be great danger in requiring landed property as a qualification since it would exclude the monied interest, whose aids may be essential in particular emergencies to the public safety.

John Dickinson of Delaware was against any recital of qualifications in the Constitution. It was impossible to make a compleat one, and a partial one would by implication tie up the hands of the Legislature from supplying the omissions. The best defence lay in the freeholders who were to elect the Legislature. Whilst this Source should remain pure, the public interest would be safe. If it ever should be corrupt, no little expedients would repel the danger. He doubted the policy of interweaving into a Republican constitution a veneration for wealth. He had always understood that a veneration for poverty & virtue, were the objects of republican encouragement. It seemed improper that any man of merit should be subjected to disabilities in a Republic where merit was understood to form the great title to public trust, honors & rewards.

Elbridge Gerry of Massachusetts: If property be one object of Government, provisions for securing it can not be improper.

James Madison of Virginia: Moved to strike out the word *landed*, before the word, "qualifications." If the proposition should be agreed to he wished the Committee to be at liberty to report the best criterion they could devise. Landed possessions were no certain evidence of real wealth. Many enjoyed them to a great extent who were more in debt than they were worth. The unjust laws of the States had proceeded more from this class of men, than any others. It had often happened that men who had acquired landed property on credit, got into the Legislatures with a view of promoting an unjust protection against their Creditors. In the next place, if a small quantity of land should be made the standard, it would be no security.—if a large one, it would exclude the proper representatives of those classes of Citizens who were not landholders. It was politic as well as just that the interests & rights of every class should be duly represented & understood in the public Councils. It was a provision every where established that the Country should be divided into districts & representatives taken from each, in order that the Legislative Assembly might equally understand & sympathise, with the rights of the people in every part of the Community. It was not less proper that every class of Citizens should have an opportunity of making their rights be felt & understood in the public Councils. The three principle classes into which our citizens were divisible, were the landed, the commercial, & the manufacturing. The 2d. & 3rd. class, bear as yet a small proportion to the first. The proportion however will daily increase. We see in the populous Countries in Europe now, what we shall be hereafter. These classes understand much less of each others interests & affairs, than men of the same class inhabiting different districts. It is particularly requisite therefore that the interests of one or two of them should not be left entirely to the care, or the impartiality of the third.... For these reasons he wished if it were possible that some other criterion than the mere possession of land should be devised. He concurred with Mr. Gouverneur Morris in thinking that qualifications in the Electors would be much more effectual than in the elected....

Gouverneur Morris 2ded. the motion.

On the Question for striking out "landed" [Ayes—10; noes—1].

On Question on 1st. part of Col. Masons proposition as to qualification of property & citizenship as so amended [Ayes—8; noes—3].

The 2d. part, for disqualifying debtors, and persons having unsettled accounts, being under consideration,

Daniel Carroll of Maryland moved to strike out "having unsettled accounts"....

James Wilson of Pennsylvania was for striking them out. They put too much power in the hands of the Auditors, who might combine with rivals in delaying settlements in order to prolong the disqualifications of particular men. We should consider that we are providing a Constitution for future generations, and not merely for the peculiar circumstances of the moment....

On question for striking out "persons having unsettled accounts with the United States" [Ayes—9; noes—2]....

On the question for agreeing to the clause disqualifying public debtors [Ayes—2; noes—9]....

The proceedings since Monday last were referred unanimously to the Committee of detail, and the Convention then unanimously Adjourned till Monday, August 6, that the Committee of detail might have time to prepare & report the Constitution.

Should Only Land Holders Be Allowed to Vote?

The Convention reconvened on August 6 and received the report of the Committee of Detail in the form of a draft Constitution that was by now beginning to resemble the final form. The Convention then adjourned to the next day "to give the members an opportunity to consider the report."

On August 7 the Convention began debate on the report. In response to the debate of July 26 (see last week's issue), the draft Constitution provided that anyone qualified to vote for members of the lower house of the state legislature could vote for members of the House of Representatives. This provision gave rise to the first extended debate over the report, when Gouverneur Morris of Pennsylvania suggested that only "freeholders," owners of land, be allowed to vote. His motion was defeated, seven states to one.

Convention Debates, 7 August 1787

(From James Madison's Notes)

James Wilson of Pennsylvania: This part of the Report was well considered by the Committee, and he did not think it could be changed for the better. It was difficult to form any uniform rule of qualifications for all the States. Unnecessary innovations he thought too should be avoided. It would be very hard & disagreeable for the same persons, at the same time, to vote for representatives in the State Legislature and to be excluded from a vote for those in the National Legislature [Congress].

Gouverneur Morris of Pennsylvania: Such a hardship would be neither great nor novel. The people are accustomed to it and not dissatisfied with it, in several of the States. In some the qualifications are different for the choice of the Governor & Representatives; In others for different Houses of the Legislature. Another objection against the clause as it stands is that it makes the qualifications of the National Legislature depend on the will of the States, which he thought not proper.

Oliver Ellsworth of Connecticut thought the qualifications of the electors stood on the most proper footing. The right of suffrage was a tender point, and strongly guarded by most of the State Constitutions. The people will not readily subscribe to the National Constitution, if it should subject them to be disfranchised. The States are the best Judges of the circumstances and temper of their own people.

George Mason of Virginia: The force of habit is certainly not attended to by those gentlemen who wish for innovations on this point. Eight or nine States have extended the right of suffrage beyond the freeholders. What will the people there say, if they should be disfranchised. A power to alter the qualifications would be a dangerous power in the hands of the Legislature.

Pierce Butler of South Carolina: There is no right of which the people are more jealous than that of suffrage. Abridgements of it tend to the same revolution as in Holland, where they have at length thrown all power into the hands of the Senates, who fill up vacancies themselves, and form a rank aristocracy.

John Dickinson of Delaware had a very different idea of the tendency of vesting the right of suffrage in the freeholders of the Country. He considered them as the best guardians of liberty. And the restriction of the right to them as a necessary defence against the dangerous influence of those multitudes without property & without principle, with which our Country like all others, will in time abound. As to the unpopularity of the innovation it was in his opinion chemirical. The great mass of our Citizens is composed at this time of freeholders, and will be pleased with it. . . .

Gouverneur Morris: He had long learned not to be the dupe of words. The sound of Aristocracy therefore, had no effect on him. It was the thing, not the name, to which he was opposed, and one of his principal objections to the Constitution as it is now before us, is that it threatens this Country with an Aristocracy. The aristocracy will grow out of the House of Representatives. Give the votes to people who have no property, and they will sell them to the rich who will be able to buy them. We should not confine our attention to the present moment. The time is not distant when this Country will abound with mechanics [skilled craftmen] & manufacturers who will receive their bread from their employers. Will such men be the secure & faithful Guardians of liberty? Will they be the impregnable barrier against aristocracy?—He was as little duped by the association of the words, "taxation & Representation"—The man who does not give his vote freely is not represented. It is the man who dictates the vote [who is represented]. Children do not vote. Why? because they want [i.e., lack] prudence. Because they have no will of their own. The ignorant & the dependent can be as little trusted with the public interest. He did not conceive the difficulty of defining "freeholders" to be insuperable. Still less that the restriction could be unpopular. 9/10 of the people are at present freeholders and these will certainly be pleased with it. As to Merchants etc. if they have wealth & value the right they can acquire it. If not they don't deserve it.

George Mason: . . . The true idea in his opinion was that every man having evidence of attachment to & permanent common interest with the Society ought to share in all its rights & privileges. . . .

James Madison of Virginia: . . . Viewing the subject in its merits alone, the freeholders of the Country would be the safest depositories of Republican liberty. In future times a great majority of the people will not only be without landed, but any other sort of, property. These will either combine under the influence of their common situation; in which case, the rights of property & the public liberty will not be secure in their hands: or which is more probable, they will become the tools of opulence & ambition, in which case there will be equal danger on another side. . . .

Benjamin Franklin of Pennsylvania: It is of great consequence that we should not depress the virtue & public spirit of our common people; of which they displayed a great deal during the war, and which contributed principally to the favorable issue of it. . . .

John Francis Mercer of Maryland: The Constitution is objectionable in many points, but in none more than the present. He objected to the footing on which the qualification was put, but particularly to the *mode of election* by the people. The people can not know & judge of the characters of Candidates. The worse possible choice will be made. . . .

John Rutledge of South Carolina thought the idea of restraining the right of suffrage to the freeholders a very unadvised one. It would create division among the people & make enemies of all those who should be excluded.

On the question for striking out as moved by Mr. Gouverneur Morris, from the word "qualifications" to the end of the III article [Ayes—1; noes—7; divided—1].

News Reports of Convention Proceedings: 18th-Century Leaks

Although the Convention debates were held in secret, attentive newspaper readers would have had a very general idea of what was going on behind closed doors.

It will be recalled that the Convention convened on May 25, when it elected George Washington president and William Jackson secretary. It then adopted rules on May 28 and 29, including a secrecy rule. On May 29, Edmund Randolph introduced the Virginia Plan, which was then debated. On June 15, William Paterson of New Jersey introduced an alternative plan, and on June 18 Alexander Hamilton discussed his plan, though he did not formally present it to the Convention as a plan. On June 19 the Convention voted to reject the Paterson Plan and to use the amended Virginia Plan as the basis of its debates. On July 16 the Convention adopted the Great Compromise which apportioned representation among the states on the basis of population for the House of Representatives and on the basis of state equality for the Senate. This bitter controversy over representation threatened the dissolution of the Convention. On July 26 the Convention adjourned to allow a Committee of Detail, consisting of John Rutledge, Edmund Randolph, Nathaniel Gorham, Oliver Ellsworth, and James Wilson, to prepare a draft Constitution. The Committee reported on August 6, and debate resumed on the next day.

Pennsylvania Herald, 30 May 1787

On Friday last [May 25] the members of the foederal convention being assembled, chose his excellency George Washington for their president, and Mr. William Jackson for their secretary. . . . When indeed we consider the critical situation of the country, the anxiety with which every good citizen regards this *dernier resorte* [last resort], and the decisive effect it must have upon the peace and prosperity of America, though every thing should certainly be given to prudence and deliberation, not a moment can be spared to useless forms or unprofitable controversy.

PENNSYLVANIA HERALD, 2 JUNE 1787

Such circumspection and secrecy mark the proceedings of the foederal convention, that the members find it difficult to acquire the habit of communication even among themselves, and are so cautious in defeating the curiosity of the public, that all debate is suspended upon the entrance of their own inferior officers. Though we readily admit the propriety of excluding an indiscriminate attendance upon the discussions of this *deliberative* council, it is hoped that the privacy of their transactions will be an additional motive for dispatch, as the anxiety of the people must be necessarily encreased, by every appearance of mystery in conducting this important business.

PENNSYLVANIA HERALD, 13 JUNE 1787

Though the particular arguments, debates, and decisions that take place in the foederal Convention, are considered as matters of secrecy, we understand, in general, that there exists a very great diversity of opinion amongst the members, and that there has been already a wonderful display of wisdom, eloquence and patriotism. Some schemes, it is said, have been projected which preserve the form, but effectually destroy the spirit of a democracy; and others, more bold, which, regarding only the necessity of a strong executive power, have openly rejected even the appearance of a popular constitution. . . .

PHILADELPHIA INDEPENDENT GAZETTEER, 16 JUNE 1787

We hear that the greatest unanimity subsists in the councils of the Federal Convention. It is to be hoped, says a correspondent, the United States will discover as much wisdom in receiving from them a suitable form of government to preserve the liberties of the people, as they did fortitude in defending them against the arbitrary and wicked attempts of Great-Britain. Nothing but Union and a vigorous Continental Government can save us from destruction.

PENNSYLVANIA GAZETTE, 18 JULY 1787

So great is the unanimity, we hear, that prevails in the Convention, upon all great foederal subjects, that it has been proposed to call the room in which they assemble—UNANIMITY HALL—In the beginning of the late war, the citizens of America looked up to a foederal government, only, for safety and protection: They were then powerful and successful at home and abroad. As soon as they set up the idol of *State Sovereignty*, they forgot the rock from whence they derived their freedom and independence, and confined their allegiance and affections only to their state governments: And hence the distress, confusion, debts and disgrace of the United States. Calamities have at last opened their eyes, and they again turn them to a foederal government for safety and protection. May the enemies of the new Confederation, whether in Rhode-Island or elsewhere, whether secret or open, meet with the fate of the disaffected [Loyalists] in the late war.

CHARLESTON COLUMBIAN HERALD, 9 AUGUST 1787

Extract of a Letter from Philadelphia, July 21

"It is expected the Convention will adjourn in September: Their proceedings are still kept secret—Three plans have been submitted to their consideration; one presented by Colonel [Alexander] Hamilton; another by Mr. Patterson, late Chief Justice of Jersey, and a third by the late Governor of Virginia [Edmund Randolph]. They are now going on with the last, and I believe, with a few alterations, it will be pretty unanimously agreed to."

PHILADELPHIA INDEPENDENT GAZETTEER, 28 JULY 1787

Thursday last, the Honorable the CONVENTION of the United States adjourned till the first Monday in August next, after having appointed the following gentlemen to act as a Committee during their recess, viz.

Mr. *Gorham* of Massachusetts, Mr. *Elseworth* of Connecticut, Mr. *Wilson* of Pennsylvania, Mr. *Randolph* of Virginia, Mr. *Rutledge* of South-Carolina.

PENNSYLVANIA HERALD, 28 JULY 1787

The Foederal Convention having resolved upon the measures necessary to discharge their important trust, adjourned till Monday week, in order to give a committee, appointed for the purpose, time to arrange and systamize the materials which that honorable body have collected. The public curiosity will soon be gratified; and it is hoped, from the universal confidence reposed in this delegation, that the minds of the people throughout the United States are prepared to receive with respect, and to try with a fortitude and perseverance, the plan which will be offered to them by men distinguished for their wisdom and patriotism.

Pennsylvania Herald, 8 August 1787

On Monday last [August 6] the Foederal Convention met, after their short adjournment; and we are told, that they are now debating by paragraphs, the plan which is to be submitted to public consideration.

Slavery and the Constitution
Part I

On August 21–22 the Constitutional Convention debated Article VII, section 4 of the Committee of Detail's draft constitution, which prohibited the federal government from taxing or banning the importation of slaves. Luther Martin of Maryland and George Mason of Virginia proposed the deletion of the prohibition so that the new Congress could ban the nefarious traffic in human bondage.

Delegates from Georgia, South Carolina, and North Carolina vehemently supported the protection for the slave trade. If the protection were deleted, Georgia and South Carolina delegates predicted that their states would never adopt the constitution.

Northerners generally acquiesced with the demands of the Georgians and South Carolinians. They argued that slavery and the slave trade were not federal issues and that the Convention should avoid measures that would drive any states to oppose the Constitution.

Convention Debates, 21–22 August 1787

(From James Madison's Notes)

Luther Martin of Maryland proposed to vary the section 4 article VII so as to allow a prohibition [of] or tax on the importation of slaves. 1. As five slaves are to be counted as 3 free men in the apportionment of Representatives; such a clause would leave an encouragement to this traffic. 2. slaves weakened one part of the Union which the other parts were bound to protect: the privilege of importing them was therefore unreasonable—3. it was inconsistent with the principles of the revolution and dishonorable to the American character to have such a feature in the Constitution.

John Rutledge of South Carolina could not see how the importation of slaves could be encouraged by this section. He was not apprehensive of [slave] insurrections and would readily exempt the other States from the obligation to protect the Southern against them.— Religion & humanity had nothing to do with this question—Interest alone is the governing principle with Nations—The true question at present is whether the Southern States shall or shall not be parties to the Union. If the Northern States consult their interest, they will not oppose the increase of Slaves which will increase the commodoties of which they will become the carriers.

Oliver Ellsworth of Connecticut was for leaving the clause as it stands. Let every State import what it pleases. The morality or wisdom of slavery are considerations belonging to the States themselves—What enriches a part enriches the whole, and the States are the best judges of their particular interest. The old confederation had not meddled with this point, and he did not see any greater necessity for bringing it within the policy of the new one.

Charles Pinckney of South Carolina: South Carolina can never receive the plan if it prohibits the slave trade. In every proposed extension of the powers of Congress, that State has expressly & watchfully excepted that of meddling with the importation of negroes. If the States be all left at liberty on this subject, South Carolina may perhaps by degrees do of herself what is wished, as Virginia & Maryland have already done.

August 22

Roger Sherman of Connecticut was for leaving the clause as it stands. He disapproved of the slave trade: yet as the States were now possessed of the right to import slaves, as the public good did not require it to be taken from them, & as it was expedient to have as few objections as possible to the proposed scheme of Government, he thought it best to leave the matter as we find it. He observed that the abolition of slavery seemed to be going on in the U.S. & that the good sense of the several States would probably by degrees compleat it. He urged on the Convention the necessity of despatching its business.

George Mason of Virginia: This infernal traffic originated in the avarice of British Merchants. The British Government constantly checked the attempts of Virginia to put a stop to it. The present question concerns not the importing States alone but the whole Union. The evil of having slaves was experienced during the late war. Had slaves been treated as they might have been by the Enemy, they would have proved dangerous instruments in their hands. But their folly dealt by the slaves, as it did by the Tories. . . . Maryland & Virginia he said had already prohibited the importation of slaves expressly. North Carolina had done the same in substance. All this would be in vain if South Carolina & Georgia be at liberty to import. The Western people are already calling out for slaves for their new lands; and will fill that Country with slaves if they can be got through South Carolina & Georgia. Slavery discourages arts & manufactures. The poor despise labor when performed by slaves. They prevent the immigration of Whites, who really enrich & strengthen a Country. They produce the most pernicious effect on manners. Every master of slaves is born a petty tyrant. They bring the judgment of heaven on a Country. As nations can not be rewarded or punished in the next world they must be in this. By an inevitable chain of causes & effects providence punishes national sins, by national calamities. He lamented that some of our Eastern [New England] brethren had from a lust of gain embarked in this nefarious traffic. As to the States being in possession of the Right to import, this was the case with many other rights, now to be properly given up. He held it essential in every point of view, that the General Government should have power to prevent the increase of slavery.

Oliver Ellsworth: As he had never owned a slave could not judge of the effects of slavery on character. He said however that if it was to be considered in a moral light we ought to go farther and free those already in the Country.—As slaves also multiply so fast in Virginia & Maryland that it is cheaper to raise than import them, whilst in the sickly rice swamps foreign supplies are necessary, if we go no farther than is urged, we shall be unjust towards South Carolina & Georgia—Let us not intermeddle. As population increases; poor laborers will be so plenty as to render slaves useless. Slavery in time will not be a speck in our Country. Provision is already made in Connecticut for abolishing it. And the abolition has already taken place in Massachusetts. As to the danger of insurrections from foreign influence, that will become a motive to kind treatment of the slaves.

SLAVERY AND THE CONSTITUTION
PART II

The debate over the slave-trade provision continued on August 22 when it was finally sent to a committee. The committee reported two days later and the Convention debated the report on August 25. The final compromise provision prohibited the federal government from banning the slave trade before 1808. James Madison reprobated the Convention's twenty-year protection: "Twenty years will produce all the mischief that can be apprehended from the liberty to import slaves. So long a term will be more dishonorable to the National character than to say nothing about it in the Constitution." The measure passed, however, 7 states to 4; and it became an important issue in the debate over the ratification of the Constitution.

CONVENTION DEBATES, 22 AUGUST 1787

(From James Madison's Notes)

Charles Pinckney of South Carolina: If slavery be wrong, it is justified by the example of all the world. He cited the case of Greece, Rome & other antient States; the sanction given by France, England, Holland & other modern States. In all ages one half of mankind have been slaves. If the Southern States were let alone they will probably of themselves stop importations. He would himself as a Citizen of South Carolina vote for it. An attempt to take away the right as proposed will produce serious objections to the Constitution which he wished to see adopted.

Charles Cotesworth Pinckney of South Carolina declared it to be his firm opinion that if himself & all his colleagues were to sign the Constitution & use their personal influence, it would be of no avail towards obtaining the assent of their Constituents. South Carolina & Georgia cannot do without slaves. As to Virginia she will gain by stopping the importations. Her slaves will rise in value, & she has more than she wants. It would be unequal to require South Carolina & Georgia to confederate on such unequal terms. He said the Royal assent [to temporary prohibitions of the slave trade] before the Revolution had never been refused to South Carolina as to Virginia. He contended that the importation of slaves would be for the interest of the whole Union. The more slaves, the more produce to employ the carrying trade; The more consumption also, and the more of this, the more of revenue for the common treasury. He admitted it to be reasonable that slaves should be dutied [taxed] like other imports, but should consider a rejection of the clause as an exclusion of South Carolina from the Union.

Abraham Baldwin of Georgia had conceived national objects alone to be before the Convention, not such as like the present were of a local nature. Georgia was decided on this point. That State has always hitherto supposed a General Government to be the pursuit of the central States who wished to have a vortex for every thing—that her distance would preclude her from equal advantage—& that she could not prudently purchase it by yielding national powers. From this it might be understood in what light she would view an attempt to abridge one of her favorite prerogatives. If left to herself, she may probably put a stop to the evil. . . .

James Wilson of Pennsylvania observed that if South Carolina & Georgia were themselves disposed to get rid of the importation of slaves in a short time as had been suggested, they would never refuse to Unite because the importation might be prohibited. As the Section now stands all articles imported are to be taxed. Slaves alone are exempt. This is in fact a bounty on that article.

Elbridge Gerry of Massachusetts thought we had nothing to do with the conduct of the States as to Slaves, but ought to be careful not to give any sanction to it.

John Dickinson of Delaware considered it as inadmissible on every principle of honor & safety that the importation of slaves should be authorized to the States by the Constitution. The true question was whether the national happiness would be promoted or impeded by the importation, and this question ought to be left to the National Government not to the States particularly interested. If England & France permit slavery [in their colonies], slaves are at the same time excluded from both those Kingdoms. Greece and Rome were made unhappy by their slaves. He could not believe that the Southern States would refuse to confederate on the account apprehended; especially as the power was not likely to be immediately exercised by the General Government.

Hugh Williamson of North Carolina stated the law of North Carolina on the subject, to wit that it did not directly prohibit the importation of slaves. It imposed a duty of 5. on each slave imported from Africa, 10. on each from elsewhere, & 50 on each from a State licensing manumission [the freeing of slaves]. He thought the Southern States could not be members of the Union if the clause should be rejected, and that it was wrong to force any thing down, not absolutely necessary, and which any State must disagree to.

Rufus King of Massachusetts thought the subject should be considered in a political light only. If two States will not agree to the Constitution as stated on one side, he could affirm with equal belief on the other, that great & equal opposition would be experienced from the other States. He remarked on the exemption of slaves from duty whilst every other import was subjected to it, as an inequality that could not fail to strike the commercial sagacity of the Northern & middle States.

John Langdon of New Hampshire was strenuous for giving the power to the General Government. He could not with a good conscience leave it with the States who could then go on with the traffic, without being restrained by the opinions here given that they will themselves cease to import slaves.

Charles Cotesworth Pinckney thought himself bound to declare candidly that he did not think South Carolina would stop her importations of slaves in any short time, but only stop them occasionally as she now does. He moved to commit the clause that slaves might be made liable to an equal tax with other imports which he thought right & which would remove one difficulty that had been started.

John Rutledge of South Carolina: If the Convention thinks that North Carolina, South Carolina & Georgia will ever agree to the plan, unless their right to import slaves be untouched, the expectation is vain. The people of those States will never be such fools as to give up so important an interest. He was strenuous against striking out the Section, and seconded the motion of General Pinckney for a commitment.

Gouverneur Morris of Pennsylvania wished the whole subject to be committed.... These things may form a bargain among the Northern & Southern States....

Roger Sherman of Connecticut said it was better to let the Southern States import slaves than to part with them, if they made that a sine qua non. He was opposed to a tax on slaves imported as making the matter worse, because it implied they were *property*. He acknowledged that if the power of prohibiting the importation should be given to the General Government that it would be exercised. He thought it would be its duty to exercise the power. . . .

Edmund Randolph of Virginia was for committing in order that some middle ground might, if possible, be found. He could never agree to the clause as it stands. He would sooner risk the constitution—He dwelt on the dilemma to which the Convention was exposed. By agreeing to the clause, it would revolt the Quakers, the Methodists, and many others in the States having no slaves. On the other hand, two States might be lost to the Union. Let us then, he said, try the chance of a commitment.

On the question for committing: Ayes—7; noes—3; absent—1.

How Should the Constitution Be Ratified?

Even before the Convention met, James Madison wrote to Thomas Jefferson that any new form of government should be founded on "such a ratification by the people themselves of the several States as will render it clearly paramount to their Legislative authorities." Accordingly, the Virginia Plan proposed that the Constitution should be ratified by state conventions "expressly chosen by the people," not by the state legislatures.

Most nationalists favored this mode of ratification because it would invest the Constitution with a legitimacy derived from the people directly and because ratification would be harder, perhaps impossible, if it depended on the legislatures.

Opponents of the Constitution argued that the ratification should be accomplished by the state legislatures, which generally ratified the Articles of Confederation. Furthermore, the Articles provided that the state legislatures should unanimously adopt any amendments to the Articles before they would go into effect.

The Convention first approved of ratification by conventions on June 12 by a vote of six states to five, and Article XXI of the Committee of Detail report of Aug. 6 provided that "The ratification of the Conventions of __ States shall be sufficient for organizing this Constitution." Article XXII expressed "the opinion" of the Convention that the Constitution should be "submitted to a Convention chosen in each State under the recommendation of its Legislature, in order to receive the ratification of such Convention." This article eventually was adopted by the Convention as a separate resolution that accompanied the Constitution.

Article XXI eventually became Article VII of the Constitution, which provided "That Ratification of the Conventions of nine States, shall be sufficient for the Establishment of this Constitution between the States so ratifying the Same."

CONVENTION DEBATES, 31 AUGUST 1787

(From James Madison's Notes)

Gouverneur Morris of Pennsylvania moved to strike out "Conventions of the" after "ratifications," leaving the States to pursue their own modes of ratification.

Daniel Carroll of Maryland mentioned the mode of altering the Constitution of Maryland pointed out therein, and that no other mode could be pursued in that State.

Rufus King of Massachusetts thought that striking out "Conventions" as the requisite mode was equivalent to giving up the business altogether. Conventions alone, which will avoid all the obstacles from the complicated formation of the Legislatures, will succeed, and if not positively required by the plan, its enemies will oppose that mode.

Gouverneur Morris said he meant to facilitate the adoption of the plan, by leaving the modes approved by the several State Constitutions to be followed.

James Madison of Virginia considered it best to require Conventions. Among other reasons for this, that the powers given to the General Government being taken from the State Governments the Legislatures would be more disinclined than conventions composed in part at least of other men; and if disinclined, they could devise modes apparently promoting, but really thwarting the ratification. The difficulty in Maryland was no greater than in other States, where no mode of change was pointed out by the Constitution, and all officers were under oath to support it. The people were in fact, the fountain of all power, and by resorting to them, all difficulties were got over. They could alter constitutions as they pleased. It was a principle in the [state] Bills of rights, that first principles might be resorted to.

James McHenry of Maryland said that the officers of Government in Maryland were under oath to support the mode of alteration prescribed by the [state] Constitution.

Nathaniel Gorham of Massachusetts urged the expediency of "Conventions" also **Charles Pinckney of South Carolina,** for reasons, formerly urged on a discussion of this question.

Luther Martin of Maryland insisted on a reference to the State Legislatures. He urged the danger of commotions from a resort to the people & to first principles in which the Governments might be on one side & the people on the other. He was apprehensive of no such consequences however in Maryland, whether the Legislature or the people should be appealed to. Both of them would be generally against the Constitution. He repeated also the peculiarity in the Maryland Constitution.

Rufus King observed that the Constitution of Massachusetts was made unalterable till the year 1790, yet this was no difficulty with him. The State must have contemplated a recurrence to first principles before they sent deputies to this Convention. . . .

On Mr. Gouverneur Morris's motion to strike out "Conventions of the," it was negatived [Ayes—4; noes—6]. . . .

Article XXII taken up . . . **Gouverneur Morris & Charles Pinckney** then moved to amend the article so as to read:

"This Constitution shall be laid before the United States in Congress assembled; and it is the opinion of this Convention that it should afterwards be submitted to a Convention chosen in each State, in order to receive the ratification of such Convention: to which end the several Legislatures ought to provide for the calling Conventions within their respective States as speedily as circumstances will permit."

Gouverneur Morris said his object was to impress in stronger terms the necessity of calling Conventions in order to prevent enemies to the plan, from giving it the go by. When it first appears, with the sanction of this Convention, the people will be favorable to it. By degrees the State officers, & those interested in the State Governments will intrigue & turn the popular current against it.

Luther Martin believed Mr. Morris to be right, that after a while the people would be against it, but for a different reason from that alledged. He believed they would not ratify it unless hurried into it by surprize.

Elbridge Gerry of Massachusetts enlarged on the idea of Mr. L. Martin in which he concurred, represented the system as full of vices, and dwelt on the impropriety of destroying the existing Confederation without the unanimous Consent of the parties to it.

Question on Mr. Gouverneur Morris's and Mr. Pinckney's motion [Ayes—4; noes—7].

Elbridge Gerry moved to postpone Article XXII.

George Mason of Virginia seconded the motion, declaring that he would sooner chop off his right hand than put it to the Constitution as it now stands. He wished to see some points not yet decided brought to a decision, before being compelled to give a final opinion on this article. Should these points be improperly settled, his wish would then be to bring the whole subject before another general Convention.

Gouverneur Morris was ready for a postponement. He had long wished for another Convention, that will have the firmness to provide a vigorous Government, which we are afraid to do. . . .

On the question for postponing [Ayes—3; noes—8].

On the question on Article XXII [Ayes—10; noes—1].

Objections Create a Moment of Peculiar Solemnity

After meeting for almost four months, the delegates to the Constitutional Convention signed the proposed new form of government. Three of the delegates in attendance on September 17 refused to sign the Constitution: Elbridge Gerry of Massachusetts and Governor Edmund Randolph and George Mason, both of Virginia.

Gerry, Mason, and Randolph had contributed much to the formulation of the Constitution during the four months of debate. But, as the Convention neared its conclusion, each of them believed that too much power had been concentrated in the federal government created by the Constitution, while the rights of the people and the sovereignty of the states were not sufficiently protected. Thus, the three men strove for the inclusion of a bill of rights and the appointment of a second general convention that would consider amendments to the Constitution proposed by the state ratifying conventions. The Convention rejected these proposals, and Gerry, Mason, and Randolph left the Convention as opponents to the Constitution they had worked so hard to draft during that eventful summer in Philadelphia.

Convention Debates, 12 September 1787

(From James Madison's Notes)

George Mason of Virginia . . . wished the plan had been prefaced with a Bill of Rights, & would second a motion if made for the purpose. It would give great quiet to the people; and with the aid of the State declarations, a bill might be prepared in a few hours.

Elbridge Gerry of Massachusetts concurred in the idea & moved for a Committee to prepare a Bill of Rights. Col. Mason seconded the motion.

Roger Sherman of Connecticut was for securing the rights of the people where requisite. The State Declarations of Rights are not repealed by this Constitution; and being in force are sufficient. . . .

Colonel Mason. The Laws of the United States are to be paramount to State Bills of Rights.

On the question for a Committee to prepare a Bill of Rights [Ayes—0; Noes—10].

CONVENTION DEBATES, 14 SEPTEMBER 1787

Charles Pinckney of South Carolina & Mr. Gerry moved to insert a declaration "that the liberty of the Press should be inviolably observed."

Mr. Sherman. It is unnecessary. The power of Congress does not extend to the Press.

On the question [Ayes—4; Noes—7].

CONVENTION DEBATES, 15 SEPTEMBER 1787

Edmund Randolph of Virginia animadverting on the indefinite and dangerous power given by the Constitution to Congress, expressing the pain he felt at differing from the body of the Convention, on the close of the great & awful subject of their labours, and anxiously wishing for some accommodating expedient which would relieve him from his embarrassments, made a motion importing "that amendments to the plan might be offered by the State Conventions, which should be submitted to and finally decided on by another general Convention." Should this proposition be disregarded, it would he said be impossible for him to put his name to the instrument. Whether he should oppose it afterwards he would not then decide but he would not deprive himself of the freedom to do so in his own State, if that course should be prescribed by his final judgment—

George Mason seconded & followed Mr. Randolph in animadversions on the dangerous power and structure of the Government, concluding that it would end either in monarchy, or a tyrannical aristocracy; which, he was in doubt, but one or the other, he was sure. This Constitution had been formed without the knowledge or idea of the people. A second Convention will know more of the sense of the people, and be able to provide a system more consonant to it. It was improper to say to the people, take this or nothing. As the Constitution now stands, he could neither give it his support or vote in Virginia; and he could not sign here what he could not support there. With the expedient of another Convention as proposed, he could sign.

Charles Pinckney. These declarations from members so respectable at the close of this important scene, gave a peculiar solemnity to the present moment. He descanted on the consequences of calling forth the deliberations & amendments of the different States on the subject of Government at large. Nothing but confusion & contraiety could spring from the experiment. The States will never agree in their plans, and the Deputies to a second Convention coming together under the discordant impressions of their Constituents, will never agree. Conventions are serious things, and ought not to be repeated. He was not without objections as well as others to the plan. He objected to the power of a majority only of Congress over Commerce. But apprehending the danger of a general confusion, and an ultimate decision by the Sword, he should give the plan his support.

Elbridge Gerry. Stated the objections which determined him to withhold his name from the Constitution. 1. the duration and re-eligibity of the Senate. 2. the power of the House of Representatives to conceal their journals. 3. the power of Congress over the places of election. 4. the unlimited power of Congress over their own compensation. 5. Massachusetts has not a due Share of Representatives allotted to her. 6. 3/5 of the Blacks are to be represented as if they were freemen. 7. *Under* the power over commerce, monopolies may be established. 8. The vice president being made head of the Senate. He could however he said get over all these, if the rights of the Citizens were not rendered insecure 1. by the general power of the Legislature to make what laws they may please to call necessary and proper. 2. raise armies and money without limit. 3. to establish a tribunal without juries, which will be a Star-Chamber as to Civil cases. Under such a view of the Constitution, the best that could be done he conceived was to provide for a second general Convention.

On the question on the proposition of Mr. Randolph. All the States answered no.

On the question to agree to the Constitution as amended. All the States ay. The Constitution was then ordered to be engrossed.

And the House adjourned.

Benjamin Franklin Appeals for Unanimity in Signing the Constitution

On September 17 the final version of the Constitution was read by the Constitutional Convention. A few last minute changes were made and Benjamin Franklin rose with a speech in his hand. Because the 81-year-old delegate could not stand for any length of time, his fellow Pennsylvania delegate James Wilson read the speech, which called for unanimity among the delegates in signing the Constitution.

Edmund Randolph of Virginia responded to Franklin by apologizing for his refusal to sign the Constitution. Randolph wanted to keep his options open and would not necessarily oppose the Constitution in his home state.

Gouverneur Morris of Pennsylvania expressed the opinion of most delegates when he said that he too had objections to the Constitution, but, on the whole, he believed that it was "the best that was to be attained." Morris also defended the paragraph that Franklin had introduced to preface the signatures of the delegates: "Done in Convention, by the unanimous consent of the States present the 17th. of Sepr." This preface, actually drafted by Morris, "related only to the fact that the States present were unanimous."

Alexander Hamilton of New York also hoped all the delegates would sign. A few influential delegates by opposing or simply refusing to sign the Constitution could "do infinite mischief by kindling the latent sparks which lurk under an enthusiasm in favor of the Convention which may soon subside." No one's ideas were more opposed to the Constitution than his, but he saw little choice "between anarchy and Convulsion on one side, and the chance of good to be expected from the plan on the other."

Despite these appeals, Randolph, George Mason and Elbridge Gerry refused to sign the Constitution. While the last of the delegates signed, Franklin expressed his opinion that the sun on the back of President Washington's chair represented a rising sun, not a setting one. The Convention had finished its work; it was now up to the people to ratify the new form of government.

Convention Debates, 17 September 1787

(From James Madison's Notes)

The engrossed Constitution being read, Doctor Franklin rose with a speech in his hand, which he had reduced to writing for his own conveniency, and which Mr. [James] Wilson read in the words following.

Mr. President, I confess that there are several parts of this constitution which I do not at present approve, but I am not sure I shall never approve them: For having lived long, I have experienced many instances of being obliged by better information or fuller consideration, to change opinions even on important subjects, which I once thought right, but found to be otherwise. It is therefore that the older I grow, the more apt I am to doubt my own judgment, and to pay more respect to the judgment of others. Most men indeed as well as most sects in Religion, think themselves in possession of all truth, and that where ever others differ from them it is so far error. Steele, a Protestant in a Dedication tells the Pope, that the only difference between our Churches in their opinions of the certainty of their doctrines is, the Church of Rome is infallible and the Church of England is never in the wrong. But though many private persons think almost as highly of their own infallibility as of that of their sect, few express it so naturally as a certain french lady, who in a dispute with her sister, said "I don't know how it happens, Sister but I meet with no body but myself, that's always in the right..."

In these sentiments, Sir, I agree to this Constitution with all its faults, if they are such; because I think a general Government necessary for us, and there is no form of Government but what may be a blessing to the people if well administered, and believe farther that this is likely to be well administered for a course of years, and can only end in Despotism, as other forms have done before it, when the people shall become so corrupted as to need despotic Government, being incapable of any other. I doubt too whether any other Convention we can obtain may be able to make a better Constitution. For when you assemble a number of men to have the advantage of their joint wisdom, you inevitably assemble with those men, all their prejudices, their passions, their errors of opinion, their local interests, and their selfish views. From such an Assembly can a perfect production be expected? It therefore astonishes me, Sir, to find this system approaching so near to perfection as it does; and I think it will astonish our enemies, who are waiting with confidence to hear that our councils are confounded like those of the Builders of Babel; and that our States are on the point of separation, only to meet hereafter for the purpose of cutting one another's throats. Thus I consent, Sir, to this Constitution because I expect no better, and because I am not sure, that it is not the best. The opinions I have had of its errors, I sacrifice to the public good—I have never whispered a syllable of them abroad—Within these walls they were born, and here they shall die—If every one of us in returning to our Constituents were to report the objections he has had to it, and endeavor to gain partizans in support of them, we might prevent its being generally received, and thereby lose all the salutary effects & great advantages resulting naturally in our favor among foreign Nations as well as among ourselves, from our real or apparent unanimity. Much of the strength & efficiency of any Government in procuring and securing happiness to the people, depends on opinion, on the general opinion of the goodness of the Government, as well as of the wisdom and integrity of its Governors. I hope therefore that for our own sakes as a part of the people, and for the sake of posterity, we shall act heartily and unanimously in recommending this Constitution (if approved by Congress & confirmed by the Conventions) wherever our influence may extend, and turn our future thoughts & endeavors to the means of having it well administered.

On the whole, Sir, I cannot help expressing a wish that every member of the Convention who may still have objections to it, would with me, on this occasion doubt a little of his own infallibility—and to make manifest our unanimity, put his name to this instrument.—He then moved that the Constitution be signed by the members and offered the following as a convenient form viz. "Done in Convention, by the unanimous consent of *the States* present the 17th. of Sepr. &c—In Witness whereof we have hereunto subscribed our names."

This ambiguous form had been drawn up by Mr. Gouverneur Morris in order to gain the dissenting members, and put into the hands of Doctor Franklin that it might have the better chance of success. . . .

Whilst the last members were signing it [the Constitution] Doctor Franklin looking towards the President's Chair, at the back of which a rising sun happened to be painted, observed to a few members near him, that Painters had found it difficult to distinguish in their art a rising from a setting sun. I have, said he, often and often in the course of the Session, and the vicissitudes of my hopes and fears as to its issue, looked at that behind the President without being able to tell whether it was rising or setting: But now at length I have the happiness to know that it is a rising and not a setting Sun.

The Constitution being signed by all the Members except Mr. Randolph, Mr. Mason, and Mr. Gerry who declined giving it the sanction of their names, the Convention dissolved itself by an Adjournment sine die.

CHAPTER 3
The Public Debate Begins

INTRODUCTION

When the Constitutional Convention adjourned on September 17, 1787, its secretary, William Jackson, took the Constitution to the Confederation Congress in New York. Congress debated the Constitution on the 26th, 27th, and 28th. Federalists hoped that Congress would endorse the Constitution and send it to the states for their consideration. But almost immediately, opposition arose. Antifederalists believed that the Convention had gone beyond its instructions, which were to revise the Articles of Confederation, not to write an entirely new constitution. They believed that the government proposed gave far too much power to the federal government and took too much from the states. Antifederalists were concerned that so powerful a government did not have in it a bill of rights. Therefore, Richard Henry Lee of Virginia, proposed amendments to the Constitution, including a bill of rights.

Federalists in Congress argued against the Antifederalist positions and strenuously opposed any amendments being added by Congress. Federalists therefore gave up on the idea of sending the Constitution to the states with an expression of approval. A simple transmittal was agreed to. But the language made it seem as if Congress unanimously supported the Constitution.

The debate over the Constitution that took place throughout the United States was vigorous and contentious. It took place in private letters, newspapers, magazines, broadsheets, and books; in coffee houses, taverns, public meetings, churches, and campaign speeches. Most of the country's 100 newspapers were Federalist and printed almost exclusively Federalist essays and news reports. Only about a dozen newspapers were either Antifederalist or were neutral and printed both sides. Many essays, usually signed by pseudonyms, were printed on both sides. Probably the finest of the Federalist essays were those called *The Federalist* and signed by "Publius."

These essays were written by Alexander Hamilton, James Madison, and John Jay. Probably the finest Antifederalist essays were written by "Federal Farmer" and "Brutus" in New York, the authors of which are still unknown today. Another Antifederalist series written in Philadelphia under the pseudonym of "Centinel" by Samuel Bryan, was a harsh attack on the new Constitution. Luther Martin, a Maryland delegate to the Constitutional Convention and state attorney general, wrote a series of essays, "Genuine Information," which were excellent discussions of the events in the Convention and the Antifederalist opposition to the Constitution.

The first five state conventions to consider the Constitution voted overwhelmingly in favor of ratification. Vigorous opposition surfaced in the Pennsylvania Convention, where Federalists refused to allow the Antifederalists to place their objections on the Convention's journals. As a result, Pennsylvania Antifederalists published their "Dissent" in newspapers and as a broadside that circulated throughout the country. When the Convention debates were finally published in a volume in 1788, only Federalist speeches were included. Feelings in Pennsylvania remained intense, and in late December violence broke out between Federalists and Antifederalists in Carlisle.

The first states ratified the Constitution overwhelmingly and in rapid succession. Delaware ratified by a vote of 30–0 on December 7, 1787; Pennsylvania by a vote of 46–23 on December 12; New Jersey by a vote of 38–0 on December 18; Georgia by a vote of 26–0 on December 31; and Connecticut by a vote of 128–40 on January 9, 1788. But when the Massachusetts Convention met on January 9, things got much more difficult for Federalists.

The Newspaper Campaign in Favor of the Constitution Begins

Eighteenth-century newspaper printers exchanged their newspapers and reprinted many items that originated elsewhere. By means of this informal news service, an article that originated in a Philadelphia newspaper, might be reprinted in 40 or 50 newspapers throughout the United States.

In 1787 and 1788, during the debate over the ratification of the Constitution, there were about 95 newspapers being published. Generally, these were weeklies, though some newspapers were published two or three times a week, and occasionally, daily (excluding Sunday). Newspapers usually consisted of a single sheet folded once, making four pages. One page was often devoted to advertisements, one-half page to foreign news, and the remainder to news from around the country and to essays.

In the debate over the Constitution, most newspapers were Federalist, and most of the articles they printed supported the Constitution. Some refused to print anything opposed to the Constitution.

The eight paragraphs below were first printed together in the weekly Philadelphia Pennsylvania Gazette, *a Federalist newspaper. The* Gazette, *which had been owned by Benjamin Franklin from 1729 to 1766, was one of the oldest, and the most widely circulated, newspapers in America. The sixth paragraph, which praised George Washington, for instance, was reprinted 44 times from Vermont to Georgia. One of the other paragraphs was reprinted 37 times, and the others were all printed at least 20 times.*

Even before the Constitutional Convention adjourned, newspapers printed articles supporting a strengthened central government. Throughout the summer of 1787, newspapers regularly printed short articles praising the Constitutional Convention. Once the Constitution was revealed, most newspapers printed a preponderance of Federalist essays thus putting Antifederalists at a great disadvantage in the debate over the Constitution.

Pennsylvania Gazette, 26 September 1787

We hear from Delaware and New-Jersey, that the federal government has been received in each of those states with universal satisfaction. And it is said a majority of the citizens of New-York, where it was made public last Friday, expressed their hearty concurrence in it.

In the city and neighbourhood of Philadelphia, a petition to our Assembly to call a Convention in order to adopt this government, has been almost unanimously signed. The zeal of our citizens in favor of this excellent constitution has never been equalled, but by their zeal for liberty in the year 1776. Republicans, Constitutionalists, Friends [Quakers], etc. have all united in signing this petition. It is expected the new government will abolish party, and make us, once more, Members of one great political Family.

The inhabitants of the old world (says a correspondent) have long been looking at America, to see whether liberty and a republican form of government are worth contending for. The United States are at last about to try the experiment. They have formed a constitution, which has all the excellencies, without any of the defects, of the European governments. This constitution has been pronounced by able judges to be the *wisest, most free* and *most efficient,* of any form of government that ancient or modern times have produced. The gratitude of ages, only, can repay the enlightened and illustrious patriots, for the toil and time they have bestowed in framing it.

The nearer the American states can bring their constitutions to the form of the federal government, the more harmony they will always have with Congress, and the more happily will they be governed. Where this is not the case, comparisons will often be drawn to the disadvantage of the state government, which will lessen the principle of obligation and obedience in its citizens. For instance,—who will not prefer, by every art, a Court to try a cause, where the Judges are appointed during *good behaviour* [for life], to *one,* in which the Judges are appointed for *three, five* or *seven* years.

It is remarkable, that while the federal government lessens the power of the *states,* it increases the privileges of *individuals.* It holds out additional security for liberty, property and life, in no less than *five* different articles, which have no place in any one of the state constitutions. It moreover provides an effectual check to the African [slave] trade, in the course of one and twenty years. How honorable to America—to have been the first Christian power that has borne a testimony against a practice, that is alike disgraceful to religion, and repugnant to the true interests and happiness of Society.

GEORGE WASHINGTON, Esquire, has already been destined, by a thousand voices, to fill the place of the first President of the United

States, under the new frame of government. While the deliverers of a nation in other countries have hewn out a way to power with the sword, or seized upon it by statagems and fraud, our illustrious Hero peaceably retired to his farm after the war, from whence it is expected he will be called, by the suffrages of three millions of people, to govern that country by his wisdom (agreeably to fixed laws) which he had previously made free by his arms.—Can Europe boast of such a man?—or can the history of the world shew an instance of such a voluntary compact between the *Deliverer* and the *delivered* of any country, as will probably soon take place in the United States.

The Americans in Europe have been remarked for *loving* their country, and hating their *governments*. They will hereafter, we hope, be distinguished for loving their country, their government, and their rulers, with the same warm and supreme affection.

Danger from the influence of GREAT MEN (concludes our Correspondent) is only to be feared in single governments, where a trifling weight often turns the scale of power. In a compound government, such as that now recommended by the Convention, the talents, ambition, and even avarice of great men, are so balanced, restrained and opposed, that they can only be employed in promoting the good of the community. Like a mill-race, it will convey off waters which would otherwise produce freshes and destruction, in such a manner as only to produce fruitfulness, beauty and plenty in the adjacent county.

A Little 18th-Century Misinformation

The day after the Constitutional Convention adjourned, secretary William Jackson left Philadelphia for New York to present the Constitution to Congress. The Constitution was read in Congress on September 20, and the 26th was assigned for its consideration.

Federalists, those who supported the Constitution, hoped that Congress would send it to the states with a statement expressing Congress's support. But Antifederalists, those opposed to the Constitution, had other ideas.

As soon as debate began on the Constitution, Antifederalist Nathan Dane of Massachusetts moved that the resolution sending the Constitution to the states express the opinion that the Constitutional Convention had exceeded its powers because instead of revising the Articles of Confederation it had proposed a totally new form of government. Others in Congress argued that it was their duty to consider the Constitution paragraph-by-paragraph before sending it to the states. Federalists were especially alarmed when Richard Henry Lee of Virginia proposed that Congress recommend amendments to the Constitution, perhaps most importantly a bill of rights, which was not in the Constitution. Lee believed that it had "been found from universal experience, that the most express declarations and reservations are necessary to protect the just rights and liberty of mankind from the silent, powerful and ever active conspiracy of those who govern."

Federalists believed that it was very important to maintain the impression that both the Convention and Congress were unanimously in favor of the Constitution. Therefore, a compromise was reached. Congress would not express its support for the Constitution, or the opinion that the Convention violated its authority, while the record of the debate in Congress would be stricken from the journals. However, the resolution of Congress was worded very cleverly to create the impression that Congress unanimously supported the Constitution, when in fact Congress was unanimous merely in transmitting the Constitution to the states. George Washington approved of this subterfuge. He wrote, "This apparent unanimity will have its effect.—Not every one has opportunities to peep behind the curtain; and as the multitude often judge from externals, the appearance of unanimity in that body, on this occasion, will be of great importance."

In the letter below, Lee explains the events in Congress to George Mason of Virginia, one of the members of the Constitutional Convention who refused to sign the Constitution.

RICHARD HENRY LEE TO GEORGE MASON
NEW YORK, 1 OCTOBER 1787

I have waited until now to answer your favor of September 18th from Philadelphia, that I might inform you how the Convention plan of Government was entertained by Congress. Your prediction of what would happen in Congress was exactly verified—It was with us, as with you, this or nothing; & this urged with a most extreme intemperance—The greatness of the powers given & the multitude of Places to be created, produces a coalition of Monarchy men, Military Men, Aristocrats, and Drones whose noise, impudence & zeal exceeds all belief—Whilst the Commercial plunder of the South stimulates the rapacious Trader. In this state of things, the Patriot voice is raised in vain for such changes and securities as Reason and Experience prove to be necessary against the encroachments of power upon the indispensable rights of human nature. Upon due consideration of the Constitution under which we now Act, some of us were clearly of opinion that the 13th article of the Confederation precluded us from giving an opinion concerning a plan subversive of the present system and eventually forming a New Confederacy of Nine instead of 13 States. The contrary doctrine was asserted with great violence in expectation of the strong majority with which they might send it forward under terms of much approbation. Having procured an opinion that Congress was qualified to consider, to amend, to approve or disapprove—the next game was to determine that tho a right to amend existed, it would be highly inexpediant, to exercise that right, but merely to transmit it with respectful marks of approbation—In this state of things I availed myself of the Right to amend, & moved the Amendments copy of which I send herewith & called the ayes & nays to fix them on the journal—This greatly alarmed the Majority & vexed them extremely—for the plan is, to push the business on with great dispatch, & with as little opposition as possible; that it may be adopted before it has stood the test of Reflection & due examination—They found it most eligible at last to transmit it merely, without approving or disapproving; provided nothing but the transmission should appear on the Journal—This compromise was settled and they took the opportunity of inserting the word *Unanimously,* which applied only to simple transmission, hoping to have it mistaken for an Unanimous approbation of the thing—It states that Congress having Received the Constitution unanimously transmit it, etc.—It is certain that no Approbation was given—This constitution has a great many excellent Regulations in it and if it could be reasonably amended would be a fine System—As it is, I think 'tis past doubt, that if it should be established, either a tyranny will result from it, or it will be prevented by a Civil war—I am clearly of opinion with you that it should be sent back with amendments Reasonable and Assent to it with held until such amendments are admitted—You are well acquainted with Mr. Stone & others of influence in Maryland—I think it will be a great point to get Maryld. & Virginia to join in the plan of Amendments & return it with them—If you are in correspondence with our Chancelor Pendleton it will be of much use to furnish him with the objections, and if he approves our plan, his opinion will have great weight with our Convention, and I am told that his relation Judge Pendleton of South Carolina has decided weight in that State & that he is sensible & independent—How important will it be then to procure his union with our plan, which might probably be the case, if our Chancelor was to write largely & pressingly to him on the subject; that if possible it may be amended there also. It is certainly the most rash and violent proceeding in the world to cram thus suddenly into Men a business of such infinite Moment to the happiness of Millions. One of your letters will go by the Packet, and one by a Merchant Ship. My compliments if you please to Your Lady & to the young Ladies & Gentlemen

[P.S.] Suppose when the Assembly recommended a Convention to consider this new Constitution they were to use some words like these—It is earnestly recommended to the good people of Virginia to send their most wise & honest Men to this Convention that it may undergo the most intense consideration before a plan shall be without amendments adopted that admits of abuses being practised by which the best interests of this Country may be injured and Civil Liberty greatly endanger'd.—This might perhaps give a decided Tone to the business—

Please to send my Son Ludwell a Copy of the Amendments proposed by me to the new Constitution sent herewith—

The Beginning of the Onslaught

The essay below was written by Samuel Bryan of Pennsylvania under the pseudonym "Centinel." It was the first of eighteen essays in the series and was the first major attack on the Constitution. It was widely reprinted throughout the United States in newspapers, broadsides, or as part of anthologies.

"Centinel" makes many of the points other Antifederalists were to make later. He criticizes the use of great names, such as Washington and Franklin, to convince people to support the Constitution. He views the general welfare clause and the supremacy clause as vast and unlimited grants of power to Congress. He cites Montesquieu for his argument that a republic cannot exist over such a large territory as the United States. He condemns the fact that the Constitution does not contain a bill of rights protecting the basic liberties of a free people. And, finally, he rejects the argument that conditions are so desperate that the Constitution must be adopted immediately exactly as the Convention proposed it. He suggests that amendments be proposed for consideration by another Constitutional Convention.

Centinel No. I
Philadelphia Independent Gazetteer, 5 Oct. 1787

The wealthy and ambitious, who in every community think they have a right to lord it over their fellow creatures . . . flatter themselves that they have lulled all distrust and jealousy of their new plan, by gaining the concurrence of the two men [George Washington and Benjamin Franklin] in whom America has the highest confidence, and now triumphantly exult in the completion of their long meditated schemes of power and aggrandisement. I would be very far from insinuating that the two illustrious personages alluded to, have not the welfare of their country at heart; but that the unsuspecting goodness and zeal of the one, has been imposed on, in a subject of which he must be necessarily inexperienced, from his other arduous engagements; and that the weakness and indecision attendant on old age, has been practised on in the other. . . .

I shall now proceed to the examination of the proposed plan of government, and I trust, shall make it appear to the meanest capacity, that it has none of the essential requisites of a free government; that it is neither founded on those balancing restraining powers, recommended by Mr. [John] Adams and attempted in the British constitution, or possessed of that responsibility to its constituents, which, in my opinion, is the only effectual security for the liberties and happiness of the people; but on the contrary, that it is a most daring attempt to establish a despotic aristocracy among freemen, that the world has ever witnessed....

By section 8 of the first Article of the proposed plan of government, "the Congress are to have power to lay and collect taxes, duties, imposts and excises, to pay the debts and provide for the common defence and *general welfare* of the United States; but all duties, imposts and excises, shall be uniform throughout the United States." Now what can be more comprehensive than these words; not content by other sections of this plan, to grant all the great executive powers of a confederation, and a STANDING ARMY IN TIME OF PEACE, that grand engine of oppression, and moreover the absolute controul over the commerce of the United States and all external objects of revenue, such as unlimited imposts [duties] upon imports, etc.—they are to be vested with every species of *internal* taxation;—whatever taxes, duties and excises that they may deem requisite for the *general welfare*, may be imposed on the citizens of these states, levied by the officers of Congress, distributed through every district in America; and the collection would be enforced by the standing army, however grievous or improper they may be. The Congress may construe every purpose for which the state legislatures now lay taxes, to be for the *general welfare*, and thereby seize upon every object of revenue....

To put the omnipotency of Congress over the state government and judicatories out of all doubt, the 6th Article ordains that "this constitution and the laws of the United States which shall be made in pursuance thereof, and all treaties made, or which shall be made under the authority of the United States, shall be the *supreme law of the land*, and the judges in every state shall be bound thereby, any thing in the constitution or laws of any state to the contrary notwithstanding."

By these sections the all-prevailing power of taxation, and such extensive legislative and judicial powers are vested in the general government, as must in their operation, necessarily absorb the state legislatures and judicatories....

If the foregoing be a just comment—if the United States are to be melted down into one empire, it becomes you to consider, whether such a government, however constructed, would be eligible in so extended a territory; and whether it would be practicable, consistent with freedom? It is the opinion of the greatest writers, that a very extensive country cannot be governed on democratical principles, on any other plan, than a confederation of a number of small republics, possessing all the powers of internal government, but united in the management of their foreign and general concerns....

The framers of it [the Constitution]; actuated by the true spirit of such a government, which ever abominates and suppresses all free enquiry and discussion, have made no provision for the *liberty of the press*, that grand *palladium of freedom*, and *scourge of tyrants;* but observed a total silence on that head. It is the opinion of some great writers, that if the liberty of the press, by an institution of religion, or otherwise, could be rendered *sacred*, even in *Turkey*, that despotism would fly before it. And it is worthy of remark, that there is no declaration of personal rights, premised in most free constitutions; and that the trial by *jury* in *civil* cases is taken away....

But our situation is represented to be so *critically* dreadful, that, however reprehensible and exceptionable the proposed plan of government may be, there is no alternative, between the adoption of it and absolute ruin.—My fellow citizens, things are not at that crisis, it is the argument of tyrants; the present distracted state of Europe secures us from injury on that quarter, and as to domestic dissentions, we have not so much to fear from them, as to precipitate us into this form of government, without it is a safe and a proper one. For remember, of all *possible* evils, that of *despotism* is the *worst* and the most to be *dreaded*.

Besides, it cannot be supposed, that the first essay on so difficult a subject, is so well digested, as it ought to be;—if the proposed plan, after a mature deliberation, should meet the approbation of the respective States, the matter will end; but if it should be found to be fraught with dangers and inconveniencies, a future general Convention being in possession of the objections, will be the better enabled to plan a suitable government.

FEDERALISTS APPEAL TO SELF-INTEREST

One of the major Federalist themes in the debate over the Constitution, was that economic conditions in America were desperate and that the Constitution would restore prosperity.

Beginning in about 1785, the United States did experience a serious postwar depression. Many people were badly hurt. The farmers suffered from a collapse of commodity prices. Workers in the city, particularly those closely associated with shipping and shipbuilding, were injured by the severe depression in international commerce, partly because the United States had been unable to negotiate commercial treaties with the large European powers, especially Great Britain.

Federalist pieces, such as these, made pointed appeals to the working people and encouraged them to support the Constitution as the way to prosperity. Their appeal was generally successful. Federalists tended to be strongest in the urban areas and in agricultural regions tied to commercial farming for export.

The item from the Boston Gazette *was reprinted in 22 newspapers from New Hampshire to South Carolina. "Marcus" was reprinted 11 times from New Hampshire to Pennsylvania.*

BOSTON GAZETTE, 15 OCTOBER 1787

A correspondent observes,—there are no objections that may be raised against the *federal Constitution,* proposed by the late Honorable Convention, but what may be urged against any form of government whatever—and to reject this constitution, is little short of reverting to a state of nature, and every man's saying, *"to your tents O Israel."*

The *husbandman* [farmer], the *mechanick* [skilled craftsmen], the *sailor,* the *labourer,* the *trader,* the *merchant* and *the man of independent fortune* are all equally concerned in forwarding the American Constitution; for nothing short of a firm efficient continental government can dissipate the gloom that involves every man's present prospect, and give permanence to any plans of business or pursuit that can be laid.—The *husbandman* finds no encouragement to encrease his stock and produce, for he finds no vent for them—the *mechanick* stands idle half his time, or gets nothing for his work but truck—*half our sailors* are out of business—the *labourer* can find no employ—our *traders* involved in debt, while they can command nothing that is due to them—our *merchants* have been sinking money ever since the peace, for want of a commercial treaty, and the wealth of those few individuals who have large sums in cash by them, lies dormant for want of encouragement to loan it, under the security of just and equal laws.— All these evils will gradually subside, till they finally disappear, if we have but wisdom and firmness to speedily adopt the New Federal Constitution.

MARCUS
NEW YORK DAILY ADVERTISER, 15 OCTOBER 1787

The INTERESTS of this STATE

It is the Interest of the Merchants to encourage the New Constitution, because Commerce may then be a national object, and nations will form treaties with us.

It is the Interest of the Mechanics to join the mercantile interest; because it is not their interest to quarrel with their *bread and butter.*

It is the Interest of the Farmer, because the prosperity of Commerce gives vent to his produce, raises the value of his lands, and commercial duties will alleviate the burthen of his taxes.

It is the Interest of the Landholder, because thousands in Europe, with moderate fortunes, will migrate to this country, if an efficient Government gives them a prospect of tranquillity.

It is the Interest of all Gentlemen and Men of Property, because they will see many low Demagogues reduced to their *tools,* whose upstart dominion insults their feelings, and whose passion for popularity will dictate laws, which ruin the minority of the Creditors, and please the majority of Debtors.

It is the Interest of all Public Creditors, because they will see the credit of the States rise, and their Securities appreciate.

It is the Interest of the American Soldier, as the military profession will then be respectable, and the Floridas may be conquered in a campaign. The spoils of the West-Indies and South-America may enrich the next generation of Cincinnati [military officers].

It is the Interest of the Lawyers who have ability and genius, because the dignities in the Supreme Court will interest professional ambition, and create emulation which is not felt now. The dignities of the State Court, a Notary or the prosecutor of a bond will not aspire to, which has cheapened their value. Men also have enjoyed them without professional knowledge, and who are only versed in the abstract and learned science of the *plough*.

It is the Interest of the Clergy, as civil tumults excite every bad passion—the soul is neglected, and the Clergy starve.

It is the interest of all men, whose education has been liberal and extensive; because there will be a theatre for the display of talents, which have no influence in the State Assemblies [legislatures], where eloquence is treated with contempt, and reason overpowered by a *silent vote*.

It is *not* the Interest of those who enjoy State consequence, which would be lost in the Assemblies of the States. These insects and worms are only seen on their own dunghill. There are minds whose narrow vision can look over the concerns of a State or Town, but cannot extend their short vision to Continental concerns. Manners are essential in such a Government, and where the Union is represented, care should be take to impress the other States with respectable opinions, and if this becomes a principle they must remain at home, and not presume to these national dignities.

"A New Combatant" Joins the Fray

This is the first of sixteen Antifederalist essays addressed "To the Citizens of the State of New-York" and signed "Brutus" that were published in the New York Journal between October 1787 and April 1788. Unfortunately, we do not know who the author was.

The "Brutus" essays were not widely reprinted, but they were reasoned and persuasive. In the essay below "Brutus" asks the people to consider carefully before granting power to the new government, and he warns that if freedom is lost in America, the "only remaining assylum for liberty," posterity will condemn the people who lost it.

Perhaps "Brutus'" most important argument is based on the received wisdom of the time, Montesquieu's belief that a republic could only exist in a small territory. "Brutus" combines this idea with the assertion that the Constitution creates a single, national government to suggest that the new government is not appropriate for America. Three days after this essay appeared, James Madison wrote that "a new Combatant . . . with considerable address & plausibility, strikes at the foundation" of the new government. And Madison's first essay as The Federalist, *his famous No. 10, responded to the argument made here that a republic could only succeed in a small territory where "the manners, sentiments, and interests of the people should be similar."*

Brutus No. I
New York Journal, 18 October 1787

Perhaps this country never saw so critical a period in their political concerns. We have felt the feebleness of the ties by which these United-States are held together, and the want [lack] of sufficient energy in our present confederation, to manage, in some instances, our general concerns. Various expedients have been proposed to remedy these evils, but none have succeeded. At length a Convention of the states has been assembled, they have formed a constitution which will now, probably, be submitted to the people to ratify or reject, who are the fountain of all power, to whom alone it of right belongs to make or unmake constitutions, or forms of government, at their pleasure. The most important question that was ever proposed to your decision, or to the decision of any people under heaven, is before you, and you are to decide upon it by men of your own election, chosen specially for this purpose. If the constitution, offered to your acceptance, be a wise one, calculated to preserve the invaluable blessings of liberty, to secure the inestimable rights of mankind, and promote human happiness, then, if you accept it, you will lay a lasting foundation of happiness for millions yet unborn; generations to come will rise up and call you blessed. You may rejoice in the prospects of this vast extended continent becoming filled with freemen, who will assert the dignity of human nature. You may solace yourselves with the idea, that society, in this favoured land, will fast advance to the highest point of perfection; the human mind will expand in knowledge and virtue, and the golden age be, in some measure, realised. But if, on the other hand, this form of government contains principles that will lead to the subversion of liberty—if it tends to establish a despotism, or, what is worse, a tyrannic aristocracy; then, if you adopt it, this only remaining assylum for liberty will be shut up, and posterity will execrate your memory.

Momentous then is the question you have to determine, and you are called upon by every motive which should influence a noble and virtuous mind, to examine it well, and to make up a wise judgment. It is insisted, indeed, that this constitution must be received, be it ever so imperfect. If it has its defects, it is said, they can be best amended when they are experienced. But remember, when the people once part with power, they can seldom or never resume it again but by force. Many instances can be produced in which the people have voluntarily increased the powers of their rulers; but few, if any, in which rulers have willingly abridged their authority. This is a sufficient reason to induce you to be careful, in the first instance, how you deposit the powers of government.

With these few introductory remarks, I shall proceed to a consideration of this constitution.

The first question that presents itself on the subject is whether a confederated government be the best for the United States or not? Or in other words, whether the thirteen United States should be reduced to one great republic, governed by one legislature, and under the direction of one executive and judicial; or whether they should continue thirteen confederated republics, under the direction and controul of a supreme federal head for certain defined national purposes only?

This enquiry is important, because, although the government reported by the convention does not go to a perfect and entire consolidation, yet it approaches so near to it, that it must, if executed, certainly and infallibly terminate in it. . . .

It is here taken for granted, that all agree in this, that whatever government we adopt, it ought to be a free one; that it should be so framed as to secure the liberty of the citizens of America, and such an one as to admit of a full, fair, and equal representation of the people. The question then will be, whether a government thus constituted, and founded on such principles, is practicable, and can be exercised over the whole United States, reduced into one state?

If respect is to be paid to the opinion of the greatest and wisest men who have ever thought or wrote on the science of government, we shall be constrained to conclude, that a free republic cannot succeed over a country of such immense extent, containing such a number of inhabitants, and these encreasing in such rapid progression as that of the whole United States. . . .

In a republic, the manners, sentiments, and interests of the people should be similar. If this be not the case, there will be a constant clashing of opinions; and the representatives of one part will be continually striving against those of the other. This will retard the operations of government, and prevent such conclusions as will promote the public good. If we apply this remark to the condition of the United States, we shall be convinced that it forbids that we should be one government. The United States includes a variety of climates. The productions of the different parts of the union are very variant, and their interests, of consequence, diverse. Their manners and habits differ as much as their climates and productions; and their sentiments are by no means coincident. The laws and customs of the several states are, in many respects, very diverse, and in some opposite; each would be in favor of its own interests and customs, and, of consequence, a legislature, formed of representatives from the respective parts, would not only be too numerous to act with any care or decision, but would be composed of such heterogenous and discordant principles, as would constantly be contending with each other.

THE FEDERALIST ESSAY NUMBER 1

This is the first of eighty-five essays entitled The Federalist *and signed "Publius," which were written by Alexander Hamilton, John Jay, and James Madison from the fall of 1787 through the spring of 1788. The essays, which appeared in the New York City newspapers and were published as two volumes in 1788, were addressed to the "People of the State of New York." They were the finest statements of Federalist principles in the ratification debate and probably the best political essays ever written in America.*

In this essay, Hamilton makes the point that in deciding on whether or not to adopt the Constitution, America was deciding whether free people were capable of establishing good government based on reason.

"Publius" suggests that the debate will likely deteriorate into name calling, because too many special interests are endangered by the Constitution. He warns that those who advocate a stronger government will be charged with favoring despotism; it will be forgotten that "dangerous ambition more often lurks behind the specious mask of zeal for the rights of the people."

"Publius" admits that he favors the Constitution. He says that he will try to answer the serious objections to the Constitution, and he lists the broad categories he will discuss.

PUBLIUS: THE FEDERALIST NO. 1 (ALEXANDER HAMILTON) NEW YORK INDEPENDENT JOURNAL, 27 OCTOBER 1787

After an unequivocal experience of the inefficacy of the subsisting Foederal Government [under the Articles of Confederation], you are called upon to deliberate on a new Constitution for the United States of America. The subject speaks its own importance; comprehending in its consequences, nothing less than the existence of the UNION, the safety and welfare of the parts of which it is composed, the fate of an empire, in many respects, the most interesting in the world. It has been frequently remarked, that it seems to have been reserved to the people of this country, by their conduct and example, to decide the important question, whether societies of men are really capable or not, of establishing good government from reflection and choice, or whether they are forever destined to depend, for their political constitutions, on accident and force. If there be any truth in the remark, the crisis, at which we are arrived, may with propriety be regarded as the aera in which that decision is to be made; and a wrong election of the part we shall act, may, in this view, deserve to be considered as the general misfortune of mankind.

This idea will add the inducements of philanthropy to those of patriotism to heighten the sollicitude, which all considerate and good men must feel for the event. Happy will it be if our choice should be decided by a judicious estimate of our true interests, unperplexed and unbiassed by considerations not connected with the public good. But this is a thing more ardently to be wished, than seriously to be expected. The plan offered to our deliberations, affects too many particular interests, innovates upon too many local institutions, not to involve in its discussion a variety of objects foreign to its merits, and of views, passions and prejudices little favourable to the discovery of truth. . . .

A torrent of angry and malignant passions will be let loose. To judge from the conduct of the opposite parties, we shall be led to conclude, that they will mutually hope to evince the justness of their opinions, and to increase the number of their converts by the loudness of their declamations, and by the bitterness of their invectives. An enlightened zeal for the energy and efficiency of government will be stigmatised, as the off-spring of a temper fond of despotic power and hostile to the principles of liberty. An overscrupulous jealousy of danger to the rights of the people, which is more commonly the fault of the head than of the heart, will be represented as mere pretence and artifice; the bait for popularity at the expence of public good. It will be forgotten, on the one hand, that jealousy is the usual comcomitant of violent love, and that the noble enthusiasm of liberty is too apt to be infected with a spirit of narrow and illiberal distrust. On the other hand, it will be equally forgotten, that the vigour of government is essential to the security of liberty; that, in the contemplation of a sound and well informed judgment, their interest can never be separated; and that a dangerous ambition more often lurks behind the specious mask of zeal for the rights of the people, than under the forbidding appearance of zeal for the firmness and efficiency of government. History will teach us, that the former has been found a much more certain road to the introduction of despotism, than the latter, and that of those men who have overturned the liberties of republics the greatest number have begun their career, by paying an obsequious court to the people, commencing Demagogues and ending Tyrants.

In the course of the preceding observations I have had an eye, my Fellow Citizens, to putting you upon your guard against all attempts, from whatever quarter, to influence your decision in a matter of the utmost moment to your welfare by any impressions other than those which may result from the evidence of truth. You will, no doubt, at the same time, have collected from the general scope of them that they proceed from a source not unfriendly to the new Constitution. Yes, my Countrymen, I own to you, that, after having given it an attentive consideration, I am clearly of opinion, it is your interest to adopt it. I am convinced, that this is the safest course for your liberty, your dignity, and your happiness. I affect not reserves, which I do not feel. I will not amuse you with an appearance of deliberation, when I have decided. I frankly acknowledge to you my convictions, and I will freely lay before you the reasons on which they are founded. The consciousness of good intentions disdains ambiguity. I shall not however multiply professions on this head. My motives must remain in the depositary of my own breast: My arguments will be open to all, and may be judged of by all. They shall at least be offered in a spirit, which will not disgrace the cause of truth.

I propose in a series of papers to discuss the following interesting particulars—*The utility of the UNION to your political prosperity—The insufficiency of the present Confederation to preserve that Union—The necessity of a government at least equally energetic with the one proposed to the attainment of this object—The conformity of the proposed Constitution to the true principles of republican government—Its analogy to your own state constitution*—and lastly, *The additional security, which its adoption will afford to the preservation of that species of government, to liberty and to property.*

In the progress of this discussion I shall endeavour to give a satisfactory answer to all the objections which shall have made their appearance that may seem to have any claim to your attention. . . .

An Antifederalist
Election-Day Appeal

On November 6, 1787, elections were held in Pennsylvania to choose delegates to its state Convention. The Convention was to decide whether the state would ratify the Constitution.

The essay below was intended to convince the people of the city and county of Philadelphia to elect an Antifederalist ticket to the Convention. The essay was signed "An Officer of the Late Continental Army," but we do not know the name of the author. It was reprinted in eight newspapers in Massachusetts, Rhode Island, Connecticut, and Pennsylvania, in a nationally circulating magazine, as a broadside, and as a pamphlet. "An Officer" summarizes many Antifederalist concerns about the Constitution.

The election resulted in an overwhelming Federalist victory. All of the Philadelphia delegates elected were Federalists, and the Convention as a whole had a two-to-one Federalist majority. Antifederalists suffered a further indignity when, at midnight on the night of November 6, after the election, a mob attacked a Philadelphia boarding house where Antifederalist assemblymen were lodging. No rioters were ever apprehended.

An Officer of the Late Continental Army
Philadelphia Independent Gazetteer, 6 Nov. 1787

With a heart full of anxiety for the preservation of your dearest rights, I presume to address you on this important occasion—In the name of sacred liberty, dearer to us than our property and our lives, I request your most earnest attention.

The proposed plan of continental government is now fully known to you. You have read it I trust with the attention it deserves—You have heard the objections that have been made to it—You have heard the answers to these objections.

If you have attended to the whole with candor and unbiassed minds, as becomes men that are possessed and deserving of freedom, you must have been alarmed at the result of your observations. Notwithstanding the splendor of names which has attended the publication of the new constitution, notwithstanding the sophistry and vain reasonings that have been urged to support its principles; alas!

you must at least have concluded that great men are not always infallible, and that patriotism itself may be led into essential errors.

The objections that have been made to the new constitution, are these. . . .

The powers of Congress extend to the *lives,* the *liberties* and the *property* of every citizen.

The *sovereignty* of the different states is *ipso facto* destroyed in its most essential parts.

What remains of it will only tend to create violent dissentions between the state governments and the Congress, and terminate in the ruin of the one or the other.

The consequence must therefore be, either that the *union* of the states will be destroyed by a violent struggle, or that their sovereignty will be swallowed up by silent encroachments into a universal aristocracy. . . .

Congress being possessed of these immense powers, the liberties of the states and of the people are not secured by a bill or DECLARATION OF RIGHTS. . . .

TRIAL BY JURY, that sacred bulwark of liberty, is ABOLISHED IN CIVIL CASES. . . .

THE LIBERTY OF THE PRESS is not secured, and the powers of congress are fully adequate to its destruction, as they are to have the trial of *libels,* or *pretended libels* against the United States, and may by a cursed abominable STAMP ACT . . . preclude you effectually from all means of information. . . .

Congress have the power of keeping up a STANDING ARMY in time of peace. . . .

The LEGISLATIVE and EXECUTIVE powers are not kept separate as every one of the American constitutions declares they ought to be; but they are mixed in a manner entirely novel and unknown, even to the constitution of Great Britain. . . .

The representation of the lower house is too small, consisting only of 65 members.

That of the *senate* is so small that it renders its extensive powers extremely dangerous: it is to consist only of 26 members. . . .

The most important branches of the EXECUTIVE DEPARTMENT are to be put into the hands of a *single magistrate,* who will be in fact an ELECTIVE KING. The MILITARY, the land and naval forces are to be entirely at his disposal. . . .

ROTATION [a limit on the number of consecutive terms for officeholders], that noble prerogative of liberty, is entirely excluded from the new system of government, and great men may and probably will be continued in office during their lives.

ANNUAL ELECTIONS are abolished, and the people are not to reassume their rights until the expiration of *two, four* and *six* years [in elections for the House, the President, and the Senate]. . . .

The importation of slaves is not to be prohibited until the year 1808, and SLAVERY will probably resume its empire in Pennsylvania.

The MILITIA is to be under the immediate command of congress, and men *conscienciously scrupulous of bearing arms,* may be compelled to perform military duty.

The new government will be EXPENSIVE beyond any we have ever experienced, the *judicial* department alone, with its concomitant train of *judges, justices, chancellors, clerks, sheriffs, coroners, escheators, state attornies and solicitors, constables, etc.* in every state and in every county in each state, will be a burden beyond the utmost abilities of the people to bear, and upon the whole,

A government partaking of MONARCHY and aristocracy will be fully and firmly established, and liberty will be but a name to adorn the *short* historic page of the halcyon days of America.

These, my countrymen, are the objections that have been made to the new proposed system of government; and if you read the system itself with attention, you will find them all to be founded in truth. . . .

Now then my fellow-citizens, my brethren, my friends; if the sacred flame of liberty be not extinguished in your breasts, if you have any regard for the happiness of yourselves, and your posterity, let me entreat you, earnestly entreat you by all that is dear and sacred to freemen, to consider well before you take an awful step which may involve in its consequences the ruin of millions yet unborn—You are on the brink of a dreadful precipice;—in the name therefore of holy liberty, for which I have fought and for which we have all suffered, I call upon you to make a solemn pause before you proceed. One step more, and perhaps the scene of freedom is closed forever in America. Let not a set of aspiring despots, *who make us* SLAVES *and tell us 'tis our* CHARTER, *wrest from you those invaluable blessings, for which the most illustrious sons of America have bled and died—but exert yourselves, like men, like freemen and like Americans, to transmit unimpaired to your latest posterity those rights, those liberties, which have ever been so dear to you, and which it is yet in your power to preserve.*

The Attack on Personalities Begins

"*Brutus, Junior," by author unknown, responds to two of the most powerful Federalist arguments. He describes the first in this way: that the members of the Constitutional Convention "were wise and experienced; that they were an illustrious band of patriots, and had the happiness of their country at heart; that they were four months deliberating on the subject, and therefore, it must be a perfect system." He responds by personal criticism of the members of the Convention. The second Federalist argument was that if the Constitution were rejected anarchy and civil war would result, and a government would be imposed by force. "Brutus, Junior" warns that if violence takes place, it will be the Federalists who will be responsible and who will suffer the consequences.*

Brutus, Junior
New York Journal, 8 November 1787

It is an invidious task, to call in question the characters of individuals, especially of such as are placed in illustrious stations. But when we are required implicitly to submit our opinions to those of others, from a consideration that they are so wise and good as not to be liable to err, and that too in an affair which involves in it the happiness of ourselves and our posterity; every honest man will justify a decent investigation of characters in plain language.

It is readily admitted, that many individuals who composed this body [the Constitutional Convention], were men of the first talents and integrity in the union. It is at the same time, well known to every man, who is but moderately acquainted with the characters of the members, that many of them are possessed of high aristocratic ideas, and the most sovereign contempt of the common people; that not a few were strongly disposed in favour of monarchy; that there were some of no small talents and of great influence, of consummate cunning, and masters of intrigue, whom the war found poor, or in embarrassed circumstances, and left with princely fortunes, acquired in public employment, who are at this day to account for many thousands of public money; that there were others who were young, ardent, and ambitious, who wished for a government corresponding with their feelings, while they were destitute of that experience which is the surest guide in political researches; that there were not a few who were gaping for posts of honour and emolument; these we find exulting in the idea of a change, which will divert places of honour, influence and emolument, into a different channel, where the confidence of the people, will not be necessary to their acquirement. It is not to be wondered at, that an assembly thus composed should produce a system liable to well founded objections, and which will require very essential alterations. We are told by one of themselves (Mr. James Wilson of Philadelphia) the plan was matter of accommodation; and it is not unreasonable to suppose, that in this accommodation, principles might be introduced which would render the liberties of the people very insecure.

I confess I think it of no importance, what are the characters of the framers of this government, and therefore should not have called them in question, if they had not been so often urged in print, and in conversation, in its favour. It ought to rest on its own intrinsic merit. If it is good, it is capable of being vindicated; if it is bad, it ought not to be supported. It is degrading to a freeman, and humiliating to a rational one, to pin his faith on the sleeve of any man, or body of men, in an affair of such momentous importance.

In answer to the second argument, I deny that we are in immediate danger of anarchy and commotions. Nothing but the passions of wicked and ambitious men, will put us in the least danger on this head: those who are anxious to precipitate a measure, will always tell us that the present is the critical moment; now is the time, the Crisis is arrived, and the present minute must be seized. Tyrants have always made use of this plea; but nothing in our circumstances can justify it.

The country is in profound peace, and we are not threatened by invasion from any quarter: the governments of the respective states are in the full exercise of their powers; and the lives, the liberty, and property of individuals are protected: all present exigencies are answered by them. It is true, the regulation of trade and a competent provision for the payment of the interest of the public debt is wanting; but no immediate commotion will arise from these; time may be taken for calm discussion and deliberate conclusions. Individuals are just recovering from the losses and embarrassments sustained by the late war: industry and frugality are taking their station, and banishing from the community, idleness and prodigality. Individuals are lessening their private debts, and several millions of the public debt is discharged by the sale of the western territory. There is no reason, therefore, why we should precipitately and rashly adopt a system, which is imperfect or insecure; we may securely deliberate and propose amendments and alterations. I know it is said we cannot change for the worse; but if we act the part of wise men, we shall take care that we change for the better: It will be labour lost, if after all our pains we are in no better circumstances than we were before.

If any tumults arise, they will be justly chargeable on those artful and ambitious men, who are determined to cram this government down the throats of the people, before they have time deliberately to examine it. All the measures of the leaders of this faction have tended to this point. . . .

The most unwearied pains has been taken, to persuade the legislatures to recommend conventions to be elected to meet at early periods, before an opportunity could be had to examine the constitution proposed; every art has been used to exasperate the people against those, who made objections to the plan. They have been told that the opposition is chiefly made by state officers, who expect to lose their places by the change, though the propagators of this falsehood, know, that very few of the state offices will be vacated by the new constitution, and are well apprized, that should it take place, it will give birth to a vast number of more lucrative and permanent appointments, which its principal advocates in every state are warmly in the pursuit of. Is it not extraordinary, that those men who are predicting, that a rejection of this constitution will lead to every evil, which anarchy and confusion can produce, should at the same moment embrace and pursue with unabating industry, every measure in their power, to rouse the passions, and thereby preclude calm and dispassionate enquiry. It would be wise in them, however, to reflect in season that should public commotion take place, they will not only be answerable for the consequences, and the blood that may be shed, but that on such an event, it is more than probable the people will discern the advocates for their liberties, from those who are aiming to enslave them, and that each will receive their just desserts.

An Antifederalist Charge: This Is a Government for the Rich

The House of Representatives was intended to be the most democratic branch of government. It was elected directly by the people, unlike the Senate or the President. But Antifederalists questioned how democratic it would be. The Constitution provided that the first House was to consist of 65 Representatives. Antifederalists believed this was far too small a number to represent the entire continent, and they believed that only the wealthy were likely to be elected. Therefore, this so-called democratic branch would in fact be controlled by an aristocracy of wealth. Rather than representing all the various classes in society, it would represent only the rich.

Brutus No. III
New York Journal, 15 November 1787

It has been observed, that the happiness of society is the end of government—that every free government is founded in compact; and that, because it is impracticable for the whole community to assemble, or when assembled, to deliberate with wisdom, and decide with dispatch, the mode of legislating by representation was devised.

The very term, representative, implies, that the person or body chosen for this purpose, should resemble those who appoint them—a representation of the people of America, if it be a true one, must be like the people. It ought to be so constituted, that a person, who is a stranger to the country, might be able to form a just idea of their character, by knowing that of their representatives. They are the sign—the people are the thing signified. It is absurd to speak of one thing being the representative of another, upon any other principle.... It is obvious, that for an assembly to be a true likeness of the people of any country, they must be considerably numerous.—One man, or a few men, cannot possibly represent the feelings, opinions, and characters of a great multitude. In this respect, the new constitution is radically defective.—

The house of assembly, which is intended as a representation of the people of America, will not, nor cannot, in the nature of things, be a proper one—sixty-five men cannot be found in the United States, who hold the sentiments, possess the feelings, or are acquainted with the wants and interests of this vast country. This extensive continent is made up of a number of different classes of people; and to have a proper representation of them, each class ought to have an opportunity of choosing their best informed men for the purpose; but this cannot possibly be the case in so small a number.

The state of New-York, on the present apportionment, will send six members to the assembly: I will venture to affirm, that number cannot be found in the state, who will bear a just resemblance to the several classes of people who compose it. In this assembly, the farmer, merchant, mechanick [skilled craftsmen], and other various orders of people, ought to be represented according to their respective weight and numbers; and the representatives ought to be intimately acquainted with the wants, understand the interests of the several orders in the society, and feel a proper sense and becoming zeal to promote their prosperity. I cannot conceive that any six men in this state can be found properly qualified in these respects to discharge such important duties: but supposing it possible to find them, is there the least degree of probability that the choice of the people will fall upon such men? According to the common course of human affairs, the natural aristocracy of the country will be elected. Wealth always creates influence, and this is generally much increased by large family connections: this class in society will for ever have a great number of dependents; besides, they will always favour each other—it is their interest to combine—they will therefore constantly unite their efforts to procure men of their own rank to be elected—they will concenter all their force in every part of the state into one point, and by acting together, will most generally carry their election.

It is probable, that but few of the merchants, and those the most opulent and ambitious, will have a representation from their body—few of them are characters sufficiently conspicuous to attact the notice of the electors of the state in so limited a representation. The great body of the yeoman [mid-sized farmers] of the country cannot expect any of their order in this assembly—the station will be too elevated for them to aspire to—the distance between the people and their representatives, will be so very great, that there is no probability that a farmer, however respectable, will be chosen—the mechanicks of every branch, must expect to be excluded from a seat in this Body—It will and must be esteemed a station too high and exalted to be filled by any but the first men in the state, in point of fortune; so that in reality there will be no part of the people represented, but the rich, even in that branch of the legislature, which is called the democratic.—The well born, and highest orders in life, as they term themselves, will be ignorant of the sentiments of the midling class of citizens, strangers to their ability, wants, and difficulties, and void of sympathy, and fellow feeling. This branch of the legislature will not only be an imperfect representation, but there will be no security in so small a body, against bribery, and corruption. . . . It will literally be a government in the hands of the few to oppress and plunder the many. You may conclude with a great degree of certainty, that it, like all others of a similar nature, will be managed by influence and corruption, and that the period is not far distant, when this will be the case, if it should be adopted; for even now there are some among us, whose characters stand high in the public estimation, and who have had a principal agency in framing this constitution, who do not scruple to say, that this is the only practicable mode of governing a people, who think with that degree of freedom which the Americans do. . . .

The more I reflect on this subject, the more firmly am I persuaded, that the representation is merely nominal—a mere burlesque; and that no security is provided against corruption and undue influence. No free people on earth, who have elected persons to legislate for them, ever reposed that confidence in so small a number. . . . The democratic branch of the legislatures of the several states in the union consists, I believe at present, of near two thousand; and this number was not thought too large for the security of liberty by the framers of our state constitutions: some of the states may have erred in this respect, but the difference between two thousand, and sixty-five, is so very great, that it will bear no comparison. . . .

JAMES MADISON TURNS REPUBLICAN THEORY UPSIDE DOWN

The tenth essay in The Federalist *was James Madison's first contribution. This is undoubtedly the most famous of the 85 essays in the series, because it was innovative and because it still applies to our modern complex and pluralistic political world.*

In this essay, Madison was responding to "Brutus" and other Antifederalists, who urged the received wisdom of the day: that a republic could not survive over a large territory with a diverse body politic. Madison argued that a large territory and a heterogeneous society were positive advantages to republican government, were a cure for the major fault of republics, the danger of faction and its ability to tyrannize the minority.

Madison believed there were many causes of faction, such as religious zealotry or the ambitions of political leaders. But the greatest cause was the different kinds of property and the unequal division of property. He wrote, "Those who hold, and those who are without property, have ever formed distinct interests in society." The different forms of property—landed, mercantile, manufacturing—form different interests, and "the regulation of these various and interfering interests forms the principal task of modern Legislation." Madison argued that the causes of faction would always exist, "and that relief is only to be sought in the means of controling its effects." This the Constitution would do.

PUBLIUS: THE FEDERALIST NO. 10 (JAMES MADISON) NEW YORK DAILY ADVERTISER, 22 NOVEMBER 1787

Among the numerous advantages promised by a well constructed Union, none deserves to be more accurately developed than its tendency to break and control the violence of faction. . . . By a faction I understand a number of citizens, whether amounting to a majority or minority of the whole, who are united and actuated by some common impulse of passion, or of interest, adverse to the rights of other citizens, or to the permanent and aggregate interests of the community.

There are two methods of curing the mischiefs of faction: the one, by removing its causes; the other, by controling its effects.

There are again two methods of removing the causes of faction: the one by destroying the liberty which is essential to its existence; the other, by giving to every citizen the same opinions, the same passions, and the same interests.

It could never be more truly said than of the first remedy, that it is worse than the disease. Liberty is to faction, what air is to fire, an aliment [element] without which it instantly expires. But it could not be a less folly to abolish liberty, which is essential to political life, because it nourishes faction, than it would be to wish the annihilation of air, which is essential to animal life, because it imparts to fire its destructive agency.

The second expedient is as impracticable, as the first would be unwise. As long as the reason of man continues fallible, and he is at liberty to exercise it, different opinions will be formed. . . .

The inference to which we are brought, is, that the *causes* of faction cannot be removed; and that relief is only to be sought in the means of controling its *effects*.

If a faction consists of less than a majority, relief is supplied by the republican principle, which enables the majority to defeat its sinister views by regular vote: It may clog the administration, it may convulse the society; but it will be unable to execute and mask its violence under the forms of the Constitution. When a majority is included in a faction, the form of popular government on the other hand enables it to sacrifice to its ruling passion or interest, both the public good and the rights of other citizens. To secure the public good, and private rights, against the danger of such a faction, and at the same time to preserve the spirit and the form of popular government, is then the great object to which our enquiries are directed: Let me add that it is the great desideratum, by which alone this form of government can be rescued from the opprobrium under which it has so long labored, and be recommended to the esteem and adoption of mankind.

By what means is this object attainable? Evidently by one of two only. Either the existence of the same passion or interest in a majority at the same time, must be prevented; or the majority, having such coexistent passion or interest, must be rendered, by their number and local situation, unable to concert and carry into effect schemes of oppression. If the impulse and the opportunity be suffered to coincide, we well know that neither moral nor religious motives can be relied on as an adequate control. . . .

The smaller the society, the fewer probably will be the distinct parties and interests composing it; the fewer the distinct parties and interests, the more frequently will a majority be found of the same party; and the smaller the number of individuals composing a majority, and the smaller the compass within which they are placed, the more easily will they concert and execute their plans of oppression. Extend the sphere, and you take in a greater variety of parties and interests; you make it less probable that a majority of the whole will have a common motive to invade the rights of other citizens; or if such a common motive exists, it will be more difficult for all who feel it to discover their own strength, and to act in unison with each other. . . .

[Under the Constitution], the influence of factious leaders may kindle a flame within their particular States, but will be unable to spread a general conflagration through the other States: a religious sect, may degenerate into a political faction in a part of the Confederacy; but the variety of sects dispersed over the entire face of it, must secure the national Councils against any danger from that source: a rage for paper money, for an abolition of debts, for an equal division of property, or for any other improper or wicked project, will be less apt to pervade the whole body of the Union, than a particular member of it; in the same proportion as such a malady is more likely to taint a particular county or district, than an entire State.

In the extent and proper structure of the Union, therefore, we behold a Republican remedy for the diseases most incident to Republican Government. And according to the degree of pleasure and pride, we feel in being Republicans, ought to be our zeal in cherishing the spirit, and supporting the character of Federalists.

ANTIFEDERALISTS CHARGE: THE REVOLUTION IS BETRAYED

This essay by "Philadelphiensis" was the third in a series of twelve probably written by Benjamin Workman, an Irish immigrant and a tutor of mathematics at the University of Pennsylvania.

The essay is noteworthy in several respects. It makes the point that the debate over the Constitution was momentous, not only for the current generation, but for mankind in general and future generations to come. The author also argues that the Constitution is really a betrayal of the Revolution and that if the Constitution were adopted, Americans would come to regret Independence. He charges that many of the Patriots of the Revolution fought not against oppressive foreign rule, but so that they could rule at home.

PHILADELPHIENSIS NO. III
PHILADELPHIA FREEMAN'S JOURNAL, 5 DECEMBER 1787

My Fellow-Citizens, Are you disposed to hear plain arguments, simple truths, and pure facts? If you are; then let me tell you, thro' the voice of reason, that the preservation of your little ones and yourselves, the love of mankind in general, and the liberty of your dear country, now demand your most serious attention. The peace, the freedom, and happiness of the present generation, and possibly many succeeding ones, are the great subjects now under discussion. Was there ever such an important time for America as this is? Can there be greater objects than these are, presented to the human understanding? I say there cannot: and I affirm it, that there is not a man in the United States, except some base assassin, or mean coward, who can be indifferent on this momentous occasion. Is there any one now among us who can remain unconcerned or neutral? If there be, I say he is not a *man;* no certainly, he is unworthy of that character; such a wretch can have no claim to the title of a free citizen of America, he is a pitiful sycophant, a cringing spaniel, a menial slave.

The independence of America, with great propriety, was thought, during our late glorious struggle, an object of such immense value, that we could scarce pay too high a price for it; an object that even dignified human nature; and that thousands of our countrymen magnanimously and cheerfully paid their blood for its purchase. But, great as this was, I say that the adoption of the new constitution is an object of much greater concern. The parents of a child may rejoice at his birth, as a happy circumstance, but his character and conduct in manhood only can give real and permanent pleasure; if these be bad, their pain is increased by disappointment; the recollection of their former joyous hopes, now augments their misery; yea, the misconduct of a son has frequently compelled his parents to curse the very day of his nativity. In this relation, the independence of America, and the new constitution exactly coincide. For if we adopt this plan of government in its present form; I say that we shall have reason to curse the day that America became independent. Horrid thought! that the greatest blessing God ever bestowed on a nation, should terminate in its misery and disgrace. Strange reverse this! that the freemen of America, *the favored of heaven*, should submit to a government so arbitrary in its embryo, that even a *bill of rights* cannot be obtained, to secure to the people their unalienable privileges.

It was a common saying among many sensible men in Great Britain and Ireland, in the time of the [Revolutionary] war, that they doubted whether the great men of America, who had taken an active part in favor of independence, were influenced by pure patriotism: that it was not the love of their country they had so much at heart, as their own private interest; that a thirst after *dominion and power,* and not to protect the *oppressed* from the *oppressor,* was the great operative principle that induced these men to oppose Britain so strenuously. This seemingly illiberal sentiment, was however generally denied by the well-hearted and unsuspecting friends of American liberty in Europe, who could not suppose that men would engage in so noble a cause through such base motives. But alas! the truth of the sentiment is now indisputably confirmed; facts are stubborn things, and these set the matter beyond controversy. The new constitution, and the conduct of its despotic advocates, shew that these men's doubts were really well founded. Unparalleled duplicity! that men should oppose tyranny under a pretence of patriotism, that they might themselves become the tyrants. How does such villainy disgrace human nature! Ah, my fellow-citizens, you have been strangely deceived indeed; when the wealthy of your own country assisted you to expel the foreign tyrant, only with a view to substitute themselves in his stead.

But we want an efficient federal government; we want an efficient federal government: this is the constant theme of the day. Well, my friends, I grant this. But what is the ultimate end of an efficient government: in what should it be efficient? I hope you anticipate my answer. The only thing in which a government should be efficient, is to protect the *liberties, lives,* and *property* of the people governed, from foreign and domestic violence. This, and this only is what every government should do effectually. For any government to do more than this is impossible, and every one that falls short of it is defective. Let us now compare the new constitution with this legitimate definition of an efficient government, and we shall find that it has scarce a particle of an efficient government in its whole composition.

In the first place then it does not protect the people in those liberties and privileges that all freemen should hold sacred—*The liberty of conscience* [freedom of religion], *the liberty of the press, the liberty of trial by jury, etc.* are all unprotected by this constitution. And in respect to protecting our *property* it can have no pretensions whatever to that; for the taxes must and will be so enormously oppressive, for supporting this expensive government, that the whole produce of our farms would not be sufficient to pay them. . . .

The Constitution Creates a Democratic Form of Government

James Wilson, a lawyer and one of the leading political figures in Pennsylvania, was one of the most important members of the Constitutional Convention in the summer of 1787. Though he had a reputation in Pennsylvania of being a haughty conservative, in the Convention he argued for the largest possible role of the people in the new government: a broad popular basis was needed because the Convention intended "raising the federal pyramid to a considerable altitude."

The Pennsylvania ratifying Convention met on November 20 and debated until December 12, when it voted to ratify the Constitution, 46–23. Wilson was the major speaker in defense of the Constitution. Three Antifederalists, William Findley, John Smilie, and Robert Whitehill, spoke effectively against the Constitution. Shorthand notes of the debates were taken and it was expected that the full debates would be published. But ultimately, the printed debates contained only the speeches of Wilson and Federalist Thomas McKean. The Antifederalist speeches were promised for a second volume, which never appeared.

In the speech printed here, Wilson rejects the charge that the Constitution would create an aristocracy and that the Constitutional Convention intended it to do so. He says that in its principles the new government would be "purely democratical" and would provide no special privileges for officeholders or the wealthy. He argues further that liberty in all the world depends on the fate of the Constitution in America, and adoption of the Constitution would "probably lay a foundation for erecting temples of liberty, in every part of the earth."

James Wilson: Speech in the Pennsylvania State Convention, 11 December 1787

We are told, and it is the last and heaviest charge, "that this government is an aristocracy, and was *intended* so to be by the late [Federal] convention;" and we are told (the truth of which is not disputed) that an aristocratical government is incompatible with freedom. I hope, before this charge is believed, some stronger reasons will be given in support of it, than any that have yet been produced.

The late convention were assembled to devise some plan for the security, safety and happiness of the people of the United States; if they have devised a plan, that robs them of their power, and constitutes an aristocracy, they are the parricides of their country, and ought to be punished as such. What part of this system is it that warrants the charge?

What is an aristocratic government? I had the honor of giving a definition of it at the beginning of our debates; it is, sir, the government of a few over the many, elected by themselves, or possessing a share in the government by inheritance, or inconsequence of territorial rights, or some quality independent of the choice of the people; this is an aristocracy, and this constitution is said to be an aristocratical form of government, and it is also said that it was intended so to be by the members of the late convention who framed it. What peculiar rights have been reserved to any class of men, on any occasion? does even the first magistrate [the President] of the United States draw to himself a single privilege, or security that does not extend to every person throughout the United States? Is there a single distinction attached to him in this system, more than there is to the lowest officer in the republic? Is there an office from which any one set of men whatsoever are excluded? Is there one of any kind in this system but is as open to the poor as to the rich? to the inhabitant of the country, as well as to the inhabitant of the city? and are the places of honor and emoluments confined to a few? and are these few the members of the late convention? Have they made any particular provisions in favor of themselves, their relations, or their posterity? If they have committed their country to the demon of aristocracy, have they not committed themselves also, with every thing they held near and dear to them?

Far, far other is the genius of this system. I have had already the honor of mentioning its general nature; but I will repeat it, sir. In its principle, it is purely democratical; but its parts are calculated in such manner, as to obtain those advantages also, which are peculiar to the other forms of government in other countries. By appointing a single magistrate, we secure strength, vigour, energy and responsibility in the executive department. By appointing a senate, the members of which are elected for six years, yet by a rotation already taken notice of, they are changing every second year, we secure the benefit of experience, while, on the other hand, we avoid the inconveniences that arise from a long and detached establishment. This body is periodically renovated from the people, like a tree, which, at the proper season, receives its nourishment from its parent earth.

In the other branch of the legislature, the house of representatives, shall we not have the advantages, of benevolence and attachment to the people, whose immediate representatives they are?

A free government has often been compared to a pyramid. This allusion is made with peculiar propriety in the system before you; it is laid on the broad basis of the people; its powers gradually rise, while they are confined, in proportion as they ascend, until they end in that most permanent of all forms. When you examine all its parts, they will invariably be found to preserve that essential mark of free governments—a chain of connection with the people. . . .

Permit me to offer one consideration more that ought to induce our acceptance of this system. I feel myself lost in the contemplation of its magnitude. By adopting this system, we shall probably lay a foundation for erecting temples of liberty, in every part of the earth. It has been thought by many, that on the success of the struggle America has made for freedom, will depend the exertions of the brave and enlightened of other nations.—The advantages resulting from this system, will not be confined to the United States, it will draw from Europe, many worthy characters, who pant for the enjoyment of freedom. It will induce princes, in order to preserve their subjects, to restore to them a portion of that liberty of which they have for many ages been deprived. It will be subservient to the great designs of providence, with regard to this globe; the multiplication of mankind, their improvement in knowledge, and their advancement in happiness.

The First Official Dissent to the Constitution

In most states, Federalists sought to have the state ratifying conventions meet as soon as possible. In Pennsylvania, for instance, Federalists in the Assembly began the process of calling a convention even before the state had officially received the Constitution from Congress. They wanted the Convention to be elected quickly and to meet quickly. Antifederalists objected to this precipitancy. They argued that the people should have time to consider the momentous step of adopting a new form of government.

In the conventions, Federalists at first refused even to consider the possibility of amendments to the Constitution. In Pennsylvania, they refused to allow the Antifederalists to place their dissent or their proposed amendments on the journal. On December 12, the Convention ratified the Constitution, 46–23. When the debates of the Convention were published, only Federalist speeches were printed.

The dissent of the minority of the Pennsylvania Convention, the first statement of opposition to the Constitution by delegates elected by the people to consider it, was published privately as a broadside and in the newspapers. It was widely reprinted and rebutted.

The Dissent of the Minority of the Pennsylvania State Convention, 18 December 1787

The proposed plan had not many hours issued forth from the womb of suspicious secrecy [the Constitutional Convention], until such as were prepared for the purpose, were carrying about petitions for people to sign, signifying their approbation of the system, and requesting the legislature to call a convention. While every measure was taken to intimidate the people against opposing it, the public papers teemed with the most violent threats against those who should dare to think for themselves, and *tar and feathers* were liberally promised to all those who would not immediately join in supporting the proposed government be it what it would. Under such circumstances petitions in favour of calling a convention were signed by great numbers in and about the city [Philadelphia], before they had leisure to read and examine the system, many of whom, now they are better acquainted with it, and have had time to investigate its principles, are heartily opposed to it. The petitions were speedily handed into the legislature.

Affairs were in this situation when on the 28th of September last a resolution was proposed to the assembly by a member of the house who had been also a member of the federal convention [George Clymer], for calling a state convention, to be elected with *ten* days for the purpose of examining and adopting the proposed constitution of the United States, though at this time the house had not received it from Congress. This attempt was opposed by a minority, who after offering every argument in this power to prevent the precipitate measure, without effect, absented themselves from the house as the only alternative left them, to prevent the measure taking place previous to their constituents being acquainted with the business—That violence and outrage which had been so often threatened was now practised; some of the members were seized the next day by a mob collected for the purpose, and forcibly dragged to the house, and there detained by force whilst the quorum of the legislature, *so formed*, compleated their resolution. . . .

The election for members of the convention was held at so early a period and the want [lack] of information was so great, that some of us did not know of it until after it was over, and we have reason to believe that great numbers of the people of Pennsylvania have not yet had an opportunity of sufficiently examining the proposed constitution.—We apprehend that no change can take place that will affect the internal government or constitution of this commonwealth, unless a majority of the people should evidence a wish for such a change; but on examining the number of votes given for members of the present state convention, we find that of upwards of *seventy thousand* freemen who are intitled to vote in Pennsylvania, the whole convention has been elected by about *thirteen thousand* voters, and though *two thirds* of the members of the convention have thought proper to ratify the proposed constitution, yet those *two thirds* were elected by the votes of only *six thousand and eight hundred* freemen. . . .

The convention met, and the same disposition was soon manifested in considering the proposed constitution, that had been exhibited in every other stage of the business. We were prohibited by an express vote of the convention, from taking any question on the separate articles of the plan, and reduced to the necessity of adopting or rejecting *in toto*. 'Tis true the majority permitted us to debate on each article, but restrained us from proposing amendments.—They also determined not to permit us to enter on the minutes our reasons of dissent against any of the articles, nor even on the final question our reasons of dissent against the whole. Thus situated we entered on the examination of the proposed system of government, and found it to be such as we could not adopt, without, as we conceived, surrendering up your dearest rights. We offered our objections to the convention, and opposed those parts of the plan, which, in our opinion, would be injurious to you, in the best manner we were able; and closed our arguments by offering the following propositions to the convention. . . .

After reading these propositions, we declared our willingness to agree to the plan, provided it was so amended as to meet those propositions, or something similar to them: and finally moved the convention to adjourn, to give the people of Pennsylvania time to consider the subject, and determine for themselves; but these were all rejected, and the final vote was taken, when our duty to you induced us to vote against the proposed plan, and to decline signing the ratification of the same.

During the discussion we met with many insults, and some personal abuse; we were not even treated with decency, during the sitting of the convention, by the persons in the gallery of the house; however, we flatter ourselves that in contending for the preservation of those invaluable rights you have thought proper to commit to our charge, we acted with a spirit becoming freemen, and being desirous that you might know the principles which actuated our conduct, and being prohibited from inserting our reasons of dissent on the minutes of the convention, we have subjoined them for your consideration, as to you alone we are accountable. It remains with you whether you will think those inestimable privileges, which you have so ably contended for, should be sacrificed at the shrine of despotism, or whether you mean to contend for them with the same spirit that has so often baffled the attempts of an aristocratic faction, to rivet the shackles of slavery on you and your unborn posterity.

ABSENT DIPLOMATS: JOHN ADAMS AND THOMAS JEFFERSON

John Adams and Thomas Jefferson were unable to attend the Constitutional Convention because they were abroad on diplomatic missions. Americans were eager to know what these two statesmen thought of the proposed Constitution. Included here are two letters giving their opinions.

JOHN ADAMS TO JOHN JAY
LONDON, 16 DECEMBER 1787

... The Public Mind cannot be occupied about a nobler Object than the proposed Plan of Government. It appears to be admirably calculated to cement all America in affection and Interest as one great Nation. A Result of accommodation and Compromise, cannot be supposed, perfectly to coincide with any ones Ideas of Perfection. But as all the great Principles necessary to order, Liberty and Safety are respected in it, and Provision is made for Corrections and Amendments as they may be found necessary, I confess I hope to hear of its adoption by all the States....

Most perfectly do I agree with you that America has nothing to fear, but a Want of Union and a Want of Government. The United States now stand in an elevated Situation, and they must and will be respected and courted, not only by France and England, but by all other Powers of Europe, while they keep themselves neutral....

THOMAS JEFFERSON TO JAMES MADISON
PARIS, 20 DECEMBER 1787

... I like the organization of the government into Legislative, Judiciary & Executive. I like the power given the Legislature to levy taxes, and for that reason solely approve of the greater house being chosen by the people directly. For tho' I think a house chosen by them will be very illy qualified to legislate for the Union, for foreign nations &c. yet this evil does not weigh against the good of preserving inviolate the fundamental principle that the people are not to be taxed but by representatives chosen immediately by themselves. I am captivated by the compromise of the opposite claims of the great & little states, of the latter to equal, and the former to proportional influence. I am much pleased too with the substitution of the method of voting by persons, instead of that of voting by states: and I like the negative given to the Executive with a third of either house, though I should have liked it better had the Judiciary been associated for that purpose, or invested with a similar and separate power. There are other good things of less moment.

I will now add what I do not like. First the omission of a bill of rights providing clearly & without the aid of sophisms for freedom of religion, freedom of the press, protection against standing armies, restriction against monopolies, the eternal & unremitting force of the habeas corpus laws, and trials by jury in all matters of fact triable by the laws of the land & not by the law of Nations. . . . Let me add that a bill of rights is what the people are entitled to against every government on earth, general or particular, & what no just government should refuse, or rest on inference.

The second feature I dislike, and greatly dislike, is the abandonment in every instance of the necessity of rotation in office, and most particularly in the case of the President. Experience concurs with reason in concluding that the first magistrate will always be re-elected if the constitution permits it. He is then an officer for life. . . .

I do not pretend to decide what would be the best method of procuring the establishment of the manifold good things in this constitution, and of getting rid of the bad. Whether by adopting it in hopes of future amendment, or, after it has been duly weighed & canvassed by the people, after seeing the parts they generally dislike, & those they generally approve, to say to them "We see now what you wish. Send together your deputies again, let them frame a constitution for you omitting what you have condemned, & establishing the powers you approve. Even these will be a great addition to the energy of your government."—At all events I hope you will not be discouraged from other trials, if the present one should fail of it's full effect.—

I have thus told you freely what I like & dislike: merely as a matter of curiosity for I know your own judgment has been formed on all these points after having heard every thing which could be urged on them. I own I am not a friend to a very energetic government. It is always oppressive. The late rebellion in Massachusetts (Shays' Rebellion) has given more alarm than I think it should have done. Calculate that one rebellion in 13 states in the course of 11 years, is but one for each state in a century & a half. No country should be so long without one. Nor will any degree of power in the hands of government prevent insurrections. France, with all it's despotism, and two or three hundred thousand men always in arms has had three insurrections in the three years I have been here in every one of which greater numbers were engaged than in Massachusetts & a great deal more blood was spilt. In Turkey, which Montesquieu supposes more despotic, insurrections are the events of every day. In England, where the hand of power is lighter than here, but heavier than with us they happen every half dozen years. Compare again the ferocious depredations of their insurgents with the order, the moderation & the almost self extinguishment of ours.—After all, it is my principle that the will of the Majority should always prevail. If they approve the proposed Constitution in all it's parts, I shall concur in it chearfully, in hopes that they will amend it whenever they shall find it works wrong. I think our governments will remain virtuous for many centuries; as long as they are chiefly agricultural; and this will be as long as there shall be vacant lands in any part of America. When they get piled upon one another in large cities, as in Europe, they will become corrupt as in Europe. Above all things I hope the education of the common people will be attended to; convinced that on their good sense we may rely with the most security for the preservation of a due degree of liberty.

P.S. The instability of our laws is really an immense evil. I think it would be well to provide in our constitutions that there shall always be a twelvemonth between the ingrossing a bill & passing it: that it should then be offered to it's passage without changing a word: and that if circumstances should be thought to require a speedier passage, it should take two thirds of both houses instead of a bare majority.

Antifederalists Riot in Carlisle, Pa.

*P*ennsylvania became the second state to ratify the Constitution on December 12, 1787, by a vote of 46 to 23 in its state convention. Federalists in Carlisle, Pa., 125 miles west of Philadelphia, planned to celebrate the state's ratification on December 26, but their celebration was interrupted by a bludgeon-wielding mob of Antifederalists who believed that the Constitution had been drafted and ratified by an aristocratic conspiracy. Demonstrations continued the next day in Carlisle as Federalists completed their celebration and Antifederalists burned effigies of state Supreme Court Chief Justice Thomas McKean and James Wilson, the two most prominent Federalists in the state convention. Reports of the events in Carlisle, printed in newspapers all over the country, raised fears that the adoption of the Constitution might split the country in two and perhaps end in civil war.

"An Old Man's" Account of the Carlisle Riot
Carlisle Gazette, 2 January 1788

About five o'clock on Wednesday afternoon [December 26], public notice being given by ringing the bell and beating the drum, a number of persons met at the public square, to testify their approbation of the proceedings of the late Convention, in the most decent and orderly manner. A piece of Artillery having been brought to the ground, and materials collected for a bonfire; a number of men armed with bludgeons, came in regular order from one quarter of the town, while others sallied forth from different streets armed in the same manner. Major James A. Wilson, (having been appointed with two other gentlemen, to make the necessary arrangements for the occasion) was preparing to have the gun loaded, when he was ordered by many of the armed party to disist, and many threats thrown out against any person who would attempt to kindle the bonfire; to which the Major replied, that those who were not disposed to rejoice, might withdraw; and that he hoped, people so pregnant with liberty as they appeared to be, would not wish to hinder their neighbours to shew marks of joy, when they were pleased.

Immediately after a number of barrels and staves were thrown at him, one of which struck him on the breast, he then sprung forward to the persons who threw at him, and struck one of them with a small pine stick, to which a piece of match rope was fixed; he was then beat down by a number of blows from six or seven persons with bludgeons, who continued beating him after he fell. They would have taken his life had not a trusty old soldier thrown himself on the Major, and received the blows aimed at him; a general confusion took place. Mr. Robert Miller, Jr., was attacked by a person who with both hands wielded a massy bludgeon, and while he was engaged with the first, received several blows from one who stood behind him.

The persons met for the purpose of the celebration, altogether unprepared for such an assault (being even without walking canes), were forced to return. The armed party having accomplished their premeditated designs of preventing the public rejoicing, proceeded to spike the cannon, and having made a large fire, committed to the flames the cannon and its carriage, together with a sledge on which it had been drawn to the ground. They then sent for an almanack, containing the federal Constitution, which was formally burned. Loud huzzas were repeated, with damnation to the 46 members, and long live the virtuous 23.

On Thursday [December 27] at 12 o'clock, I understand that the friends to government intended to carry into execution their resolution of the celebration of the event from which, the evening before they had been so violently prevented. I went to the place, found them at the courthouse armed chiefly with muskets and bayonets; they discovered every pacific disposition, but at the same time the most determined resolution to repel, at the risque of their lives any attack which might be made on them. A bonfire was made, and the ratification of the Constitution by this state was read, accompanied by the acclamations of all the people present, repeated vollies of musketry and firing of cannon.

I cannot help giving my praise to the good order and coolness and determined spirit with which the business was conducted, although the mob made their appearance in several places, armed with guns and bludgeons, and even came close to where the Federalists were firing the cannon, and used threatning language, which was treated with every possible contempt, and no violence offered to them. The Federalists remained 2 hours on the ground, testified their joy, with every appearance of harmony and good humour, and returned without any disturbances to their homes.

Immediately after a drum beat—the mob gathered—collected barrels, and proceeded to the court-house with noise and tumult, when there was brought from an adjacent lot two effigies with labels on their breasts, THOMAS MCKEAN, Chief Justice, and JAMES WILSON the Calledonian.—They formed in order, had the effigies carried in front, preceded only by a noted Captain of militia, who declared he was inspired from Heaven, paraded the streets, and with shouts and most dreadful execrations committed them to the flames. . . . Every lover of good order must lament the wound the dignity of the state has received in burning in the public street, in one of the largest towns in open day, the effigy of the first magistrate of the commonwealth. Proceedings of this kind are really alarming, directly tend to the dissolution of all governments, and must receive the reprobation of every honest citizen.

AN ADDRESS TO THE MINORITY OF THE PENNSYLVANIA CONVENTION, CARLISLE GAZETTE, 2 JANUARY 1788

The history of mankind is pregnant with frequent, bloody and almost imperceptible transitions from freedom to slavery. Rome, after she had been long distracted by the fury of the patrician and plebian parties, at length found herself reduced to the most abject slavery under a Nero, a Caligula, etc. The successive convulsions, which happened at Rome, were the immediate consequence of the aspiring ambition of a few great men, and the very organization and construction of the government itself. The republic of Venice, by the progressive and almost imperceptible encroachments of the nobles, has at length denegrated into an odious and permanent aristocracy. This we are convinced by indubitable demonstration, will be the final consequence of the proposed Federal Constitution; and because we prize the felicity and freedom of our posterity equally with our own, we esteem it our indispensible duty to oppose it with that determined resolution and spirit that becomes freemen. That fire for liberty which was kindled in every patriotic breast during the late glorious contention, though in a latent state, will be easily rekindled; and upon the contact of a very spark will devour by its direful explosion, not only the enemies of liberty, but both parties promiscuously. Discontent, indignation and revenge already begins to be visible in every patriotic countenance; and civil discord already raises her sneaky head: And we are well convinced that nothing less than a total recantation and annihilation of the proposed aristocratic delusion will appease the insulted and enraged defenders of liberty. If the lazy and great wish to ride, they may lay it down as an indubitable position or axiom, that the people of America will make very refractory and restiff hackneys. Although the designing and artful Federalists have effected their scheme so far as to have the Constitution adopted in this state by surprize, notwithstanding the people are pretty generally convinced of their delusion, and little less than the lives of their betrayers will satiate their revenge. Not even the authority of the clergy, who seem generally to have been a set of men decidedly opposed to popular freedom, can give sanction to such a government. The people of America understand their rights better than, by adopting such a Constitution, to rivet the fetters of slavery; or to sacrifice their liberty at the shrine of aristocracy or arbitrary government. . . .

POLITICAL PRESSURE APPLIED TO SAM ADAMS

On Thursday, January 4, 1788, ten of Boston's twelve delegates to the forthcoming state Convention dined with former governor James Bowdoin (Governor John Hancock and John Winthrop did not attend). They discussed the Constitution. Christopher Gore, a Federalist delegate, reported that Sam Adams, the great leader of the Revolution, "was open & decided against it." Adams argued that the Constitution "would never answer and ought not to be adopted, but on condition of such amendments as would destroy it." Winthrop and others were reported to be saying that the tradesmen of Boston were opposed to the Constitution.

Adams's opposition and Winthrop's remark led the tradesmen to call a meeting, where they would express their strong support for the Constitution and urge their delegates to support it in the state Convention. Gore and others worried that Adams "unless affected by some such steps as these will be indefatigable & constant in all ways & means to defeat the adoption of the proposed form of Government."

The meeting was held at the Green Dragon Tavern on January 7. John Lucas, commissary of pensions for Massachusetts, Paul Revere, a goldsmith and revolutionary hero, and Benjamin Russell, printer of the Massachusetts Centinel were chosen to draft resolutions (which may have been prepared well before). These resolutions were adopted unanimously and appeared in the newspapers.

Sam Adams played a minor role in the Convention. Eventually, he spoke and voted in favor of the compromise by which the Convention voted to ratify the Constitution and proposed recommendatory amendments to the Constitution.

MASSACHUSETTS GAZETTE, 8 JANUARY 1788

Agreeable to an advertisement inserted in the papers of this day, the Tradesmen of this town convened at Mason's-hall, Green Dragon, when John Lucas, Esquire, Paul Revere, Esquire, and Mr. Benjamin Russell, were chosen to draft certain resolutions, expressive of the sense of this body. The committee, after having retired for that purpose, returned, and reported the following—which, being read, was

Unanimously accepted, and ordered to be printed in the several public papers—viz.

Whereas some persons, intending to injure the reputation of the tradesmen of this town, have asserted, that they were unfriendly and adverse to the adoption of the constitution of the United States of America, as proposed on the 17th September last, by the Convention of the United States assembled in Philadelphia: Therefore, to manifest the falsehood of such assertions, and to discover to the world our sentiments of the proposed frame of government,

Be it Resolved:

1. That such assertions are false and groundless; and it is the sense of this body, that all those, who propagate such reports, have no other view than the injury of our reputation, in the attainment of their own wicked purposes, on base and false grounds.

2. That, in the judgment of this body, the proposed frame of government, is well calculated to secure the liberties, protect the property, and guard the rights of the citizens of America; and it is our warmest wish and prayer that the same should be adopted by the commonwealth.

3. That, it is our opinion, if said constitution should be adopted by the United States of America, trade and navigation will revive and increase, employ and subsistence will be afforded to many of our townsmen, who are now suffering from want of the necessaries of life; that it will promote industry and morality; render us respectable as a nation; and procure us all the blessings to which we are entitled from the natural wealth of our country; our capacity for improvement, from our industry, our freedom and independence.

4. That it is the sense of this body, that if the proposed frame of government should be rejected, the small remains of commerce yet left us, will be annihilated, the various trades and handicrafts dependent thereon, must decay; our poor will be increased, and many of our worthy and skilful mechanicks compelled to seek employ and subsistence in strange lands.

5. That, in the late election of delegates to represent this town in Convention, it was our design, and the opinion of this body, the design of every good man in town, to elect such men, and such only, as would exert their utmost ability to promote the adoption of the proposed frame of government in all its parts, without any conditions, pretended amendments, or alterations whatever: and that such,

and such only, will truly represent the feelings, wishes, and desires of their constituents: and if any of the delegates of this town should oppose the adoption of said frame of government in gross, or under pretence of making amendments, or alterations of any kind, or of annexing conditions to their acceptance, such delegate or delegates will act contrary to their best interest, the strongest feelings, and warmest wishes of the Tradesmen of the town of Boston. . . .

It was with pleasure, says a correspondent, he observed the perfect order, unanimity, and intelligence, that pervaded the body of respectable Tradesmen which met last evening at the Green-Dragon. Notwithstanding the number exceeded three hundred and eighty, as appeared by an enumeration made at the time of their retiring from the Hall, as much regularity and propriety were discovered throughout all their proceedings, and deliberations, as ever were observed in any legislative body.

MASSACHUSETTS CENTINEL, 9 JANUARY 1788

At about six o'clock, near four hundred of the most respectable *real* Tradesmen of this town—men who obtain their support from the sweat of their brow, and the labour of their hands—men who are constantly employed in the hive of the Commonwealth for their own subsistence and the dignity of the state, met at the Green-Dragon—when the subsequent spirited and patriotick proceedings took place. Although convened together at a short notice, and forming a large body when met, the whole business was conducted with as much propriety and regularity, we venture to say, as ever marked the proceedings of the best organized and well regulated assembly whatever. . . .

The resolves of so respectable a body as were convened on the evening of Monday last, can leave no doubt of their sentiments—and although they do not wish to preclude a fair discussion of the great subject—yet they are convinced that the *unbiassed, unprejudiced* and *truly patriotick* members of the honourable Convention will join with them in determining that the blessings of Independence are suspended on the adoption of the new Federal Constitution.

THE CONSTITUTION CREATES A REPUBLICAN FORM OF GOVERNMENT

In the debate over the ratification of the Constitution, Antifederalists made several telling arguments that compelled Federalists to reply. In the essay below, James Madison assures the public that the Constitution creates a republican form of government, rather than a monarchy or an aristocracy. The term republican government was somewhat obscure then, as it still is today. Madison defined it as "a government which derives all its power directly or indirectly from the great body of the people" and in which the officeholders had limits on their terms.

Madison had some explaining to do. Except for the House of Representatives, the people's will was expressed only indirectly, and the two-year term for congressmen was longer than in most states. The President was elected by electors. Senators were elected by the state legislatures for six-year terms. The judges were appointed by the President for life terms. Madison argued that there was nothing extraordinary about this: that these provisions could all be found in the state constitutions that most Antifederalists claimed to prefer to the new Constitution.

This suggests an important point: very little in the Constitution was new. Most of its provisions were taken from the various state constitutions. The innovation of the Constitution was its concept of federalism, the division of power between the state and federal governments.

PUBLIUS: THE FEDERALIST NO. 39 (JAMES MADISON) NEW YORK INDEPENDENT JOURNAL, 16 JANUARY 1788

The first question that offers itself is, whether the general form and aspect of the government be strictly republican? It is evident that no other form would be reconcileable with the genius of the people of America; with the fundamental principles of the revolution; or with that honorable determination, which animates every votary of freedom, to rest all our political experiments on the capacity of mankind for self-government. If the plan of the Convention therefore be found to depart from the republican character, its advocates must abandon it as no longer defensible.

What then are the distinctive characters of the republican form? Were an answer to this question to be sought, not by recurring to principles, but in the application of the term by political writers, to the constitutions of different States, no satisfactory one would ever be found. . . .

If we resort for a criterion, to the different principles on which different forms of government are established, we may define a republic to be, or at least may bestow that name on, a government which derives all its powers directly or indirectly from the great body of the people; and is administered by persons holding their offices during pleasure, for a limited period, or during good behaviour. It is *essential* to such a government, that it be derived from the great body of the society, not from an inconsiderable proportion, or a favored class of it; otherwise a handful of tyrannical nobles, exercising their oppressions by a delegation of their powers, might aspire to the rank of republicans, and claim for their government the honorable title of republic. It is *sufficient* for such a government, that the persons administering it be appointed, either directly or indirectly, by the people; and that they hold their appointments by either of the tenures just specified; otherwise every government in the United States, as well as every other popular government that has been or can be well organized or well executed, would be degraded from the republican character. According to the Constitution of every State in the Union, some or other of the officers of government are appointed indirectly only by the people. According to most of them the chief magistrate [governor] himself is so appointed. And according to one [Maryland], this mode of appointment is extended to one of the coordinate branches of the legislature. According to all the Constitutions also, the tenure of the highest offices is extended to a definite period, and in many instances, both within the legislative and executive departments, to a period of years. According to the provisions of most of the constitutions, again, as well as according to the most respectable and received opinions on the subject, the members of the judiciary department are to retain their offices by the firm tenure of good behaviour [life tenure].

On comparing the Constitution planned by the Convention, with the standard here fixed, we perceive at once that it is in the most rigid sense conformable to it. The House of Representatives, like that of one branch at least of all the State Legislatures, is elected immediately by the great body of the people. The Senate, like the present Congress, and the Senate of Maryland, derives its appointment indirectly from the people. The President is indirectly derived from the choice of the people, according to the example in most of the States. Even the judges, with all other officers of the Union, will, as in the several States, be the choice, though a remote choice, of the people themselves. The duration of the appointments is equally conformable to the republican standard, and to the model of the State Constitutions. The House of Representatives is periodically elective as in all the States: and for the period of two years as in the Senate of South-Carolina. The Senate is elective for the period of six years; which is but one year more than the period of the Senate of Maryland; and but two more than the Senates of New-York and Virginia. The President is to continue in office for the period of four years; as in New-York and Delaware, the chief magistrate is elected for three years, and in South-Carolina for two years. In the other States the election is annual. In several of the States however, no constitutional provision is made for the impeachment of the Chief Magistrate. And in Delaware and Virginia, he is not impeachable till out of office. The President of the United States is impeachable at any time during his continuance in office. The tenure by which the Judges are to hold their places, is, as it unquestionably ought to be, that of good behaviour. The tenure of the ministerial [cabinet] offices generally will be a subject of legal regulation, conformably to the reason of the case, and the example of the State Constitutions.

Could any further proof be required of the republican complextion of this system, the most decisive one might be found in its absolute prohibition of titles of nobility, both under the Federal and the State Governments; and in its express guarantee of the republican form to each of the latter.

The Constitution and the Foreign Slave Trade: An Insult to God

Luther Martin, attorney general of Maryland, had been a member of the Constitutional Convention, where he came to oppose the strong national government being created. He left the Convention before Sept. 17, but he would have refused to sign the Constitution had he been there.

The Maryland legislature called its delegates to the Convention to appear and give "information of the proceedings" of the Convention. Martin addressed the Assembly on Nov. 29, 1787. He later expanded his remarks for publication in the newspapers and as a pamphlet entitled Genuine Information.

In the excerpts below Martin discusses the debate in the Constitutional Convention on the issue of the slave trade. The Committee of Detail had provided that the federal government could not prohibit the importation of slaves. The Convention rejected this provision, but delegates from Georgia and South Carolina declared that their states could never agree to the Constitution if it allowed the banning of the slave trade. This then became the subject of a compromise proposed by a committee of all the states, of which Martin was a member. The committee proposed that the importation of slaves could not be prohibited until 1800. This was extended by the Convention to 1808.

Luther Martin's Genuine Information
Baltimore Maryland Gazette, 18, 22 January 1788

This report [of the committee] was adopted by a majority of the convention, but not without considerable opposition.—It was said, that we had but just assumed a place among independent nations, in consequence of our opposition to the attempts of Great-Britain to enslave us—that this opposition was grounded upon the preservation of those rights, to which God and Nature had entitled us, not in particular, but in common with all the rest of mankind—That we had appealed to the Supreme Being for his assistance, as the God of freedom, who could not but approve our efforts to preserve the rights which he had thus imparted to his creatures—that now, when we scarcely had risen from our knees, from supplicating his aid and protection—in forming our government over a free people, a government formed pretendedly on the principles of liberty and for its preservation;—in that government to have a provision, not only putting it out of its power to restrain and prevent the slave trade, but even encouraging that most infamous traffic, by giving the States power and influence in the union, in proportion as they cruelly and wantonly sport with the rights of their fellow creatures, ought to be considered as a solemn mockery of, and insult to, that God whose protection we had then implored, and could not fail to hold us up in detestation, and render us contemptible to every true friend of liberty in the world.—It was said [by George Mason of Virginia], it ought to be considered that national crimes can only be, and frequently are, punished in this world by national punishments, and that the continuance of the slave trade, and thus giving it a national sanction and encouragement, ought to be considered as justly exposing us to the displeasure and vengeance of Him, who is equal Lord of all, and who views with equal eye, the poor African slave and his American master!

[January 22] It was urged that by this system, we were giving the general government full and absolute power to regulate commerce, under which general power it would have a right to restrain, or totally prohibit the slave trade—it must appear to the world absurd and disgraceful to the last degree, that we should except from the exercise of that power, the only branch of commerce, which is unjustifiable in its nature, and contrary to the rights of mankind—That on the contrary, we ought rather to prohibit expressly in our constitution, the further importation of slaves; and to authorize the general government from time to time, to make such regulations as should be thought most advantageous for the gradual abolition of slavery, and the emancipation of the slaves which are already in the States.

That slavery is inconsistent with the genius of republicanism, and has a tendency to destroy those principles on which it is supported, as it lessens the sense of the equal rights of mankind, and habituates us to tyranny and oppression.—It was further urged, that by this system of government, every State is to be protected both from foreign invasion and from domestic insurrections; that from this consideration, it was of the utmost importance it should have a power to restrain the importation of slaves, since in proportion as the number of slaves were encreased in any State, in the same proportion the State is weakened and exposed to foreign invasion, or domestic insurrection, and by so much the less will it be able to protect itself against either; and therefore will by so much the more, want aid from, and be a burthen to, the union.—It was further said, that as in this system we were giving the general government a power under the idea of national character, or national interest, to regulate even our weights and measures, and have prohibited all possibility of emitting paper money, and passing instalment laws [to protect creditors], etc.—It must appear still more extraordinary, that we should prohibit the government from interfering with the slave trade, than which nothing could so materially affect both our national honour and interest.—These reasons influenced me both on the committee and in convention, most decidedly to oppose and vote against the clause, as it now makes a part of the system.

You will perceive, Sir, not only that the general government is prohibited from interfering in the slave trade before the year eighteen hundred and eight, but that there is no provision in the constitution that it shall afterwards be prohibited, nor any security that such prohibition will ever take place—and I think there is great reason to believe that if the importation of slaves is permitted until the year eighteen hundred and eight, it will not be prohibited afterwards—At this time we do not generally hold this commerce in so great abhorrence as we have done.—When our own liberties were at stake, we warmly felt for the common rights of men—The danger being thought to be past, which threatened ourselves, we are daily growing more insensible to those rights—In those States who have restrained or prohibited the importation of slaves, it is only done by legislative acts which may be repealed—When those States find that they must in their national character and connection suffer in the disgrace, and share in the inconveniences attendant upon that detestable and iniquitous traffic, they may be desirous also to share in the benefits arising from it, and the odium attending it will be greatly effaced by the sanction which is given to it in the general government.

CHAPTER 4

The People Decide

INTRODUCTION

By January 9, 1788, five of the nine states needed for the adoption of the Constitution had ratified overwhelmingly, including Pennsylvania, one of the "large" states. The next large state to consider the Constitution was Massachusetts, which was of critical importance. It was known that there was strong opposition in Rhode Island, New York, Virginia, and North Carolina. A rejection by Massachusetts would embolden the opposition in these states, and if all of them failed to ratify, the Constitution would be defeated.

After three weeks' debate, it was clear that there was not a majority for ratification. Therefore, Federalists arranged a compromise. Governor John Hancock would propose that the Convention ratify the Constitution unconditionally, but the Convention would instruct its future representatives and senators to propose amendments to the Constitution in the first federal Congress. This compromise won enough delegates so that Massachusetts ratified the Constitution on February 6, 1788, by a vote of 187–168. All of the remaining states adopted this form of unconditional ratification with recommended amendments, except for Maryland, which did not propose amendments, North Carolina, which refused to ratify until amendments were adopted, and Rhode Island, which did not hold its convention until 1790.

Maryland ratified the Constitution on April 26, by a vote of 63–11. South Carolina ratified on May 23, by a vote of 149–73, and New Hampshire, on June 21, by a vote of 57–47. New Hampshire was the ninth state to ratify, thereby putting the Constitution into effect among the ratifying states. But that still left New York, Virginia, North Carolina, and Rhode Island.

Strong opposition existed in each of these states and powerful attacks were made against ratification in the newspapers and elsewhere by such writers as Luther Martin, Mercy Otis Warren, "Brutus," "Federal Farmer," and "A Plebeian." George Washington, for one, felt that many of these criticisms were unjustified. Other Federalist defenders were Alexander Hamilton and James Madison writing as "Publius" and John Jay writing as "A Citizen of New York." Federalists and Antifederalists in New York and Virginia made efforts to coordinate their efforts to support or defeat the Constitution.

On June 25, 1788, after a month of difficult debate, Virginia ratified the Constitution unconditionally, 89–79, but called for the adoption of extensive amendments, including a comprehensive bill of rights. On July 26, New York ratified by a vote of 30–27; it too called for many amendments and went further by adopting a circular letter to the other states that proposed a second constitutional convention to consider amendments to the Constitution. Finally, on August 2, 1788, the North Carolina Convention refused to ratify until amendments were adopted. North Carolina did not adopt the Constitution until November 1789, and Rhode Island remained obstinate and out of the Union until May 1790.

THE OLD PATRIOTS OF '75
DEBATE THE CONSTITUTION

The Massachusetts Convention met on January 9 with a majority of its delegates opposed to the Constitution. Two weeks into the debate, thirty-year-old Fisher Ames of Dedham asked the Old Patriots of 1775 to unite in favor of the Constitution. Amos Singletary, a sixty-six-year-old delegate from Sutton, answered Ames by attacking the lawyers, monied men, and men of learning who had drafted the Constitution and sought only to be elected to Congress so that they could oppress the people with dry taxes (taxes on land) as well as import duties (imposts) and excises.

When Singletary finished his diatribe, forty-eight-year-old Jonathan Smith of Lanesborough responded. Smith, a farmer who had risen to the rank of colonel in the Massachusetts militia during the Revolution, recalled the horror and anarchy of Shays' Rebellion that had divided the state from August 1786 to February 1787. Without a strong government, according to Smith, anarchy would occur and naturally lead to tyranny. Smith also appealed to his fellow farmers to trust the lawyers, monied men, and men of learning who supported the Constitution. Those who had suspicion in their hearts were the ones not to be trusted.

The account of these speeches first appeared in the Massachusetts Centinel *on February 13 and was reprinted sixteen times in newspapers throughout the country.*

MASSACHUSETTS CONVENTION DEBATES
25 JANUARY 1788

Fisher Ames, in a short discourse, called on those who stood forth in 1775, to stand forth now—to throw aside all interested and party views—to have one purse, and one heart for the whole—and to consider, that as it was necessary then, so was it necessary now to UNITE, or DIE we must.

Amos Singletary. Mr. President, I should not have troubled the Convention again if some gentleman had not called upon them that were on the stage, in the beginning of our troubles, in the year 1775.—I was one of them—I have had the honour to be a member of the Court [the state legislature, the General Court] all the time, Mr.

President, and I say, that if any body had proposed such a Constitution as this, in that day, it would have been thrown away at once—it would not have been looked at. We contended with Great-Britain—some said for a threepenny duty on tea, but it was not that—it was because they claimed a right to tax us and bind us in all cases whatever—and does not this Constitution do the same—does it not take all we have—all our property—does it not lay *all* taxes, duties, imposts and excises—and what more have we to give? They tell us Congress won't lay dry [land] taxes upon us, but collect all the money they want by impost—I say there has always been a difficulty about impost—Whenever the General Court was a going to lay an impost, they would tell us it was more than trade could bear, that it hurt the fair trader, and encouraged smuggling—and there will always be the same objection—they won't be able to raise money enough by impost, and then they will lay it on the land, and take all we have got. These lawyers, and men of learning, and monied men, that talk so finely and gloss over matters so smoothly, to make us poor, illiterate people, swallow down the pill—they expect to get into Congress themselves—they expect to be the managers of this Constitution and get all the power and all the money into their own hands, and then they will swallow up all us little folks, like the great *Leviathan*, Mr. President, yes, just as the whale swallowed up *Jonah*. This is what I am afraid of—but I won't say any more at present, but reserve the rest to another opportunity.

Jonathan Smith. Mr. President, I am a plain man, and get my living by the plough. I am not used to speak in publick, but I beg your leave to say a few words to my brother plough-joggers, in this house. I have lived in a part of the country where I have known the worth of good government by the want of it. There was a black cloud that rose in the east last winter, and spread over the west.

(*Here Mr. William Widgery interrupted. Mr. President, I wish to know what the gentleman means by the east.*)

I mean, Sir, the county of Bristol—the cloud rose there and burst upon us, and produced a dreadful effect. It brought on a state of *anarchy*, and that leads to *tyranny*. I say it brought anarchy.—People that used to live peaceably, with, and were before good neighbours, got distracted and took up arms against government.

(Here Mr. Kingsley called to order, and asked what had the history of last winter to do with the Constitution? Several gentlemen, and among the rest the Hon. Mr. Samuel Adams, said the gentleman was in order—let him go on in his own way.)

I am a going, Mr. President, and you my brother Farmers, to shew what were the effects of anarchy, that you may see the reasons why I wish for good government. People, I say, took up arms, and then if you went to speak to them you had the *musquet of death* presented to your breast. They would rob you of your property, threaten to burn your houses—oblige you to be on your guard night and day—alarms spread from town to town—families were broken up—the tender mother would cry, O my son is among them! What shall I do for my child! Some were taken captive—children were taken out of their schools and carried away. Then we should hear of an *action,* and the poor prisoners were *set in the front*, to be killed by their own friends. How dreadful, how distressing, was this! Our distress was so great that we should have been glad to catch at any thing that looked like government for protection. Had any person, that was able to protect us, come and set up his standard we should all have flocked to it, even if it had been a *monarch*—and that monarch might have proved a tyrant—so that you see anarchy leads to tyranny, and better have *one* tyrant than so many at once.

Now, Mr. President, when I saw this Constitution, I found it was a cure for these disorders. It was just such a thing as we wanted. I got a copy of it and read it over and over—I had been a member of the Convention to form our own State Constitution, and had learnt something of the checks and ballances of power, and I found them all here. I did not go to any lawyer, to ask his opinion—we have no lawyer in our town, and we do well enough without.—I formed my own opinion, and was pleased with this Constitution. My Hon. old Daddy, there *(pointing to Mr. Singletary)* won't think that I expect to be a Congress-man, and swallow up the liberties of the people. I never had any post, nor do I want one, and before I have done you will think I don't deserve one. But I don't think the worse of the Constitution because lawyers, and men of learning and monied men, are fond of it. I don't suspect that they want to get into Congress and abuse their power. I am not of such a jealous make—they that are honest themselves are not apt to suspect other people. I don't know why our constituents have not as good a right to be jealous of us, as we seem to be of the Congress—and I think those gentlemen who are so very suspicious, that as soon as a man gets into power, he turns *rogue*, had better look *at home.*

We are by this Constitution allowed to send *ten* members to Congress. Have we not more than that number, fit to go? I dare say if we pick out ten, we shall have another ten left, and I hope ten times ten, and will not these be a check upon those that go? Will they go to Congress and abuse their power and do mischief, when they know they must return and look the other ten in the face, and be called to account for their conduct? Some gentlemen think that our liberty and property is not safe in the hands of monied men, and men of learning—I am not of that mind.

Brother Farmers, let us suppose a case now—suppose you had a farm of 50 acres, and your title was disputed, and there was a farm of 5000 acres, joined to you that belonged to a man of learning, and his title was involved in the same difficulty—would not you be glad to have him for your friend, rather than to stand alone in the dispute? Well the case is the same—these lawyers, these monied men, these men of learning, are all embarked in the same cause with us—and we must all swim or sink together—and shall we throw the Constitution over-board, because it does not please us all alike? Suppose two or three of you had been at the pains to break up a piece of rough land, and sow it with wheat—would you let it lie waste, because you could not agree what *sort* of a fence to make? Would it not be better to put up a fence that did not please every one's fancy rather than not fence it at all, or keep disputing about it, until the wild beasts came in and devoured it. Some gentlemen say, don't take a leap in the dark.—I say take things *in* time—gather fruit when it is ripe. There is a time to sow and a time to reap—we sowed our seed when we sent men to the federal Convention, now is the harvest, now is the time to reap the fruit of our labour, and if we don't do it now, I am afraid we shall never have another opportunity.

MASSACHUSETTS RATIFIES THE CONSTITUTION

On February 6, 1788, Massachusetts became the sixth state to ratify the Constitution. In the last speech given before the final vote was taken, Governor John Hancock advocated a policy of conciliation. Hancock had been elected president of the convention, but was unable to attend the debates for the first three weeks because of illness. (Some people believed that Hancock found it convenient to be ill until he saw which way the majority would swing.) After the convention voted to ratify the Constitution, several leaders of the opposition publicly stated that they would cease their opposition and bow to the wishes of the majority. The victory in Massachusetts was a turning point in the struggle to ratify the Constitution.

MASSACHUSETTS CONVENTION, 6 FEBRUARY 1788

John Hancock: Gentlemen, Being now called upon to bring the subject under debate to a decision, by bringing forward the question, I beg your indulgence to close the business with a few words. I am happy that my health has been so far restored, that I am rendered able to meet my fellow citizens, as represented in this Convention. I should have considered it as one of the most distressing misfortunes of my life, to be deprived of giving my aid and support to a system, which if amended (as I feel assured it will be) according to your proposals, cannot fail to give the people of the United States, a greater degree of political freedom, and eventually as much national dignity, as falls to the lot of any nation on the earth. I have not since I had the honor to be in this place, said much on the important subject before us: All the ideas appertaining to the system, as well those which are against as for it, have been debated upon with so much learning and ability, that the subject is quite exhausted.

But you will permit me, Gentlemen, to close the whole with one or two general observations. This I request, not expecting to throw any new light upon the subject, but because it may possibly prevent uneasiness and discordance, from taking place amongst us and amongst our constituents.

That a general system of government is indispensably necessary to save our country from ruin is agreed upon all sides. That the one now to be decided upon has its defects all agree; but when we consider the variety of interests, and the different habits of the men it is intended for, it would be very singular to have an entire union of sentiment respecting it. Were the people of the United States to delegate the powers proposed to be given, to men who were not dependent on them frequently for elections, to men whose interests either from rank, or title, would differ from that of their fellow citizens in common, the task of delegating authority would be vastly more difficult; but as the matter now stands, the powers reserved by the people render them secure, and until they themselves become corrupt, they will always have upright and able rulers. I give my assent to the Constitution in full confidence that the amendments proposed will soon become a part of the system, these amendments being in no wise local, but calculated to give security and ease alike to all the States, I think that all will agree to them.

Suffer me to add that let the question be decided as it may, there can be no triumph on the one side, or chagrin on the other. Should there be a great division, every good man, every one who loves his country, will be so far from exhibiting extraordinary marks of joy, that he will sincerely lament the want of unanimity, and strenuously endeavour to cultivate a spirit of conciliation, both in Convention, and at home. The people of this Commonwealth are a people of great light, of great intelligence in publick business; they know that we have none of us an interest separate from theirs; that it must be our happiness to conduce to theirs, and that we must all rise or fall together: They will never, therefore, forsake the first principle of society, that of being governed by the voice of the majority; and should it be that the proposed form of government should be rejected, they will zealously attempt another. Should it by the vote now to be taken be ratified, they will quietly acquiesce, and where they see a want of perfection in it, endeavour in a constitutional way to have it amended.

The question now before you is such as no nation on earth, without the limits of America, have ever had the privilege of deciding upon. As the Supreme Ruler of the Universe has seen fit to bestow upon us this glorious opportunity, let us decide upon it, appealing to him for the rectitude of our intentions, and in humble confidence that he will yet continue to bless and save our country.

The question was then put ... and the yeas and nays being taken thereon, there were: Yeas 187; Nays 168. Majority, 19.

... **Abraham White** rose, and said, that notwithstanding he had opposed the adoption of the Constitution, upon the idea that it would endanger the liberties of his country, yet, as a majority had seen fit to adopt it, he should use his utmost exertions to induce his constituents to live in peace under, and chearfully submit to it.

He was followed by **William Widgery,** who said, that he should return to his constituents, and inform them, that he had opposed the adoption of this Constitution, but that he had been overruled, and that he had been carried by a majority of wise and understanding men: that he should endeavour to sow the seeds of union and peace among the people he represented—and that he hoped, and believed, that no person would wish for, or suggest the measure of a PROTEST; for, said he, we must consider that this body is as full a representation of the people, as can be conceived.—After expressing his thanks for the civility which the inhabitants of this town [Boston] have shewn to the convention, and declaring, as his opinion, that they had not in the least influenced the decision; he concluded by saying he should support, as much as in him lay, the Constitution, and believed, as this state had adopted it, not only 9, but the whole 13 would come into the measure.

Daniel Cooley (Amherst) said, that he endeavoured to govern himself by the principles of reason, that he was directed to vote against the adoption of the Constitution, and that in so doing, he had not only complied with his directions, but had acted according to the dictates of his own conscience; but that as it has been agreed to by a majority, he should endeavour to convince his constituents of the propriety of its adoption.

John Taylor, also said, he had uniformly opposed the Constitution, that he found himself fairly beat, and expressed his determination to go home, and endeavour to insure a spirit of harmony and love, among the people.

George Washington Defends the Constitution

George Washington was proud of the work of the Constitutional Convention and of the Constitution it produced. He sincerely believed that it would provide a strong government, but one that would assure the liberties of the people.

Washington did not participate extensively in the public debate over ratifying the Constitution. He did, however, write many letters to friends and former associates. He was especially close to a few people, such as the Marquis de Lafayette. The letter below offers a glimpse of Washington's affection for Lafayette and an insight into his private thinking about government and America.

Washington believed that under the Constitution America would be free so long as the people retained their civic virtue. Of course, there was nothing that could protect against unlawful seizures of power, but the Constitution's checks and balances provided protection against tyranny within the constitutional limits.

Many opponents of the Constitution disagreed. They sought amendments to the Constitution before it went into effect. Washington opposed these efforts as misguided.

George Washington to the Marquis de Lafayette
Mount Vernon, 7 February 1788

You know it always gives me the sincerest pleasure to hear from you, my dear Marquis, and therefore I need only say that your two kind letters of the 9th and 15th of October so replete with personal affection and confidential intelligence, afforded me inexpressible satisfaction....

You appear to be, as might be expected from a real friend to this Country, anxiously concerned about its present political situation. So far as I am able I shall be happy in gratifying that friendly solicitude. As to my sentiments with respect to the merits of the new Constitution, I will disclose them without reserve (although by passing through the Post offices they should become known to all the world) for, in truth, I have nothing to conceal on that subject. It appears to me, then, little short of a miracle, that the Delegates from so many different States (which States you know are also different from each other in their manners, circumstances and prejudices) should unite in forming a system of national Government, so little liable to well founded objections. Nor am I yet such an enthusiastic, partial or undiscriminating admirer of it, as not to perceive it is tinctured with some real (though not radical) defects. The limits of a letter would not suffer me to go fully into an examination of them; nor would the discussion be entertaining or profitable, I therefore forbear to touch upon it. With regard to the two great points (the pivots on which the whole machine must move) my Creed is simply:—

1st.—That the general Government is not invested with more Powers than are indispensably necessary to perform the functions of a good Government; and, consequently, that no objection ought to be made against the quantity of Power delegated to it:

2ly.—That these Powers (as the appointment of all Rulers will forever arise from, and, at short stated intervals, recur to the free suffrage of the People) are so distributed among the Legislative, Executive, and Judicial Branches, into which the general Government is arranged, that it can never be in danger of degenerating into a monarchy, an Oligarchy, an Aristocracy, or any other despotic or oppressive form; so long as there shall remain any virtue in the body of the People.—

I would not be understood my dear Marquis to speak of consequences which may be produced, in the revolution of ages, by corruption of morals, profligacy of manners, and listlessness for the preservation of the natural and unalienable rights of mankind; nor of the successful usurpations that may be established at such an unpropitious juncture, upon the ruins of liberty, however providently guarded and secured, as these are contingencies against which no human prudence can effectually provide. It will at least be a recommendation to the proposed Constitution that it is provided with more checks and barriers against the introduction of Tyranny, & those of a nature less liable to be surmounted, than any Government hitherto instituted among mortals, hath possessed. We are not to expect perfection in this world: but mankind, in modern times, have apparently made some progress in the science of Government.—Should that which is now offered to the People of America, be found on experiment less perfect than it can be made—a Constitutional door is left open for its amelioration. Some respectable characters have wished that the States, after having pointed out whatever alterations and amendments may be judged necessary, would appoint another federal Convention to modify it upon those documents. For myself I have wondered that sensible men should not see the impracticability of the scheme. The members would go fortified with such Instructions that nothing but discordant ideas could prevail. Had I but slightly suspected (at the time when the late Convention was in session) that another Convention would not be likely to agree upon a better form of Government, I should now be confirmed in the fixed belief that they would not be able to agree upon any System whatever:—So many, I may add, such contradictory, and, in my opinion, unfounded objections have been urged against the System in contemplation; many of which would operate equally against every efficient Government that might be proposed. I will only add, as a farther opinion founded on the maturest deliberation, that there is no alternative—no hope of alteration—no intermediate resting place—between the adoption of this and a recurrence to an unqualified state of Anarchy, with all its deplorable consequences.—

A Federalist Satire

The item below is a Federalist satire of one of the most acerbic of the Antifederalist essayists, Pennsylvanian Samuel Bryan, who wrote eighteen essays under the pseudonym "Centinel."

This satire pretends to ask the people why they have not been aroused by the danger of tyranny created by the Constitution. It portrays the Antifederalists as really anarchists, who believe that "all government is tyrannical and oppressive." The essay asks why there has been little or no violent reaction to the Constitution, such as the Antifederalist mob that broke up a Federalist celebration in Carlisle, Pa., and it compares Antifederalists with the Shaysites of Massachusetts.

This essay was very popular with Federalists. It was reprinted in whole or part sixteen times from New Hampshire to South Carolina. Most of these newspapers had printed none of the real "Centinel" essays. Antifederalist printer Eleazer Oswald, of the Philadelphia Independent Gazetteer, *refused to print this satire, declaring that it was "spurious."*

Centinel No. XV (Spurious)
Pennsylvania Mercury, 16 February 1788

Friends, Countrymen, and Fellow-citizens! You have fought, you have bled, and you have conquered.—You have established your independence, and you ought to be free—But, behold! a set of aristocrats, demagogues, conspirators, and tyrants, have arisen up, and say you shall be governed—Is this to be endured by freemen,—men, who have lain in the open air, exposed to cold and hunger,—men who have worn out their health and constitutions in marches and countermarches from one end of the continent to the other; and after they have attained the noble prize, for which they contended, are they to sit down tamely and be governed? Of what service is a man's liberty to him, unless he can do as he pleases? And what man can do as he pleases, who lives under a government?—The very end of government is to bind men down to certain rules and duties; therefore, 'tis only fit for slaves and vassals.—Every freeman ought to govern himself, and then he will be governed most to his own mind.

Thus, my friends, you see all government is tyrannical and oppressive. In the next place it is insulting: It is as much as to tell us, we know not how to take care of ourselves, and therefore should submit to be directed by others, who are appointed as guardians over so many wards. Now, of what use can our reason be to us, if after we have come (or ought to have come) to years of discretion, we are still to be led, guided, and bandied about by those who pretend to know better than we?—And, who pray are those who are to be thus led, guided, and bandied about? Why, the people!—Strange! that three millions of people should be led, guided, and bandied about by ninety or an hundred aristocratical, demagogical, tyrannical conspirators!—Would it not be more according to order, propriety, and the nature of things, that the ninety or an hundred conspirators should be led, guided, and bandied about by the three millions of people.

In the third place, all government is expensive; for these ninety or an hundred conspirators will not govern us for nothing, they must be paid for it.—Think on that, my countrymen, we must not only be governed, be insulted by being governed, but we must pay these demagogues for coming from all parts of the continent, to lay their heads together how to govern us most effectually—for this, we must pay them mileage, pay them wages, fill their purses, supply their tables to keep them in idleness to riot on the fat of the land, to plot, contrive, and juggle us into good order and government. Now all this money might be saved to the public, by each man governing himself, and doing as he pleased, which by nature he has a right to do.

Oh my countrymen! my bowels yearn with affliction, when I think to what a pass we are likely to come—When I think, after all we have done and suffered for dear liberty, we must still be kept in order, and governed.—I had hoped, after our glorious struggle, this country would be an asylum for all those noble, untamed spirits, who were desirous of flying from all law, gospel, and government.—But alas! after all I have said and written, after all the inventions I have racked my brain for, and horrible descriptions I have laid before you, you are still unroused, and I have made no impression on any, except a few of those choice spirits at Carlisle.—And how have these been treated by the conspirators and federalists—they have been called insurgents, rioters, and British deserters—true, many of them were deserters, and to their credit be it spoken,—they deserted from king and country, friends and relations, wives and children, to come here and be free—they expected we were to be a free people, and they have come among us to live at large, and do as they please—Think then how disappointed they must be, and how peculiarly hard their case is, either to stay here and be governed, or to return and be hanged.

Rouse then, my friends, my countrymen, my fellow-citizens!—Rouse, ye Shayites, Dayites, and Shattuckites [all leaders of Shays' Rebellion in Massachusetts]!—Ye insurgents, rioters, and deserters! Ye tories, refugees, and antifoederalists! Rouse, and kick up a dust before it is too late!—Be not such a parcel of stupid, dunder-headed, blunder-headed, muddle-headed, puddle-headed blockheads—Such a tribe of snivelling, drivelling, sneaking, slinking, moping, poking, mumping, pitiful, pimping, pettifogging, poltrons,—such a set of nincumpoops, ninnyhammers, mushrooms, jackasses, jackanapeses, p-ssab-ds—Rouse!—awaken!—rub your eyes!—Do not you see the aristocrats, monocrats, demagogues, pedagogues, gogmagogs, brobdingnags, conspirators, and foederal hobgoblins, are preparing to govern you, to enslave you, enthral you, and bemaul you.—If you submit to them, they will rob you of your liberties—they will tie you hand and foot,—they will play hob with you, play the dickens with you, and play the d-v-l with you—they will put halters round your necks, and hold your noses to the grindstone—they will purge you and bleed you, glister you and blister you, drench you and vomit you—they will tread on your toes, break your shins, dock your tails, draw your teeth, tear your hair and scratch out your eyes,—they will pull your noses, lug your ears, punch you in the guts, and kick you in the breech—ZOUNDS! will nothing rouse you!

JOHN HANCOCK DEFENDS THE MASSACHUSETTS CONVENTION

On February 6, 1788, the Massachusetts Convention ratified the Constitution by a vote of 187 to 168. This Federalist victory would have been impossible, except for the compromise which provided that the Convention would vote to ratify the Constitution unconditionally, but would also call upon the first Congress under the Constitution to adopt some of the amendments Antifederalists had advocated. Antifederalists had argued that the Constitution should not be ratified until the amendments were added.

Federalists devised this compromise and they persuaded Governor Hancock to present it to the Convention as his own. The nature of the compromise and Hancock's prestige persuaded enough Convention delegates to vote for ratification to win the day. After the vote, several minority delegates declared that they accepted the result and would seek to unify the people and make the new system work.

When the legislature convened in February, Hancock addressed a joint session and submitted the result of the Convention. As called for by tradition, the legislature attempted to write a polite response. But this turned into a row between Federalists and Antifederalists. Finally, it was decided to lay the matter aside, and no response was made. The minority's proposed answer, below, suggests why Federalists decided to let the matter lie.

GOVERNOR JOHN HANCOCK'S SPEECH TO THE MASSACHUSETTS LEGISLATURE, 27 FEBRUARY 1788

The Convention which you appointed to deliberate upon that important subject [the Constitution], have concluded their Session, after having adopted & ratified the proposed plan, according to their resolution, a copy whereof, I have directed the Secretary to lay before you.

The obvious imbecility of the Confederation of the United States, has too long given pain to our friends, and pleasure to our enemies; but the forming a new System of Government, for so numerous a people, of very different views, and habits, spread upon such a vast extent of Territory, containing such a great variety of soils, and under such extremes of climate, was a task, which nothing less than the dreadful apprehension of losing our national existence, could have compelled the people to undertake.

We can be known to the world, only under the appellation of the *United States;* if we are robbed of the idea of our Union, we immediately become seperate nations, independent of each other, and no less liable to the depredations of foreign powers, than to wars and bloody contentions amongst ourselves. To pretend to exist as a nation without possessing those powers of coerce, which are necessarily incident to the national Character, would prove a fatal solecism in politicks. The objects of the proposed Constitution, are defence against external enemies, and the promotion of tranquility and happiness amongst the States. Whether it is well calculated for those important purposes, has been the subject of extensive and learned discussion in the Convention which you appointed. I believe there was never a body of men assembled, with greater purity of intention, or with higher zeal for the public interest. And although when the momentous Question was decided, there was a greater division than some expected, yet there appeared a candour, and a spirit of Conciliation, in the minority, which did them great honor, and afforded an happy presage of unanimity amongst the people at large. Tho' so many of the members of the late Convention could not feel themselves convinced that they ought to vote for the ratification of this System, yet their opposition was conducted with a candid and manly firmness, and with such marks of integrity and real regard to the public interest, as did them the highest honor, and leaves no reason to suppose that the peace, and good order of the Government is not their object.

The amendments proposed by the Convention, are intended to obtain a constitutional security of the principles to which they refer themselves, and must meet the wishes of all the States. I feel myself assured, that they will very early become a part of the Constitution; and when they shall be added to the proposed plan, I shall consider it the most perfect System of government, as to the objects it embraces, that has been known amongst mankind.

Gentlemen, As that BEING, in whose hands is the government of all the Nations of the Earth, and who putteth down one, and raiseth up another according to His Sovereign Pleasure, has given to the People of these States, a rich and an extensive Country; has in a marvellous manner, given them, a name and a standing among the Nations of the

World—has blessed them with external Peace, and internal Tranquility;—I hope and pray, that the gratitude of their Hearts may be expressed by a proper use of those inestimable blessings,—by the greatest exertions of Patriotism,—by forming and supporting Institutions for cultivating the human Understanding, and for the greatest Progress of the Arts and Sciences,—by establishing Laws for the support of Piety, Religion and Morality, as well as for punishing Vice and Wickedness,—and by exibiting in the great Theatre of the World, those social, public and private Virtues, which give more Dignity to a People, possessing their own Sovereignty, than Crowns and Diadems afford to Sovereign Princes. . . .

Proposed Minority Response to Governor Hancock
5 March 1788

In confederation and union with our sister states, we have happily baffled the intrigues and defeated the force of Great-Britain, have supported the rights of mankind, and secured the freedom and independence of America. While we wish to preserve the union entire, and are fully sensible of the ill consequences of an interruption of it, we are sorry to differ from your Excellency in the mode of effecting the first and avoiding the last.—Every good government should have for its objects defence against external enemies, and the promotion of internal tranquility and happiness. While we suspend our opinion of the purity of intention, and of the great zeal for the interest and welfare with which the late convention assembled, we are in justice to our constituents constrained to say that the result of their deliberations does not seem well calculated for those valuable purposes. We shall, under this head, only add, that the rights and liberties of a great country should stand on firmer ground than that of mere probability. If the amendments proposed with the ratification of the late convention, had been made a condition of ratification, they would have gone some way, though not fully, to a conciliation of our minds to the system, but your Excellency will permit us to say, that, as they now stand, they neither comport with the dignity or safety of the Commonwealth.

MERCY WARREN SEES DANGER IN THE CONSTITUTION

It was once generally believed that the essay below was written by Elbridge Gerry, a leading Antifederalist and one of three delegates to the Constitutional Convention who refused to sign the Constitution. But in 1930, the great constitutional historian Charles Warren discovered family papers that demonstrated that the author was Mercy Otis Warren.

Mercy Warren (1728–1814) was an historian, playwright, and poet. As a leading Revolutionary (her brother was James Otis) she published three plays between 1772 and 1775 that satirized the royal establishment in Massachusetts. By 1788 she had already begun writing her history of the Revolution, which was published in 1805.

Warren opposed the Constitution because she believed it was a tool of the aristocracy to destroy democracy, that it endangered freedom of religion, of the press, and trial by jury, that it did not honor the principle of separation of powers between the executive and legislative branches, and that it would create a consolidated government that would annihilate the states.

"A Columbian Patriot" was published as a nineteen-page pamphlet in Boston in February 1788. It was reprinted as a pamphlet and in a newspaper in New York and in two Philadelphia newspapers, and was widely distributed by Antifederalists.

In the excerpt below, Warren argues for continued opposition to the Constitution even though six of the nine required states had already ratified. She is especially bitter that the Massachusetts Convention ratified, and she compares Governor John Hancock, who helped achieve ratification, unfavorably with Virginia Governor Edmund Randolph. Hancock introduced the proposal that the Massachusetts Convention adopted, providing that the Convention would ratify the Constitution but would ask that amendments to be added after the new government went into effect. Antifederalists had demanded that amendments be adopted before ratification, and Warren is scornful of Hancock's compromise.

Warren attacks the idea that the country needs the "reigns of government" drawn more tightly. The country, despite Shays' Rebellion, was at peace. The Constitution was not needed, and if the people were not hurried into adopting it, they would realize that it was not only unnecessary but dangerous.

A Columbian Patriot (Mercy Otis Warren)
Observations on the Constitution

Though several State Conventions have assented to, and ratified, yet the voice of the people appears at present strong against the adoption of the Constitution.—By the chicanery, intrigue, and false colouring of those who plume themselves, more on their education and abilities, than their political, patriotic, or private virtues—by the imbecility of some, and the duplicity of others, a majority of the Convention of Massachusetts have been flattered with the ideas of amendments, when it will be too late to complain—While several very worthy characters, too timid for their situation, magnified the hopeless alternative, between the dissolution of the bands of all government, and receiving the proffered system *in toto,* after long endeavouring to reconcile it to their consciences, swallowed the indigestible penacea, and in a kind of sudden desperation lent their signature to the dereliction of the honorable station they held in the Union, and have broken over the solemn compact, by which they were bound to support their own excellent constitution till the period of revision.—

Yet Virginia, equally large and respectable, and who have done honour to themselves, by their vigorous exertions from the first dawn of independence, have not yet acted upon the question; they have wisely taken time to consider before they introduce innovations of a most dangerous nature:—her inhabitants are brave, her burgesses are free, and they have a Governor who dares to think for himself, and to speak his opinion (without first pouring libations on the alter of popularity) though it should militate with some of the most accomplished and illustrious characters. . . .

It is true this country lately armed in opposition to regal despotism—impoverished by the expences of a long war, and unable immediately to fulfil their public or private engagements, have appeared in some instances, with a boldness of spirit that seemed to set at defiance all authority, government, or order, on the one hand; while on the other, there has been, not only a secret wish, but an open avowal of the necessity of drawing the reigns of government much too taut, not only for republicanism, but for a wise and limited monarchy.—But the character of this people is not averse to a degree of subordination: the truth of this appears from the easy restoration of tranquility, after a dangerous insurrection in one of the states; this also evinces the little necessity of a complete revolution of government throughout the union. But it is a republican principle that the majority should rule; and if a spirit of moderation could be cultivated on both sides, till the voice of the people at large could be fairly heard it should be held sacred.—And if, on such a scrutiny, the proposed constitution should appear repugnant to their character and wishes; if they, in the language of a late elegant pen, should acknowledge that "no confusion in my mind, is more terrible to them than the stern disciplined regularity and vaunted police of arbitrary governments, where every heart is depraved by fear, where mankind dare not assume their natural characters, where the free spirit must crouch to the slave in office, where genius must repress her effusions, or like the Egyptian worshippers, offer them in sacrifice to the calves in power, and where the human mind, always in shackles, shrinks from every generous effort." Who would then have the effrontery to say, it ought not to be thrown out with indignation, however some respectable names have appeared to support it.—But if after all, on a dispassionate and fair discussion, the people generally give their voice for a voluntary dereliction of their privileges, let every individual who chooses the active scenes of life, strive to support the peace and unanimity of his country, though every other blessing may expire—And while the statesman is plodding for power, and the courtier practising the arts of dissimulation without check—while the rapacious are growing rich by oppression, and fortune throwing her gifts into the lap of fools, let the sublimer characters, the philosophic lovers of freedom who have wept over her exit, retire to the calm shades of contemplation, there they may look down with pity on the inconsistency of human nature, the revolutions of states, the rise of kingdoms, and the fall of empires.

A Defense of the Electoral College

Every four years Americans elect a President, and every four years considerable debate is generated over the method we use in that election. The people do not elect the President directly, nor does the Congress or the state legislatures elect the President. Rather, the people vote for electors in each state, who then cast their ballots for the President and Vice President.

Because of a tie vote between Thomas Jefferson and Aaron Burr in the presidential election of 1800, some changes were instituted in the method of electing the President. The rise of political parties and improvements in communications have also changed the nature of presidential elections; but, the electoral college established by the Founding Fathers still remains intact today. In The Federalist *No. 68, Alexander Hamilton explained why the Constitution provides for this indirect election of our chief executive.*

PUBLIUS: THE FEDERALIST NO. 68 (ALEXANDER HAMILTON) NEW YORK INDEPENDENT JOURNAL, 12 MARCH 1788

The mode of appointment of the chief magistrate of the United States is almost the only part of the system, of any consequence, which has escaped without severe censure, or which has received the slightest mark of approbation from its opponents. The most plausible of these [the Federal Farmer], who has appeared in print, has even deigned to admit, that the election of the president is pretty well guarded. I venture somewhat further; and hesitate not to affirm, that if the manner of it be not perfect, it is at least excellent. It unites in an eminent degree all the advantages; the union of which was to be desired.

It was desirable, that the sense of the people should operate in the choice of the person to whom so important a trust was to be confided. This end will be answered by committing the right of making it, not to any pre-established body [i.e., Congress or the state legislatures], but to men, chosen by the people for the special purpose, and at the particular conjuncture.

It was equally desirable, that the immediate election should be made by men most capable of analyzing the qualities adapted to the station, and acting under circumstances favourable to deliberation and to a judicious combination of all the reasons and inducements, which were proper to govern their choice. A small number of persons, selected by their fellow citizens from the general mass, will be most likely to possess the information and discernment requisite to such complicated investigations.

It was also peculiarly desirable, to afford as little opportunity as possible to tumult and disorder. This evil was not least to be dreaded in the election of a magistrate, who was to have so important an agency in the administration of the government, as the president of the United States. But the precautions which have been so happily concerted in the system under consideration, promise an effectual security against this mischief. The choice of *several* to form an intermediate body of electors, will be much less apt to convulse the community, with any extraordinary or violent movements, than the choice of *one* who was himself to be the final object of the public wishes. And as the electors, chosen in each state, are to assemble and vote in the state, in which they are chosen, this detached and divided situation will expose them much less to heats and ferments, which might be communicated from them to the people, than if they were all to be convened at one time, in one place.

Nothing was more to be desired, than that every practicable obstacle should be opposed to cabal, intrigue and corruption. These most deadly adversaries of republican government might naturally have been expected to make their approaches from more than one quarter, but chiefly from the desire in foreign powers to gain an improper ascendant in our councils. How could they better gratify this, than by raising a creature of their own to the chief magistracy of the union? But the convention have guarded against all danger of this sort with the most provident and judicious attention. They have not made the appointment of the president to depend on any pre-existing bodies of men who might be tampered with before hand to prostitue their votes; but they have referred it in the first instance to an immediate act of the people of America, to be exerted in the choice of persons for the temporary and sole purpose of making the appointment. And they have excluded from eligibility to this trust, all those who from situation might be suspected of too great devotion to the president in office. No senator, representative, or other person holding a place of trust or profit under the United States, can be of the number of the electors. Thus, without corrupting the body of the people, the immediate agents in the election will at least enter upon the task, free from any sinister bias. Their transient existence, and their detached situation, already taken notice of, afford a satisfactory prospect of their continuing so, to the conclusion of it. . . .

All these advantages will be happily combined in the plan devised by the convention; which is, that the people of each state shall choose a number of persons as electors, equal to the number of senators and representatives of such state in the national government, who shall assemble within the state and vote for some fit person as president. Their votes, thus given, are to be transmitted to the seat of the national government; and the person who may happen to have a majority of the whole number of votes will be the president. . . .

This process of election affords a moral certainty, that the office of president, will seldom fall to the lot of any man, who is not in an eminent degree endowed with the requisite qualifications. Talents for low intrigue and the little arts of popularity may alone suffice to elevate a man to the first honors in a single state; but it will require other talents and a different kind of merit to establish him in the esteem and confidence of the whole union, or of so considerable a portion of it as would be necessary to make him a successful candidate for the distinguished office of president of the United States. It will not be too strong to say, that there will be a constant probability of seeing the station filled by characters pre-eminent for ability and virtue. And this will be thought no inconsiderable recommendation of the constitution, by those, who are able to estimate the share, which the executive in every government must necessarily have in its good or ill administration. . . .

Property and Liberty Both Secured by the Constitution

The essay below was probably written by George Nicholas, a Virginia lawyer. He was elected to the Virginia state ratifying Convention, where he voted in favor of the Constitution in June 1788.

In the essay, Nicholas returned to one of the most important themes in Federalist thinking—the close connection between liberty and property and the need for a government that could protect both. Nicholas tackled the main Antifederalist objection, that the Constitution would endanger liberty. He turned this around a little by arguing that liberty without justice and security is an empty ideal. He called for a government that could withstand the whims of the people yet would still operate under proper restraints.

Nicholas believed that the government under the Constitution would be unable to deprive the people of their personal and property rights, that it could not tax some people or property more than others, and that its justice system would be equally open to all. One major benefit of the Constitution, was that it would prevent the states from abusing their power in such a way as to endanger property rights, as they had done in recent years.

The State Soldier (George Nicholas)
Virginia Independent Chronicle, 19 March 1788

All the objections to the constitution appear to be contained under two heads—the one respects our liberties, the other our interests. To those which respect our liberties, only, I mean to reply in this paper; and in order the more effectually to do that, I shall head this first class of objections under that assertion, which holds forth, that *by the adoption of this constitution we shall be deprived of our liberties.*

And considering that as the *ne plus ultra* of antifoederal workmanship, I shall, after viewing it in the light of a slender fabrick built in air, and filled with imaginary bugbears, first examine into its foundation as a general assertion; and then prove its feebleness by trying the arguments on which it depends for support.

The only desirable purpose of any government, is, the security of mens persons and property; and that which advances farthest that way, is not only the most perfect, but the most free.

Chimerical and speculative enjoyments, may amuse the imagination; but justice and safety alone can ensure real happiness—and liberty without happiness is but emptiness and sound.

The more independent a government is therefore of the people, under proper restraints, the more likely it is to produce that justice; and the more substantial and efficient under such restraints, the better calculated to protect both the persons and property of mankind. And the efficiency and energy, of this government being acknowledged, in this *general objection* itself, the only necessary enquiry will be, whether the restraints are sufficient to prevent its becoming too formidable in the end.

In respect to restraints on government, there are but three things necessary to be guarded against, the first is a power to deprive men of their personal rights or property by direct laws; the second, is, a power to depress those natural rights into a meanness of person by preventing men from acquiring property from loading them unequally with the public burthens of the state; and the third is, a power to destroy the equality of right by a partial administration of justice. That government which is guarded against those powers, may be said to have all the restraints necessary to constitute a rational happiness under any society.

Let us examine then how far the proposed constitution may be valued on that head.

Under this government neither the Congress nor state legislature could, by direct laws, deprive us of any property we might hold under the general law of the land, or punish us for any offence committed previous to the passage of such laws, since they are prohibited from passing ex post facto laws. Nor could they injure the value of any species of property by partial taxes, since from the proportion laid down in that government, to affect the value of slaves, for instance, in this state, they must ruin all the free persons in several others. Nor could they injure the property of an individual in any state, since the same proportion must be observed throughout a part as well as the whole.

Neither could they in the third instance destroy the equality of right, or injure the value of property in a particular state, or belonging to any individual by a partial administration of justice, since the same doors of one general tribunal would be opened to all—which would on the contrary enhance the value of all property on the continent by giving confidence to foreign creditors, and an equal security to citizens of every state. . . .

That from what has been said already on either side, it may I think be concluded that our liberties so far from being diminished, will be increased by the adoption of the new constitution, as it will be a means of depriving the states of the right of exercising the most unbounded acts of injustice, under which, both the persons and property of men are insecure; and under such insecurity, every earthly consideration is lessened in its value. Whence, as there is no species of liberty but what is connected either with the person or property of mankind, so there is no species of it also but what is increased by adding confidence and safety to the one, and permanence and value to the other. And that government therefore which is best calculated to ensure both, is most consistent with every rational idea of liberty and happiness.

The Constitution Is What the Court Says It Is

The power of the Supreme Court to declare acts of Congress unconstitutional is well established in law today. But in the early days of the Republic this was in dispute. The first exercise of this power took place in 1803 in the case of Marbury v. Madison. *At that time, President Thomas Jefferson and Secretary of State James Madison (the defendant) questioned whether the court had such a power, though in 1788 both would have agreed that it did. The Court did not declare another act of Congress unconstitutional until 1857, in the infamous Dred Scott decision. Since then, the court has struck down many acts of Congress. Historians and political scientists, however, still debate whether this power of judicial review was intended by the Framers of the Constitution.*

The essay below, by the great Antifederalist essayist who signed his name "Brutus" (we do not know who he was), clearly indicates that Antifederalists understood that the court would have such power, and they objected to it as another restraint on the power of the people. The judges were appointed, not elected, and they held their offices for life (good behavior), but they had the power to strike down legislation. Antifederalists viewed this as antidemocratic and another reason to oppose the Constitution.

Brutus No. XV
New York Journal, 20 March 1788

I said in my last number, that the supreme court under this constitution would be exalted above all other power in the government, and subject to no controul. The business of this paper will be to illustrate this, and to shew the danger that will result from it. I question whether the world ever saw, in any period of it, a court of justice invested with such immense powers, and yet placed in a situation so little responsible. Certain it is, that in England, and in the several states, where we have been taught to believe, the courts of law are put upon the most prudent establishment, they are on a very different footing.

The judges in England, it is true, hold their offices during their good behaviour, but then their determinations are subject to correction by the house of lords; and their power is by no means so extensive as that of the proposed supreme court of the union.—I believe they in no instance assume the authority to set aside an act of parliament under the idea that it is inconsistent with their constitution. They consider themselves bound to decide according to the existing laws of the land, and never undertake to controul them by adjudging that they are inconsistent with the constitution—much less are they vested with the power of giving an *equitable* construction to the constitution.

The judges in England are under the controul of the legislature, for they are bound to determine according to the laws passed by them. But the judges under this constitution will controul the legislature, for the supreme court are authorised in the last resort, to determine what is the extent of the powers of the Congress; they are to give the constitution an explanation, and there is no power above them to set aside their judgment. The framers of this constitution appear to have followed that of the British, in rendering the judges independent, by granting them their offices during good behaviour, without following the constitution of England, in instituting a tribunal in which their errors may be corrected; and without adverting to this, that the judicial under this system have a power which is above the legislative, and which indeed transcends any power before given to a judicial by any free government under heaven.

. . . There is no power above them, to controul any of their decisions. There is no authority that can remove them, and they cannot be controuled by the laws of the legislature. In short, they are independent of the people, of the legislature, and of every power under heaven. Men placed in this situation will generally soon feel themselves independent of heaven itself.

I have said that the judges under this system will be *independent* in the strict sense of the word: To prove this I will shew—That there is no power above them that can controul their decisions, or correct their errors. There is no authority that can remove them from office for any errors or want of capacity, or lower their salaries, and in many cases their power is superior to that of the legislature.

1st. There is no power above them that can correct their errors or controul their decisions—The adjudications of this court are final and irreversible, for there is no court above them to which appeals can lie, either in error or on the merits.—In this respect it differs from the courts in England, for there the house of lords is the highest court, to whom appeals, in error, are carried from the highest of the courts of law.

2d. They cannot be removed from office or suffer a dimunition of their salaries, for any error in judgement or want of capacity.

It is expressly declared by the constitution,—"That they shall at stated times receive a compensation for their services which shall not be diminished during their continuance in office."

3d. The power of this court is in many cases superior to that of the legislature. I have shewed, in a former paper, that this court will be authorised to decide upon the meaning of the constitution, and that, not only according to the natural and obvious meaning of the words, but also according to the spirit and intention of it. In the exercise of this power they will not be subordinate to, but above the legislature. For all the departments of this government will receive their powers, so far as they are expressed in the constitution, from the people immediately, who are the source of power. The legislature can only exercise such powers as are given them by the constitution, they cannot assume any of the rights annexed to the judicial, for this plain reason, that the same authority which vested the legislature with their powers, vested the judicial with theirs—both are derived from the same source, both therefore are equally valid, and the judicial hold their powers independently of the legislature, as the legislature do of the judicial.—The supreme court then have a right, independent of the legislature, to give a construction to the constitution and every part of it, and there is no power provided in this system to correct their construction or do it away. If, therefore, the legislature pass any laws, inconsistent with the sense the judges put upon the constitution, they will declare it void; and therefore in this respect their power is superior to that of the legislature.

THE PUBLICATION OF THE BOOK VERSION OF *THE FEDERALIST*

B<i>eginning on October 27, 1787, a remarkable series of eighty-five essays began appearing in New York City newspapers. These essays, entitled</i> The Federalist, *were written under the pen name "Publius" by Alexander Hamilton, James Madison and John Jay. Over the last 200 years, these essays have been recognized as the single most important American contribution to the study of government.*

Around December 1, 1787, New York City printers John and Archibald M'Lean were commissioned by Alexander Hamilton and a committee of gentlemen to produce 500 copies of a pamphlet containing 20 to 25 essays, at a total cost of £30. The M'Leans first announced their publication plans on January 2, 1788, in John M'Lean's New York Independent Journal. *In general, the work would be "printed on a fine Paper and good Type" in a duodecimo volume, although "a few Copies" would be printed on "superfine Royal Writing Paper," at ten shillings a volume. Printers and booksellers throughout America were authorized to accept subscriptions. From January to March, the M'Lean advertisement was run several times in the* Independent Journal *and the* New York Packet *and one or more times in the New York* Daily Advertiser, *the* Poughkeepsie Country Journal, *the Richmond* Virginia Independent Chronicle, *and John M'Lean's* Norfolk and Portsmouth Journal *in Norfolk, Va.*

On March 19 the New York Independent Journal *announced that "Those Gentlemen, who were intrusted with Subscription Lists for the* FEDERALIST, *are requested to send them to the Printing-Office, No. 41, Hanover-Square, as the first Volume of that Valuable Work will be published on Saturday next."*

On 22 March, the Independent Journal *informed its readers that the first volume of* The Federalist *had just been published and was selling for three shillings to subscribers, who were asked to send for their copies. The* Journal *also stated that a second volume was in press.*

Volume I, over 230 pages long, contains the preface below; a table of contents giving descriptive titles for each essay; and the texts of the first thirty-six essays. The unsigned preface below was written by Alexander Hamilton only five days before the volume was offered for sale. Hamilton also served as editor and corrected a number of the essays.

John and Archibald M'Lean were not satisfied with their compensation as printers of The Federalist. *On October 14, 1788, four and a half months after the appearance of Volume II, Archibald M'Lean sent a bill to the New York committee that had commissioned the publication. M'Lean stated that when he and his brother first agreed to print the pamphlet edition, they anticipated one volume of no more than twenty-five essays, for which they planned to charge six shillings. However, "The Work encreased from 25 Numbers to 85, so that instead of giving the Subscribers one vollume containing 200 Pages for six shillings, I was obliged to give them two vollumes containing upwards of 600 pages.*

"The Money expended for Printing Paper, Journeymens Wages and Binding was upwards of two hundred and seventy Pounds; of which sum I have charged Coll: Hamilton with 144 Pounds, which is not three shillings per Vol: I have several hundred Copies remaining on hand, and even allowing they were all sold, at the low Price I am obliged to sell them at, I would not clear five Pounds on the whole impression." On May 22 and August 14, 1789, Archibald M'Lean advertised in his New York Daily Gazette *(a successor to the* Independent Journal*) "that a few Copies" of* The Federalist *remained for sale. In 1799 the remaining copies of the M'Lean edition were republished by John Tiebout of New York City with new title pages.*

Soon after its appearance, Volume I of The Federalist *was reviewed in the March and April issues of the New York* American Magazine. *The reviewer, probably editor Noah Webster, summarized the essays and asserted that "it would be difficult to find a treatise, which, in so small a compass, contains so much valuable information, or in which the true principles of republican government are unfolded with such precision." Volume II of* The Federalist *was reviewed in the May and June issues of the* Magazine.

Advertisement, New York Independent Journal
22 March 1788

A desire to throw full light upon so interesting a subject has led, in a great measure unavoidably, to a more copious discussion than was at first intended; and the undertaking not being yet completed, it is judged adviseable to divide the collection into two Volumes.

The several matters which are contained in these Papers, are immediately interwoven with the very existence of this new Empire, and ought to be well understood by every Citizen of America. The Editor entertains no doubt that they will be thought by the judicious reader, the cheapest as well as most valuable publication ever offered to the American Public.

The second Volume is in the Press, and will be published with all possible expedition.

Subscribers will be pleased to send for their Copies, to the Printing-Office, No. 41, Hanover-Square, four Doors from the Old-Slip.

Those Gentlemen who were intrusted with Subscription Lists, will please to return them to the Printers; and those in the Country are desired to forward theirs immediately.

Preface to Volume I of The Federalist

It is supposed that a collection of the papers which have made their appearance, in the Gazettes of this City, under the Title of the Federalist, may not be without effect in assisting the public judgment on the momentous question of the Constitution for the United States, now under the consideration of the people of America. A desire to throw full light upon so interesting a subject has led, in a great measure unavoidably, to a more copious discussion than was at first intended. And the undertaking not being yet completed, it is judged adviseable to divide the collection into two Volumes, of which the ensuing Numbers constitute the first. The second Volume will follow as speedily as the Editor can get it ready for publication.

The particular circumstances under which these papers have been written, have rendered it impracticable to avoid violations of method and repetitions of ideas which cannot but displease a critical reader. The latter defect has even been intentionally indulged, in order the better to impress particular arguments which were most material to the general scope of the reasoning. Respect for public opinion, not anxiety for the literary character of the performance, dictates this remark. The great wish is, that it may promote the cause of truth, and lead to a right judgment of the true interests of the community.

Was There a Conspiracy to Stop Antifederalist Newspapers?

In the eighteenth century, the press was considered "the great palladium of freedom," and it was believed that so long as the press was free there could be no tyranny. Conversely, one of the first steps an incipient tyrant would take would be to shackle the press.

Printers in America maintained the fiction that their presses were open to all sides of a public issue. But in fact, newspaper printers generally sided with one political faction or the other, and the articles they printed tended to support the faction they favored.

In the debate over the Constitution, the vast majority of printers were Federalists. Antifederalists printed their articles in a few newspapers, the American Herald *in Boston, the* New York Journal, *the* Independent Gazetteer *and the* Freeman's Journal *in Philadelphia, and a few other papers, like the Winchester* Virginia Gazette. *These articles tended to be reprinted in other newspapers far less often than Federalist articles.*

Antifederalists became alarmed in early 1788 when the post office announced a new policy prohibiting newspaper printers from exchanging their newspapers postage free. Printers would now have to contract directly with post riders who carried the mail between towns. Printers soon noticed that the circulation of newspapers from printer to printer through the mails was becoming intermittent. Antifederalist leaders had long suspected that their letters were being intercepted in the post office; now they believed that the newspapers were not being delivered, thereby isolating the printing centers from the rest of the country. In the articles below, Matthias Bartgis, printer of the Winchester Virginia Gazette *expressed his outrage at the stoppage of the mails. Some of his readers disagreed with him.*

The Editors, 26 March 1788

The Editors of this Paper, feel with their brother Printers throughout the United States, the ill-consequences of a *late* regulation at the general Post-Office, for stopping the circulation of the news-papers through the medium of the mails, they not having received any Northern papers, except by transcient conveyance, for several months past. Whatever *secret views* the promoters of this diabolical plan may have, we hope the guardians of our liberty and future safety, will be vigilant in frustrating so dangerous a measure, which may eventually lead us blindfold to the rivets of slavery. If this is a *sample* of what we *may expect* from the establishment of the Federal Constitution, may we not with propriety say, from *such a government, "Good Lord, deliver us."*

A FEDERALIST: TO THE EDITORS, 2 APRIL 1788

Of all the anti-federal productions which have yet appeared, the paragraph in your last paper, respecting the stoppage of the circulation of news-papers is the most extraordinary. If the fact be as there stated, it is a grievance which ought to be redressed, but it is inconsistency in the extreme to charge a government which is not in existence, with the mal-administration of the present government. If Congress authorise the abuse, it affords an additional reason for their dissolution, and for the establishment of a government on more liberal principles, in which our rulers will be chosen by the people at large, and consequently we may expect them to be more attentive to our interests, and more vigilant guardians of our liberties, than the members of the present Congress.

THE EDITORS, 2 APRIL 1788

The Editors sincerely wish that the new Constitution had been so framed, that *every paragraph* published on that important subject, could have been truly federal, but when opinions vary, and it is submitted to the People for free discussion, to see *men in public office* taking undue measures to establish it, without a thorough investigation, and by means which not only grossly infringes on the liberties of the people, but strikes a fatal blow at their very political existence, the Editors think it a duty incumbent on them as Printers of a public paper, to give the alarm. It ever has been (even under the tyrannical government of Britain) an invariable privilege to suffer, for the public good, a free passage for news-papers in the mails, but of late, for reasons which the Editors wish not to suggest, they are prohibited. Whatever may be the views of *public men* at the present day, if they should be continued in office (which it is more than probable they will, unless from their present conduct they are well guarded against) may we not expect the same measures? which, if practised, we may bid adieu to that *scourge to tyrants, an unrestrained Press.*

The most distant view of injuring the Constitution did not exist by publishing the paragraph above referred to, but, that due notice might be taken of so daring a breach of public confidence.

ONE OF THE PEOPLE, 9 APRIL 1788

Extract of a letter from a gentleman in the country dated March 31, to his friend in town.

"From Messi'rs Bartgis & Company's addresses to the public, in their papers of the 7th and 14th instant, I was led to believe that they were party men. But from their piece in the last *Winchester Gazette,* [April 2], I take them to be strong anti-federalists: be that as it may, I am clear of opinion, every man has a right to enjoy his own opinion. But I am also of opinion that they, nor no other man can, with propriety, lay the blame of their not receiving the northern papers, to the Federal Constitution, when every body knows, that Constitution has not taken place, and of course can have no effect. If the Post-Master-General, his deputy, his deputy's deputy, or any other, has stop'd the circulation of news, as they have set forth in their piece, the Post-Master-General, his deputy, &c. are liable to public censure, and ought to be exposed, then their prayer would [have] been with more propriety thus: From our present, or any other government, which will suffer the Post-Master-General, his deputy, his deputy's deputy, or any other person whatever to stop the press, "Good Lord, deliver us."

THE EDITORS, 9 APRIL 1788

The Editors with the greatest reluctance again trouble their readers with a defence of their public conduct, as Printers:—they have before asserted, that no intention existed with them of injuring the constitution:—they wish to expose every secret attempted to effect a *partial* [biased] circulation of observations wrote on the subject, *by men who are looking for continuations of lucrative offices.* Had an effort been made by those *opposed* to the constitution, to wrest from the public eye, *the means of information,* they would as readily have exposed them. They conceive it *their duty* to be watchful of every attempt to destroy our dear-earn'd freedom, let the design come from what man, or set of men, it may.

Whatever the *private sentiments* of the Editors may be, on political subjects, they ever have endeavoured to demonstrate a *strict equality* of publications on the new government: *unbiassed by party, and unawed by frowns, they are determined to be free.*

Absolute Power Corrupts Absolutely

Luther Martin, attorney general of Maryland and a former member of the Constitutional Convention, was one of the major Antifederalist essayists. In the piece below, he demonstrates a common trait of Antifederalists: he looks at history as a cautionary tale warning against granting undefined or excessive power to any person or government.

Martin believed that government should have only so much power as was absolutely necessary and no more. His view of human nature was hardly flattering. Man was hungry for power, and when once he had it, he used it to oppress his fellows.

Martin's description of the Federalist argument, that the people should trust their leaders, is a caricature of a more complex position. But suspicion of power led Antifederalists to oppose the Constitution, because it granted too much power to the federal government, and to demand the addition of a Bill of Rights before the Constitution was adopted.

Luther Martin's Address
Maryland Journal, 1 April 1788

Power absolute and unlimited, united with unerring wisdom and unbounded goodness, is the government of the Deity over the universe!—But remember, my fellow-citizens, that the persons to whom you are about to delegate authority, are and will be weak, erring mortals, subject to the same passions, prejudices and infirmities with yourselves; and let it be deeply engraven on your hearts, that from the first history of government to the present time, if we begin with Nimrod, and trace down the rulers of nations to those who are *now* invested with supreme power, we shall find few, very few, who have made the beneficent Governor of the Universe the model of their conduct, while many are they who, on the contrary, have imitated the demons of darkness.

We have no right to expect that our rulers will be more wise, more virtuous, or more perfect than those of other nations have been, or that they will not be equally under the influence of ambition, avarice, and all that train of baleful passions, which have so generally proved the curse of our unhappy race.

We must consider mankind such as they really are,—such as experience has shewn them to be heretofore, and bids us to expect to find them hereafter, and not suffer ourselves to be misled by interested deceivers or enthusiastick visionaries; and therefore in forming a system of government, to delegate no greater power than is *clearly* and *certainly necessary*, ought to be the first principle with every people who are influenced by reason and a regard for their safety, and in doing this, they ought most solicitously to endeavour so to qualify even that power, by such checks and restraints, as to produce a perfect responsibility in those who are to exercise it, and prevent them from its abuse with a chance of impunity;—since such is the nature of man, that he has a propensity to abuse authority and to tyrannize over the rights of his fellow-men;—and to whomsoever power is given, not content with the actual deposit, they will ever strive to obtain an increase.

Those who would wish to excite and keep awake your jealousy and distrust, are your truest friends;—while they, who speak peace to you when there is no peace—who would lull you into security, and wish you to repose blind confidence in your future governors, are your most dangerous enemies.—Jealousy and distrust are the guardian angels who watch over liberty:—security and confidence are the forerunners of slavery.

But the advocates for the system tell you that we who oppose it, endeavour to terrify you with mere possibilities, which may never be realized, that all our objections consist in saying government *may* do this, and government *may* do that.—

I will, for argument sake, admit the justice of this remark, and yet maintain that the objections are insurmountable.—I consider it an incontrovertible truth, that whatever by the constitution government even *may* do, if it relates to the abuse of power, by acts tyrannical and oppressive, it some time or other *will* do.—Such is the ambition of man, and his lust for domination, that no power less than that which fixed its bounds to the ocean, can say, to them, "thus far shall ye go and no farther." . . . Those who tell you the government by this constitution *may* keep up a *standing army*,—abolish the trial by jury,—oppress the citizens of the states by its powers over the militia,—destroy the freedom of the press,—infringe the liberty of conscience [religion], and do a number of other acts injurious to and destructive of your rights, yet that it *never will do so;* and that you safely may accept such a constitution, and be perfectly at ease and secure that your rulers will always be so good, so wise, and so virtuous—such emanations of the Deity, that they will never use their power but for your interest and your happiness—contradict the uniform experience of ages, and betray a total ignorance of human nature, or a total want [lack] of ingenuity.

Look back, my fellow citizens, to your conduct but a few years past [during the Revolution], and let that instruct you what ought to be your conduct at this time. . . .

You are not now called upon to make an equal sacrifice—you are not now requested to beat your ploughshares into swords, or your pruning hooks into spears—to leave your peaceful habitations, and exchange domestic tranquility for the horrors of war;—peaceably, quietly and orderly to give this system of slavery your negative, is all that is asked by the advocates of freedom—to pronounce the single monosyllable *no,* is all they entreat;—shall they entreat you in vain?—when by this it is to be determined, whether our independence, for obtaining which we have been accustomed to bow the knee with reverential gratitude to Heaven, shall be our greatest curse—and when on this it depends whether we shall be subjected to a government, of which the little finger will be thicker than the loins of that of Great-Britain.

But there are also persons who pretend that your situation is at present so bad, that it cannot be worse, and urge that as an argument why we should embrace any remedy proposed, however desperate it may appear. . . .

Should the citizens of America, in a fit of desperation, be induced to commit this fatal act of political *suicide,* to which by such arguments they are stimulated, the day will come when labouring under more than Egyptian bondage, compelled to furnish their quota of brick, though destitute of straw and of mortar; galled with your chains, and worn down by oppression, you will, by sad experience, be convinced (when that conviction shall be too late) that there is a difference in evils, and that the buzzing of gnats is more supportable than the sting of a serpent.

The Senate Criticized

The Senate under the new Constitution most nearly resembled the old Confederation Congress.

The states were equally represented in both bodies and members of both were elected by the state legislatures (until the 17th Amendment provided for popular election of U.S. Senators in 1913).

The equality of the states in the Senate was applauded by the small states and by those people who favored a confederation of states as opposed to a consolidated national government that might one day abolish the states. Many Americans also objected to the senators' six-year term.

No other public official in America had as long a term—in fact, before the Constitution, no official's term was longer than three years. The six-year term, coupled with the abolition of the mandatory rotation in office and the power of states to recall their congressmen, caused many Americans to fear that senators would no longer adequately represent their constituents.

Many of these fears were expressed by "Brutus," one of the country's leading Antifederalist essayists.

Brutus No. XVI
New York Journal, 10 April 1788

The apportionment of members of the Senate among the States is not according to numbers, or the importance of the States; but is equal. This, on the plan of a consolidated government, is unequal and improper; but is proper on the system of confederation—on this principle I approve of it.

It is indeed the only feature of any importance in the constitution of a confederated government. It was obtained after a vigorous struggle of that part of the Convention who were in favor of preserving the state governments.

It is to be regretted, that they were not able to have infused other principles into the plan, to have secured the government of the respective states, and to have marked with sufficient precision the line between them and the general government.

The term for which the senate are to be chosen, is in my judgment too long, and no provision being made for a rotation will, I conceive, be of dangerous consequence. It is difficult to fix the precise period for which the senate should be chosen. It is a matter of opinion, and our sentiments on the matter must be formed, by attending to certain principles.

Some of the duties which are to be performed by the senate, seem evidently to point out the propriety of their term of service extended beyond the period of the assembly (i.e., the House of Representatives).

Besides as they are designed to represent the aristocracy of the country, it seems fit they should possess more stability, and so continue a longer period than that branch who represent the democracy.

The business of making treaties and some other which it will be proper to commit to the senate, requires that they should have experience, and therefore that they should remain some time in office to acquire it.

But still it is of equal importance that they should not be so long in office as to be likely to forget the hand that formed them, or be insensible of their interests. Men long in office are very apt to feel themselves independent. To form and pursue interests separate from those who appointed them.

And this is more likely to be the case with the senate, as they will for the most part of the time be absent from the state they represent, and associate with such company as will possess very little of the feelings of the middling class of people.

For it is to be remembered that there is to be a *federal* city, and the inhabitants of it will be the great and the mighty of the earth. For these reasons I would shorten the term of their service to four years.

Six years is too long a period for a man to be absent from his home, it would have a tendency to wean him from his constituents. A rotation in the senate, would also in my opinion be of great use. It is probable that senators once chosen for a state will, as the system now stands, continue in office for life.

The office will be honorable if not lucrative. The persons who occupy it will probably wish to continue it, and therefore use all their influence and that of their friends to continue in office.—Their friends will be numerous and powerful, for they (i.e., the Senators) will have it in their power to confer great favors; besides it will before long be considered as disgraceful not to be re-elected.

It will therefore be considered as a matter of delicacy to the character of the senator not to return him again. Everybody acquainted with public affairs knows how difficult it is to remove from office a person who has long been in it.

It is seldom done except in cases of gross misconduct. It is rare that want (i.e., lack) of competent ability procures it. To prevent this inconvenience, I conceive it would be wise to determine, that a senator should not be eligible after he had served for the period assigned by the constitution for a certain number of years; perhaps three would be sufficient.

A farther benefit would be derived from such an arrangement; it would give opportunity to bring forward a greater number of men to serve their country, and would return those, who had served, to their state, and afford them the advantage of becoming better acquainted with the condition and politics of their constituents.

It farther appears to me proper, that the legislatures should retain the right which they now hold under the confederation, of recalling their members.

It seems an evident dictate of reason, that when a person authorizes another to do a piece of business for him, he should retain the power to displace him, when he does not conduct according to his pleasure.

This power in the state legislatures, under the confederation, has not been exercised to the injury of the government, nor do I see any danger of its being so exercised under the new system. It may operate much to the public benefit.

These brief remarks are all I shall make on the organization of the senate.

Point and Counterpoint

Two of the finest essays on the Constitution were published in New York in mid-April 1788, two weeks before the state was to elect delegates to its ratifying Convention. The first, signed with the pseudonym "A Citizen of New York," was written by John Jay. Jay had been influential in writing the New York constitution in 1777, had written five of The Federalist *essays, and was Secretary for Foreign Affairs. He was to become the first Chief Justice of the United States in 1789.*

The second pamphlet, signed by "A Plebeian," was published soon after. In a postscript, the author, who is unknown, noted the recent publication of Jay's pamphlet and commented that it "appears to contain little more than declamation and observations that have been often repeated by the advocates of the new constitution." Nevertheless he responded to some of Jay's arguments.

Two of the most potent Antifederalist objections were that the Constitution did not guarantee the freedom of the press and that the Constitution, while it guaranteed jury trials in criminal cases, said nothing about civil cases. Jay points out that the New York constitution, which Antifederalists praised, protected neither right. Jay also reiterates a frequently invoked Federalist argument which was that the people should support the Constitution because it was recommended by the great men of the Constitutional Convention, including Washington and Franklin. "A Plebeian" is not persuaded.

A Citizen of New York (John Jay)
New York, ca. 15 April 1788

We are told, among other strange things, that the liberty of the press is left insecure by the proposed Constitution, and yet that Constitution says neither more nor less about it, than the Constitution of the State of New-York does. We are told that it deprives us of trial by jury, whereas the fact is, that it expressly secures it in certain cases, and takes it away in none—it is absurd to construe the silence of this, or of our own Constitution, relative to a great number of our rights, into a total extinction of them—silence and blank paper neither grant nor take away any thing. Complaints are also made that the proposed Constitution is not accompanied by a bill of rights; and yet they who make these complaints, know and are content that no bill of rights accompanied the Constitution of this state. In days and countries where Monarchs and their subjects were frequently disputing about prerogative and privileges, the latter often found it necessary, as it were to run out the line between them, and oblige the former to admit by solemn acts, called bills of rights, that certain enumerated rights belonged to the people, and were not comprehended in the royal prerogative. But thank God we have no such disputes—we have no Monarchs to contend with, or demand admissions from—the proposed Government is to be the government of the people—all its officers are to be their officers, and to exercise no rights but such as the people commit to them. . . .

Reflect that the present plan comes recommended to you by men and fellow-citizens, who have given you the highest proofs that men can give, of their justice, their love for liberty and their country, of the prudence, of their application, and of their talents. They tell you it is the best that they could form; and that in their opinion, it is necessary to redeem you from those calamities which already begin to be heavy upon us all. You find that not only those men, but others of similar characters, and of whom you have also had very ample experience, advise you to adopt it. . . . We must in the business of Government as well as in all other business, have some degree of confidence, as well as a great degree of caution. Who on a sick bed would refuse medicines from a physician, merely because it is as much in his power to administer deadly poisons, as salutary remedies.

A Plebeian
New York, 17 April 1788

It may be a strange thing to this author to hear the people of America anxious for the preservation of their rights, but those who understand the true principles of liberty, are no strangers to their importance. The man who supposes the constitution, in any part of it, is like a blank piece of paper, has very erroneous ideas of it. He may be assured every clause has a meaning, and many of them such extensive meaning, as would take a volume to unfold. The suggestion, that the liberty of the press is secure, because it is not in express words spoken of in the constitution, and that the trial by jury is not taken away, because it is not said in so many words and letters it is so, is puerile and unworthy of a man who pretends to reason. We contend, that by the indefinite powers granted to the general government, the liberty of the press may be restricted by duties [taxes], etc. and therefore the constitution ought to have stipulated for its freedom....

The author manifests equal levity in referring to the constitution of this state, to shew that it was useless to stipulate for the liberty of the press, or to insert a bill of rights in the constitution. With regard to the first, it is perhaps an imperfection in our constitution that the liberty of the press is not expressly reserved; but still there was not equal necessity of making this reservation in our State as in the general Constitution, for the common and statute law of England, and the laws of the colony are established, in which this privilege is fully defined and secured. It is true, a bill of rights is not prefixed to our constitution, as it is in some of the states; but still this author knows, that many essential rights are reserved in the body of it; and I will promise, that every opposer of this system will be satisfied, if the stipulations that they contend for are agreed to, whether they are prefixed, affixed, or inserted in the body of the constitution, and that they will not contend which way this is done, if it be but done.

I shall add but one remark, and that is upon the hackneyed argument introduced by the author, drawn from the character and ability of the framers of the new constitution. The favourers of this system are not very prudent in bringing this forward. It provokes to an investigation of characters, which is an invidious task. I do not wish to detract from their merits, but I will venture to affirm, that twenty assemblies of equal numbers might be collected, equally respectable both in point of ability, integrity, and patriotism. Some of the characters which compose it I revere; others I consider as of small consequence, and a number are suspected of being great public defaulters, and to have been guilty of notorious peculation and fraud, with regard to public property in the hour of our distress. I will not descend to personalities, nor would I have said so much on the subject, had it not been in self defence. Let the constitution stand on its own merits. If it be good, it stands not in need of great men's names to support it. If it be bad, their names ought not to sanction it.

WASHINGTON REFLECTS ON THE PRESENT AND FUTURE

In the letter below, to John Armstrong of Pennsylvania, George Washington reveals a lot about himself. He explains that he reluctantly attended the Constitutional Convention the previous year partly because a refusal to serve would be interpreted by others not only as a dereliction of duty but as something worse, by which he probably meant that people would think that he hoped for a collapse of the tottering Confederation government so that his leadership would be required to restore order.

As for Armstrong's hint that Washington would once again be called upon, this time to be the first President under the Constitution, Washington expresses his preference to stay at Mount Vernon, but does not say he will refuse to serve. Washington agrees that the first people elected under the new Constitution will play a critical role in restoring public confidence in government.

Washington is also concerned about the nature of the opposition to the Constitution. He believes the Antifederalists appealed to the passions rather than the mind. But Washington was an optimistic man. Even if the opposition was poor, it had a good effect because it forced the Federalists to explain themselves better and this resulted in great works such as The Federalist.

Washington's optimism is apparent in his view of the future. Once the new government is installed and prosperity restored, America, where "equal liberty is enjoyed, where every man may reap his own harvest," would be "the happiest people upon earth."

GEORGE WASHINGTON TO JOHN ARMSTRONG
MOUNT VERNON, 25 APRIL 1788

I well remember the observation you made in your letter to me of last year, "that my domestic retirement must suffer an interruption.—" This took place [when Washington attended the Constitutional Convention in Philadelphia], notwithstanding it was utterly repugnant to my feelings, my interest and my wishes; I sacrificed every private consideration and personal enjoyment to the earnest and pressing solicitations of those who saw and knew the alarming situation of our public concerns, and had no other end in view but to promote the interest of their Country; and conceiving that under these circumstances, and at so critical a moment, an absolute refusal to act, might, on my part, be construed as a total dereliction of my Country, if imputed to no worse motives.—Altho' you say the same motives induce you to think that another tour of duty of this kind will fall to my lot, I cannot but hope that you will be disappointed, for I am so wedded to a state of retirement; and find the occupations of a rural life so congenial; with my feelings, that to be drawn unto public at the advanced age, would be a sacrifice that could admit of no compensation.

Your remarks on the impressions which will be made on the manners and sentiments of the people by the example of those who are first called to act under the proposed Government are very Just; and I have no doubt but (if the proposed Constitution obtains) those persons who are chosen to administer it will have wisdom enough to discern the influence which their examples as rulers and legislators may have on the body of the people, and will have virtue enough to pursue that line of conduct which will most conduce to the happiness of their Country;—and as the first transactions of a nation, like those of an individual upon his enterance into life, make the deepest impression and are to form the leading traits in its character, they will undoubtedly pursue those measures which will best lead to the restoration of public and private faith and of consequence promote our national respectibility and individual welfare. . . .

I am very glad to find that the opposition in your State however formidable it has been represented, is, generally speaking, composed of such characters as cannot have an extensive influence; their forte, as well as that of those of the same class in other States seems to lie in misrepresentation, and a desire to inflame the passions and to alarm the fears by noisy declamation rather than to convince the understanding by some arguments or fair and impartial statements—Baffled in their attacks upon the constitution they have attempted to vilify and debase the Characters who formed it, but even here I trust they will not succeed.—Upon the whole I doubt whether the opposition to the Constitution will not ultimately be productive of more good than evil; it has called forth, in its defence, abilities (which would not perhaps have been otherwise exerted) that have thrown new lights upon the science of Government, they have given the rights of men a full and fair discussion, and have explained them in so clear and forcible a manner as cannot fail to make a lasting impression upon those who read the best publications on the subject, and particularly the pieces under the signiture of Publius [*The Federalist*].—There will be a greater weight of abilities opposed to the system in the convention of this State [Virginia] than there has been in any other, but notwithstanding the unwearied pains which have been taken, and the vigorous efforts which will be made in the Convention to prevent its adoption, I have not the smallest doubt but it will obtain here.—

I am sorry to hear that the College [Dickinson College] in your neighbourhood is in so declining a state as you represent it, and that it is likely to suffer a farther injury by the loss of Dr. Nisbet whom you are afraid you shall not be able to support in a proper manner on account of the scarcity of Cash which prevents parents from sending their Children hither. This is one of the numerous evils which arise from the want of a general regulating power [national government], for in a Country like this where equal liberty is enjoyed, where every man may reap his own harvest, which by proper attention will afford him much more than what is necessary for his own consumption, and where there is so ample a field for every mercantile and mechanical exertion, if there can not be money found to answer the common purpose of education, not to mention the necessary commercial circulation, it is evident that there is something amiss in the ruling political power which requires a steady, regulating and energetic hand to connect and control.—That money is not to be had, every man's experience tells him, and the great fall in the price of property is an unequivocal, and melancholy proof of it; when, if that property was well secured—faith and Justice well preserved—a stable government well administered,—and confidence restored,—the tide of population and wealth would flow to us, from every part of the globe, and, with a due sense of the blessing, make us the happiest people upon earth.

AMERICAN RIGHTS MUST BE SPELLED OUT

In early November 1787, an anonymous Antifederal pamphlet signed "Federal Farmer" appeared. Hailed as the most reasoned piece against the Constitution, this pamphlet went through four separate printings and was distributed and read throughout the country. A sequel appeared on May 2, 1788.

Both "Federal Farmer" pamphlets were composed of letters written by the "Farmer" to "A Republican." The sequel, following the example of the original, refrained from the vindictiveness and acerbic language of many political essays of the day. In the excerpt that follows from the sequel, "Federal Farmer" argued that amendments to the Constitution were needed to limit the power of government and to guarantee the unalienable rights of the people.

FEDERAL FARMER: LETTERS TO A REPUBLICAN
2 MAY 1788

Three states have now adopted the constitution without amendments; these, and other circumstances, ought to have their weight in deciding the question, whether we will put the system into operation, adopt it, enumerate and recommend the necessary amendments, which afterwards, by three-fourths of the states, may be ingrafted into the system, or whether we will make the amendments prior to the adoption—I only undertake to shew amendments are essential and necessary—how far it is practicable to ingraft them into the plan, prior to the adoption, the state conventions must determine. Our situation is critical, and we have but our choice of evils—We may hazard much by adopting the constitution in its present form—we may hazard more by rejecting it wholly—we may hazard much by long contending about amendments prior to the adoption. The greatest political evils that can befall us, are discords and civil wars—the greatest blessings we can wish for, are peace, union, and industry, under a mild, free, and steady government. Amendments recommended will tend to guard and direct the administration—but there will be danger that the people, after the system shall be adopted, will become inattentive to amendments—Their attention is now awake—

the discussion of the subject, which has already taken place, has had a happy effect—it has called forth the able advocates of liberty, and tends to renew, in the minds of the people, their true republican jealousy and vigilance, the strongest guard against the abuses of power; but the vigilance of the people is not sufficiently constant to be depended on—Fortunate it is for the body of a people, if they can continue attentive to their liberties, long enough to erect for them a temple, and constitutional barriers for their permanent security: when they are well fixed between the powers of the rulers and the rights of the people, they become visible boundaries, constantly seen by all, and any transgression of them is immediately discovered: they serve as centinels for the people at all times, and especially in those unavoidable intervals of inattention.

Some of the advocates [of the Constitution], I believe, will agree to recommend good amendments; but some of them will only consent to recommend indefinite, specious, but unimportant ones; and this only with a view to keep the door open for obtaining, in some favourable moment, their main object, a complete consolidation of the states, and a government much higher toned, less republican and free than the one proposed. If necessity, therefore, should ever oblige us to adopt the system, and recommend amendments, the true friends of a federal republic must see they are well defined, and well calculated, not only to prevent our system of government moving further from republican principles and equality, but to bring it back nearer to them—they must be constantly on their guard against the address, flattery, and maneuvres of their adversaries. . . .

Good government is generally the result of experience and gradual improvements, and a punctual execution of the laws is essential to the preservation of life, liberty, and property . . . ; the quantity of power delegated ought to be compensated by the brevity of the time of holding it, in order to prevent the possessors increasing it. The supreme power is in the people, and rulers possess only that portion which is expressly given them; yet the wisest people have often declared this is the case on proper occasions, and have carefully formed stipulation to fix the extent, and limit the exercise of the power given. . . .

A free and mild government is that in which no laws can be made without the formal and free consent of the people, or of their constitutional representatives; that is, of a substantial representative branch. Liberty, in its genuine sense, is security to enjoy the effects of our honest industry and labours, in a free and mild government, and personal security from all illegal restraints.

Of rights, some are natural and unalienable, of which even the people cannot deprive individuals. . . . The following, I think, will be allowed to be unalienable or fundamental rights in the United States:—

No man, demeaning himself peaceably, shall be molested on account of his religion or mode of worship—The people have a right to hold and enjoy their property according to known standing laws, and which cannot be taken from them without their consent, or the consent of their representatives; and whenever taken in the pressing urgencies of government, they are to receive a reasonable compensation for it—Individual security consists in having free recourse to the laws—The people are subject to no laws or taxes not assented to by their representatives constitutionally assembled—They are at all times intitled to the benefits of the writ of habeas corpus, the trial by jury in criminal and civil causes—They have a right, when charged, to a speedy trial in the vicinage; to be heard by themselves or counsel, not to be compelled to furnish evidence against themselves, to have witnesses face to face, and to confront their adversaries before the judge—No man is held to answer a crime charged upon him till it be substantially described to him; and he is subject to no unreasonable searches or seizures of his person, papers or effects—The people have a right to assemble in an orderly manner, and petition the government for a redress of wrongs—The freedom of the press ought not to be restrained—No emoluments, except for actual service—No hereditary honors, or orders of nobility, ought to be allowed—The military ought to be subordinate to the civil authority, and no soldier be quartered on the citizens without their consent—The militia ought always to be armed and disciplined, and the usual defence of the country—The supreme power is in the people, and power delegated ought to return to them at stated periods, and frequently—The legislative, executive, and judicial powers, ought always to be kept distinct—others perhaps might be added.

THE POLITICAL NAME CALLING GETS ROUGH

On April 26, 1788, Maryland became the seventh state to ratify the Constitution, when its Convention voted, 63 to 11 in favor. However, nine states were needed to put the Constitution into effect, and, of the remaining six states, only South Carolina seemed certain to vote for ratification. Rhode Island and New York seemed certain to reject the Constitution, while Virginia's prospects were unclear. North Carolina would probably follow Virginia's lead. In Pennsylvania, which had ratified in December, Antifederalists were threatening to call another convention to undo the state's ratification. Throughout the country, sentiment was probably evenly balanced between the two sides. The battle was far from over.

Despite this, Federalists argued that the Constitution was overwhelmingly popular, based on the votes of the conventions that had already met. They claimed that Antifederalists were coming over to support the Constitution. In the essay below, Antifederalists were courted. But Antifederalist leaders, such as Maryland attorney general Luther Martin, a prolific writer against the Constitution, were attacked. Most of those who remained opposed to the Constitution were described not merely as mistaken, but as unpatriotic and seditious.

A PATRIOTIC CITIZEN
PENNSYLVANIA MERCURY, 10 MAY 1788

To the Well-Meaning Few who are opposed to the new plan of federal government.

Gentlemen: As a friend, a fellow-citizen, and a patriot, I now address you.—That six-sevenths of the people of the United States are firm friends to the proposed system [the Constitution], is a well-known fact. But, though this ensures the ratification of the constitution, by a very respectable majority, and there is no doubt but that a few revolving months will set this masterpiece of political wisdom in motion, yet something still is wanting to complete the great work—I wish for the concurrence of *every real whig* [Patriot during the Revolution], of *every honest citizen* amongst us; as for individuals who are antifederal from interested motives, and designing incendiaries who are enemies to the peace and rising greatness of America, we have very small reason, to hope that the former will sacrifice their paltry pelf, or the latter their infamous principles, for the general good: we ought, however, to guard against their weak but desperate efforts, by warning our fellow-citizens of the base motives which actuate those sons of sedition.

When men err through mistake, the criminality of the act ought, in my opinion, to be much extenuated, if not entirely pardoned, because of the honesty of the intention: your conduct, therefore, my worthy fellow-citizens, is only reprehensible in this; that you have suffered yourselves to be imposed on by the scurrilous declamations of designing men; that you have mistaken falsehood for truth, and defamation for argument; and that you have refused to place a reasonable confidence in the chosen patriots of your country, while you have reposed a mistaken and unlimitted one in men who, under the borrowed mask of patriotism, have strained every nerve to destroy private reputation, to sow sedition through the land, and to force the wounds of civil discord, which have been so recently healed, to bleed afresh.

But it is not yet too late to retrieve your lost honor, and to come in for a share of that endless fame, which the enlightened citizens of America shall acquire by the transactions of 1787 and 1788. Suffer yourselves to be deceived no longer, dare to act like men, be your own advisers, let reason resume its place, and I will venture to affirm, that you will act the part of good citizens, in giving your support to a system which is approved of by a truly respectable majority of the people, such as we never before had an instance of.

This circumstance alone should procure the acquiescence of every honest, of every reasonable man; for as the very basis of republican government is, that a majority, even a bare majority, shall govern, how absurd is it to suppose that *one seventh* of the people should pretend to controul *six sevenths!*

Had the writers opposed to the constitution confined their strictures to the system itself, and pointed out its defects (or what they thought its defects) with manly candor and decency, they had merited the thanks of their country, and clearly evinced that they were actuated by patriotism, not by that self-interested, turbulent and seditious spirit which uniformly chacterises their inflammatory essays.

Finding this constitution proof against all attacks, by argument, they have cautiously avoided reasoning on the subject; but have asserted, in plain English, that the framers of it, and those who have ratified it, are all villainous conspirators, and consequently that this plan of government is calculated to enslave the people of America, to make them hewers of wood and drawers of water, and to force them to make bricks without straw. What an insult to the freemen of America! "They chose delegates to the federal convention who are traitors and conspirators against their liberties!—They are abettors of the treason in approving of the conspirators conduct!" The degrading insult has been felt, and has rendered the incendiaries infamous in the eyes of many, who were at first wavering, but are now decidedly federal. . . .

Blush, ye well-meaning citizens, who have associated with such men as are the ringleaders of anti-federalism (*alias* sedition) in the United States. Who are they? Let us examine—We must pass over the three states of Delaware, New-Jersey and Georgia; not even one opposer of the constitution having been found in the conventions of those states—In Connecticut nearly one-third were against it; but these like peaceable citizens and good republicans immediately acquiesced in the decision of the majority—In Massachusetts a considerable part of the minority have acted the same praise-worthy part, and none now persevere in anti-federalism but a few, who were, not long since, enrolled under the banners of SHAYS.—Who were the opposers of federal measures in Maryland? None but *Luther Martin* and his *ten* followers—Thus we perceive, that in six of the states which have adopted the constitution, the opposition, comparatively speaking, is almost nothing—In the convention of Pennsylvania, 'tis true, we have had *twenty-three* dissentients, who are well known to be the mere echoes and tools of a few individuals in Philadelphia, who are apprehensive that their loaves and fishes are in danger. . . .

With these, then, and the respectable group of Rhode-Island, you are joined in opposing the almost unanimous voice of United America. Let the idea of being connected with such be no longer harboured in your bosoms. Turn with indignation from them, and their infamous principles. And join the patriotic sons of freedom, who are now about to complete the glory and independence of America.

Interstate Efforts to Influence the Course of Ratification

*S*outh Carolina's ratifying convention was scheduled to meet on May 12, 1788, and it was expected to vote in favor of the Constitution, making it the eighth state. Nine states were needed to put the Constitution into effect. Three state ratifying conventions were scheduled to convene in June: Virginia, New York, and New Hampshire. North Carolina's convention was to assemble in July.

New Yorker John Lamb, chairman of the Antifederalist "Federal Republican Committee," wrote letters to Antifederalists in these states, such as Richard Henry Lee of Virginia, seeking collaboration among the conventions to oppose ratification. On the other hand, New York Federalist Alexander Hamilton was sending copies of The Federalist to Virginia Governor Edmund Randolph and was arranging for express riders to speed the news of Virginia and New Hampshire ratification to New York. The climax of the constitutional struggle was at hand, and both sides redoubled their efforts.

John Lamb to Richard Henry Lee
New York, 18 May 1788

The Importance of the Subject upon which we address you, we trust will be a sufficient Apology for the Liberty we take.

The System of Government proposed by the late Convention to the respective States for their Adoption, involves in it Questions and Consequences in the highest Degree interesting to the People of these States.

While we see, in common with our Brethren of the other States, the Necessity of making Alterations in the present existing federal Government, we cannot but apprehend that the one proposed in its Room contains in it Principles dangerous to public Liberty and Safety.

It would far exceed the Bounds of a Letter to detail to you our Objections to the proposed Constitution. And it is the less necessary that we should do it, as they are well stated in a Publication, which we take the Liberty of transmitting you in a series of Letters from the Federal Farmer to the Republican. WE renounce all Ideas of local Objections and confine ourselves to such only as affect the Cause of general Liberty, and are drawn from those genuine Republican Principles and Maxims, which we consider as the Glory of our Country, and which gave rise to the late glorious Revolution and supported the Patriots of America in supporting it.

Impressed with these Sentiments we hold it a Duty we owe our Country our Posterity and the Rights of Mankind to use our best Endeavours to procure Amendments to the System previous to its Adoption—

To accomplish this desireable Event it is of Importance that those States who have not yet acceded to the Plan should open a correspondence, and maintain a Communication—That they should understand one another on the Subject and unite in the Amendments they propose—

With this View we address you on the Subject and request a free Correspondence may be opened between such Gentlemen in your State as are of Opinion with us on the Subject of Amendments—WE request your Opinion on the Matter and that you would state such Amendments as you judge necessary to be made.

I think it would conduce very much to promote Union and prevent Discord and an Hostile Disposition among the States, if a Correspondence could be brought about between the Conventions of your State, New Hampshire and this, who we presume will be in Session at the same time—WE have the highest Hopes that such a Measure would produce the happiest Effects—We shall write to New Hampshire and propose it and wish your Convention may be inclined to agree to it—We have every Reason to believe it will be agreeable to ours.—

It is not yet declared who are the Members elected for our Convention. The Ballots are to be counted the last Tuesday in this Month—But by the best Information received from the different Counties we have not a Doubt of there being a decided Majority returned who will be opposed to the Constitution in its present Form. A number of the leading and influential Characters who will compose the Opposition in our Convention are associated with us. WE are anxious to form a Union with our Friends in the other States, and to manifest to the Continent and to the World, that our Opposition to this Constitution does not arise from an Impatience under the Restraint of good Government from local or State Attachments, from interested Motives or Party Prejudice—but from the purer Sentiments of the Love of Liberty, an Attachment to Republican Principles and an Adherence to those Ideas which prevailed at the Commencement of the late Revolution, and which animated the most illustrious Patriots to undertake and persevere in the glorious and arduous Contest.

In behalf of the federal republican Committee I have the honour to be Sir, Your most obedient servant, John Lamb, Chairman.

ALEXANDER HAMILTON TO JAMES MADISON
NEW YORK, 19 MAY 1788

Some days since I wrote to you, My Dear Sir.... I then mentioned to you that the question of a majority for or against the constitution would depend upon the County of Albany. By the latter accounts from that quarter I fear much that the issue there has been against us.

As [Governor George] Clinton is truly the leader of his party, and is inflexibly obstinate I count little on overcoming opposition by reason. Our only chances will be the previous ratification by Nine states, which may shake the firmness of his followers; and a change in the sentiments of the people which have been for some time travelling towards the constitution, though the first impressions made by every species of influence and artifice were too strong to be eradicated in time to give a decisive turn to the elections. We shall leave nothing undone to cultivate a favourable disposition in the Citizens at large.

The language of the Antifederalists is that if all the other states adopt, New York ought still to hold out—I have the most direct intelligence, but in a manner, which forbids a public use being made of it, that Clinton has in several conversations declared his opinion of the *inutility* of the UNION. Tis an unhappy reflection, that the friends to it should by quarrelling for straws among themselves promote the designs of its adversaries—

We think here that the situation of your state is critical—Let me know what you now think of it—I believe you meet nearly at the time we do—It will be of vast importance that an exact communication should be kept up between us at that period; and the moment *any decisive* question is taken, if favorable, I request you to dispatch an express to me with pointed orders to make all possible diligence, by changing horses etc. All expences shall be thankfully and liberally paid.

I executed your commands respecting the first vol. of the Foederalist—I sent 40 of the common copies & twelve of the finer ones addressed to the care of [Virginia] Governor Randolph. The Printer announces the second vol in a day or two, when an equal number of the two kinds shall also be forwarded.

NO BILL OF RIGHTS IS NEEDED SAYS THE FEDERALIST

On May 28, 1788, the second volume of The Federalist *appeared. Most of the essays had already been printed in three New York City newspapers. But this volume also contained eight new essays numbered 78–85.*

One of the most successful and persuasive arguments the Antifederalists used against the Constitution was that it lacked a bill of rights and was, therefore, dangerous to liberty. Despite, or perhaps because of, the potency of this charge, The Federalist *did not respond to it in a major way until the 84th essay.*

In this essay, Alexander Hamilton expressed some of the reasons Federalists used to justify the absence of a bill of rights in the Constitution. He pointed out that the Constitution already protected against the suspension of the writ of habeas corpus, prohibited bills of attainder and ex post facto laws, and guaranteed trial by jury in criminal cases. But more importantly, Hamilton questioned the need or the value of a bill of rights in a government of the people and by the people.

PUBLIUS: THE FEDERALIST NO. 84 (ALEXANDER HAMILTON) NEW YORK, 28 MAY 1788

In the course of the foregoing review of the constitution I have taken notice of, and endeavoured to answer, most of the objections which have appeared against it. There however remain a few which either did not fall naturally under any particular head, or were forgotten in their proper places. These shall now be discussed; but as the subject has been drawn into great length, I shall so far consult brevity as to comprise all my observations on these miscellaneous points in a single paper.

The most considerable of these remaining objections is, that the plan of the convention contains no bill of rights. . . . It has been several times truly remarked, that bills of rights are in their origin, stipulations between kings and their subjects, abridgements of prerogative in favor of privilege, reservations of rights not surrendered to the prince. Such was MAGNA CHARTA, obtained by the Barons, sword in hand, from king John. Such were the subsequent confirmations of that charter by subsequent princes. Such was the *petition of right* assented to by Charles the First, in the beginning of his reign [1628]. Such also was the declaration of right presented by the lords and commons to the prince of Orange in 1688, and afterwards thrown into the form of an act of parliament, called the bill of rights [1689]. It is evident, therefore, that according to their primitive signification, they have no application to constitutions professedly founded upon the power of the people, and executed by their immediate representatives and servants. Here [under the Constitution], in strictness, the people surrender nothing, and as they retain every thing, they have no need of particular reservations. "WE THE PEOPLE of the United States, to secure the blessings of liberty to ourselves and our posterity, do *ordain* and *establish* this constitution for the United States of America." Here is a better recognition of popular rights than volumes of those aphorisms which make the principal figure in several of our state bills of rights, and which would sound much better in a treatise of ethics than in a constitution of government. . . .

I go further, and affirm that bills of rights, in the sense and in the extent in which they are contended for, are not only unnecessary in the proposed constitution, but would even be dangerous. They would contain various exceptions to powers which are not granted; and on this very account, would afford a colourable pretext to claim more than were granted. For why declare that things shall not be done which there is no power to do? Why for instance, should it be said, that the liberty of the press shall not be restrained, when no power is given by which restrictions may be imposed? I will not contend that such a provision would confer a regulating power; but it is evident that it would furnish, to men disposed to usurp, a plausible pretence for claiming that power. They might urge with a semblance of reason, that the constitution ought not to be charged with the absurdity of providing against the abuse of an authority, which was not given, and that the provision against restraining the liberty of the press afforded a clear implication, that a power to prescribe proper regulations concerning it, was intended to be vested in the national government. . . .

On the subject of the liberty of the press, as much has been said, I cannot forbear adding a remark or two: In the first place, I observe that there is not a syllable concerning it in the constitution of this state [New York], and in the next, I contend that whatever has been said about it in that of any other state, amounts to nothing. What signifies a declaration that "the liberty of the press shall be inviolably preserved?" What is the liberty of the press? Who can give it any definition which would not leave the utmost latitude for evasion? I hold it to be impracticable; and from this, I infer, that its security, whatever fine declarations may be inserted in any constitution respecting it, must altogether depend on public opinion, and on the general spirit of the people and of the government. And here, after all, as intimated upon another occasion, must we seek for the only solid basis of all our rights.

There remains but one other view of this matter to conclude the point. The truth is, after all the declamation we have heard, that the constitution is itself in every rational sense, and to every useful purpose, A BILL OF RIGHTS. The several bills of rights, in Great-Britain, form its constitution, and conversely the constitution of each state is its bill of rights. And the proposed constitution, if adopted, will be the bill of rights of the union. Is it one object of a bill of rights to declare and specify the political privileges of the citizens in the structure and administration of the government? This is done in the most ample and precise manner in the plan of the convention, comprehending various precautions for the public security, which are not to be found in any of the state constitutions. Is another object of a bill of rights to define certain immunities and modes of proceeding, which are relative to personal and private concerns? This we have seen has also been attended to, in a variety of cases, in the same plan. Adverting therefore to the substantial meaning of a bill of rights, it is absurd to allege that it is not to be found in the work of the convention. It may be said that it does not go far enough though it will not be easy to make this appear; but it can, with no propriety be contended that there is no such thing. It certainly must be immaterial what mode is observed as to the order of declaring the rights of the citizens, if they are to be found in any part of the instrument which establishes the government. And hence it must be apparent that much of what has been said on this subject rests merely on verbal and nominal distinctions, which are entirely foreign from the substance of the thing.

The Virginia Convention Begins

The Virginia Convention opened on June 2, 1788, and the debates began two days later. The sides were closely balanced, no one was certain whether the Constitution would prevail or be defeated. There was a stellar cast. On the Antifederalist side, the leader was Patrick Henry, the great orator of the American Revolution, ably supported by George Mason, the author of the Virginia Declaration of Rights and the state constitution, and one of three members of the Federal Convention who had refused to sign the Constitution. A young James Monroe assisted in the attack.

On the Federalist side, James Madison was the dominant force. He was assisted by Governor Edmund Randolph, who had also refused to sign the Constitution, but who had by now come to support the Constitution. Joining them were Edmund Pendleton, a legal giant of the day in Virginia, and John Marshall, still a young man, but destined to become the greatest Chief Justice in the history of the United States.

In the debates below, the profound disagreement between the two sides is apparent. They differ on whether the nation was contented and peaceful or was suffering from political diseases that required drastic reform.

Virginia Convention Debates, 4 and 5 June 1788

Patrick Henry, June 4: Mr. Chairman.—The public mind, as well as my own, is extremely uneasy at the proposed change of Government. Give me leave to form one of the number of those who wish to be thoroughly acquainted with the reasons of this perilous and uneasy situation—and why we are brought hither to decide on this great national question. I consider myself as the servant of the people of this Commonwealth, as a centinel over their rights, liberty, and happiness. I represent their feelings when I say, that they are exceedingly uneasy, being brought from that state of full security, which they enjoyed, to the present delusive appearance of things. A year ago the minds of our citizens were at perfect repose. Before the meeting of the Federal Convention at Philadelphia, a general peace, and an universal tranquillity prevailed in this country;—but since that period they are exceedingly uneasy and disquieted. When I wished for an appointment to this [state] Convention, my mind was extremely agitated for the situation of public affairs. I conceive the republic to be in extreme danger. If our situation be thus uneasy, whence has arisen this fearful jeopardy? It arises from this fatal system—it arises from a proposal to change our government:—A proposal that goes to the utter annihilation of the most solemn engagements of the States. . . . Was our civil polity, or public justice, endangered or sapped? Was the real existence of the country threatened—or was this preceded by a mournful progression of events? This proposal of altering our Federal Government is of a most alarming nature: Make the best of this new Government—say it is composed by any thing but inspiration—you ought to be extremely cautious, watchful, jealous of your liberty; for instead of securing your rights you may lose them forever. If a wrong step be now made, the Republic may be lost forever. If this new Government will not come up to the expectation of the people, and they should be disappointed—their liberty will be lost, and tyranny must and will arise. I repeat it again, and I beg Gentlemen to consider, that a wrong step made now will plunge us into misery, and our Republic will be lost. It will be necessary for this Convention to have a faithful historical detail of the facts, that preceded the session of the Federal Convention, and the reasons that actuated its members in proposing an entire alteration of Government—and demonstrate the dangers that awaited us: If they were of such awful magnitude, as to warrant a proposal so extremely perilous as this, I must assert, that this Convention has an absolute right to a thorough discovery of every circumstance relative to this great event. . . . Disorders have arisen in other parts of America, but here, Sir, no dangers, no insurrection or tumult, has happened—every thing has been calm and tranquil. But notwithstanding this, we are wandering on the great ocean of human affairs. I see no landmark to guide us. We are running we know not whither. Difference in opinion has gone to a degree of inflammatory resentment in different parts of the country—which has been occasioned by this perilous innovation.

Edmund Pendleton, June 5: Mr. Chairman—My worthy friend (Mr. Henry) has expressed great uneasiness in his own mind, and informed us, that a great many of our citizens are also extremely uneasy, at the proposal of changing our government: But that a year ago, before this fatal system was thought of, the public mind was at perfect repose. It is necessary to inquire, whether the public mind was at ease on the subject, and if it be since disturbed: What was the cause; what was the situation of this country, before the meeting of the Federal Convention? Our General Government was totally inadequate to the purpose of its institution; our commerce decayed; our finances deranged; public and private credit destroyed: These, and many other national evils, rendered necessary the meeting of that Convention. If the public mind was then at ease, it did not result from a conviction of being in a happy and easy situation: It must have been an inactive unaccountable stupor. The Federal Convention devised the paper on your table, as a remedy to remove our political diseases. What has created the public uneasiness since? Not public reports, which are not to be depended upon; but mistaken apprehensions of danger, drawn from observations on governments which do not apply to us. . . . Where is the cause of alarm? We, the people, possessing all power, form a Government, such as we think will secure happiness: And suppose in adopting this plan we should be mistaken in the end; where is the cause of alarm on that quarter? In the same plan we point out an easy and quiet method of reforming what may be found amiss [the amendment process]. No but, say Gentlemen, we have put the introduction of that method in the hands of our servants; who will interrupt it from motives of self-interest. What then?—We will resist—did my friend say, conveying an idea of force? Who shall dare to resist the people? No,—we will assemble in Convention; wholly recall our delegated powers, or reform them so as to prevent such abuse; and punish those servants, who have perverted powers designed for our happiness, to their own emolument. We ought to be extremely cautious not to be drawn into dispute with regular Government, by faction and turbulence, its natural enemies. Here, then, Sir, there is no cause of alarm on this side; but on the other side, rejecting of Government and dissolving of the Union, produce confusion and despotism.

An Antifederalist Effort to Stave Off Civil War

*A*lthough there were still many Antifederalists determined to oppose the Constitution at all costs, once eight states had ratified, some Antifederalists believed that adoption of the Constitution was inevitable. They believed that further efforts to prevent the Constitution from going into effect would be a terrible mistake: it might lead to civil war, it would prevent those states not ratifying from participating in the organization of the new government, and it would limit Antifederal influence in the effort to adopt amendments to the Constitution.

In the letter below Charles Pettit, a Philadelphia Antifederalist and a former member of Congress, made some of these points to Robert Whitehill of Cumberland County in backcountry Pennsylvania. Whitehill had led the Antifederalists in the state Convention. Opposition to the Constitution was still strong in Pennsylvania; in fact, there had been a petition campaign to undo the state's ratification. Pettit urged Whitehill to work with moderate Federalists who also supported amendments after the government under the Constitution went into effect. Similar arguments persuaded Antifederalists in the Virginia and New York conventions to support ratification.

Charles Pettit to Robert Whitehill
Philadelphia, 5 June 1788

I am among those who find much to approve in the proposed Constitution, and who think it may be so amended as to make it a better plan than we shall be likely to agree upon again if it should be wholly rejected: At the same Time I consider some Amendments necessary to the safety of the People, as well as to the operation of the Plan as a System of Government. I should have been better pleased if I could percieve that the Temper of the Times would admit of making the necessary Amendments previously to it's Adoption of the Organization of the Government under it; but it now appears to me that this cannot be safely attempted....

Eight States have already voted an Adoption of the new Plan, & most of the rest are as likely to carry it in the same Manner as some of those who have given it their Fiat. And tho' many of the People in some of the adopting States may be far from satisfied with the Determination, yet the Decisions of their Conventions will throw into that side of the Scales most of the Doubtful, the Wavering & the Negligent, who form a large Proportion of the People in every State. Hence direct Opposition, however well founded in just principles, may become imprudent Rebellion, and produce greater Hazards and more certain Mischeifs than any real Patriot would wish to see his Country involved in. In this View of the Matter it becomes a Question worthy of the serious attention of those who wish for Amendments, whether the most likely way to obtain the End, be not by directing their Efforts to a point after the Adoption of nine States or upwards. Many who are zealous Advocates for the Adoption will also be Advocates for Amendments. I am not unaware, however, that a considerable proportion of those who profess to be of this Class may want [lack] Sincerity; that their professions are intended to deceive by lulling the Opposition for the present, and that when the Adoption shall be attained, they will become Adherents *in toto,* and express great Apprehensions of the Danger of attempting Amendments at present. . . .

If then difficulties will certainly oppose Amendments in any Mode in which they can be proposed, it seems to be the part of Prudence to choose that Mode in which such Difficulties may be most likely to be overcome—that Mode which is most likely to succeed;—and that Mode which is least likely in the Experiment to produce Anarchy, or the still more dreadful Event—a Civil War. Should the latter take place I make no Calculation of the Probability of success on either side of the question: Victory on either side would be destructive.

The Mode that appears to me most eligible, all things considered, is to endeavour to combine the Friends to Amendments in some plan in which they may confidently draw together, and by which they may increase the Probability of Success. This Plan, I take it, must be so moderate in its object as to obtain the Approbation of the moderate part of those who call themselves Federalists; that is, of those who on a supposition that no Modification could be made between the full Adoption and the total Rejection of the proposed system, prefer the former to the latter. Of these I believe a large Proportion are desirous of having Amendments made, tho' many of them have not digested in their own Minds precisely what those Amendments should be. The Convention of Massachusetts have defined the principles on which Amendments satisfactory to them may be made. The Convention of South Carolina have done the same, and some other state Conventions will probably express their Opinions in like manner at the Time of their Adoption. I should therefore wish that the States who have adopted the System without suggesting Amendments, would by their Assemblies propose such Amendments as would be pleasing to them, and Instruct their Members of Congress at their first Meeting to take into early Consideration *all* such Amendments as are or shall be proposed by any State in its collective Capacity, either by its Convention or Assembly, and recommend it to the several States to elect (by the People at large in every State) Members to meet in general Convention with full Power to Adopt all or any of the Amendments so proposed....

Indeed I am of Opinion that nine States or upwards will shortly have adopted; and whenever that shall be the Case they will proceed to the Arrangements under the new Constitution—And tho' they may not proceed to Legislate for, nor to exercise Jurisdiction over such States as shall have rejected, they may nevertheless choose all the Officers and make all the necessary Arrangements without the aid or participation of the non-adopting States, tho' such Arrangements and Appointments will be binding on them when they do accede to the Plan, either on farther consideration, or on obtaining satisfactory Amendments. Hence it appears to me most advisable for all the States to entitle themselves to a full participation in the first Arrangement and organization of the Government, and, indeed, the most likely way to obtain the Amendments necessary to the safety and Satisfaction of the People. It will be considered that the Adherents to the System, whether amended or not, act under a kind of legitimate Authority. They will therefore derive weight from Organization and Systematic order. The Opposers will have none of these Advantages; they will be moreover weakened by falling into various Classes from differing in opinion as to the Amendments they desire, and from their dispersed Situation; and be more likely to counteract each other in effect, if not directly, than to Act in general Concert.

Slavery Debated in the Virginia Convention

The Constitution did not mention the word "slaves," but it dealt with the issue in several ways. First, for purposes of representation and taxation, slaves were counted as three-fifths of a person. Second, it provided that slaves who escaped to free states were not free but had to be returned. Third, it did not allow Congress to prohibit the foreign slave trade until 1808, and the Constitution could not be amended to allow such a prohibition.

Nearly all Virginians opposed the slave trade as barbaric, and the state had prohibited the importation of slaves. Many Virginians also opposed slavery itself. In the Constitutional Convention George Mason had spoken movingly of the evils of slavery and had warned prophetically of the divine punishment the nation would suffer for tolerating such an evil. But in the Virginia Convention, he criticized the Constitution for not protecting slavery, and James Madison assured the Convention that the Constitution provided greater protection for slavery than existed under the Articles of Confederation.

Virginia Convention Debates, 17 June 1788

George Mason: Mr. Chairman.—This is a fatal section, which has created more dangers than any other.—The first clause, allows the importation of slaves for twenty years. . . . Its exclusion has been a principal object of this State, and most of the States in the Union. The augmentation of slaves weakens the States; and such a trade is diabolical in itself, and disgraceful to mankind. Yet by this Constitution it is continued for twenty years. As much as I value an union of all the States, I would not admit the Southern States into the Union, unless they agreed to the discontinuance of this disgraceful trade, because it would bring weakness and not strength to the Union. And though this infamous traffic be continued, we have no security for the property of that kind [slaves] which we have already. There is no clause in this Constitution to secure it; for they may lay such a tax as will amount to manumission [emancipation]. And should the Government be amended, still this detestable kind of commerce cannot be discontinued till after the expiration of twenty years.—For the fifth article, which provides for amendments, expressly excepts this clause. I have ever looked upon this as a most disgraceful thing to America. I cannot express my detestation of it. Yet they have not secured us the property of the slaves we have already. So that "They have done what they ought not to have done, and have left undone what they ought to have done."

James Madison: Mr. Chairman.—I should conceive this clause to be impolitic, if it were one of those things which could be excluded without encountering greater evils.—The Southern States would not have entered into the Union of America, without the temporary permission of that trade. And if they were excluded from the Union, the consequences might be dreadful to them and to us. We are not in a worse situation than before. That traffic is prohibited by our [state] laws, and we may continue the prohibition. The Union in general is not in a worse situation. Under the articles of Confederation, it might be continued forever: But by this clause an end may be put to it after twenty years. There is therefore a melioration of our circumstances. A tax may be laid in the mean time [on the importation of slaves]; but it is limited, otherwise Congress might lay such a tax as would amount to a prohibition. From the mode of representation and taxation, Congress cannot lay such a tax on slaves as will amount to manumission. Another clause secures us that property which we now possess. At present, if any slave elopes to any of those States where slaves are free, he becomes emancipated by their laws. For the laws of the States are uncharitable to one another in this respect. But in this Constitution, "No person held to service, or labor, in one State, under the laws thereof, escaping into another, shall in consequence of any law or regulation therein, be discharged from such service or labor; but shall be delivered up on claim of the party to whom such service or labour may be due."—This clause was expressly inserted to enable owners of slaves to reclaim them. This is a better security than any that now exists. No power is given to the General Government to interpose with respect to the property in slaves now held by the States. The taxation of this State being equal only to its representation, such a tax cannot be laid as he supposes. They cannot prevent the importation of slaves for twenty years; but after that period they can. The Gentlemen from South-Carolina and Georgia [in the Constitutional Convention] argued in this manner:—"We have now liberty to import this species of property, and much of the property now possessed, has been purchased, or otherwise acquired, in contemplation of improving it by the assistance of imported slaves. What would be the consequence of hindering us from it? The slaves of Virginia would rise in value, and we would be obliged to go to your markets." I need not expatiate on this subject. Great as the evil is, a dismemberment of the Union would be worse. If those States should disunite from the other States, for not indulging them in the temporary continuance of this traffic, they might solicit and obtain aid from foreign powers. . . .

Patrick Henry: . . . He considered the clause which had been adduced by the Gentleman [James Madison] as a security for this property [slaves], as no security at all. It was no more than this—That a run-away negro could be taken up in Maryland or New-York. This could not prevent Congress from interfering with that property by laying a grievous and enormous tax on it, so as to compel owners to emancipate their slaves rather than pay the tax. He apprehended it would be productive of much stock-jobbing, and that they would play into one another's hands in such a manner as that this property would be lost to this country.

George Nicholas wondered that Gentlemen who were against slavery, would be opposed to this clause, as after that period the slave trade would be done away. He asked, if Gentlemen did not see the inconsistency of their arguments? They object, says he, to the Constitution, because the slave trade is laid open for twenty odd years; and yet they tell you, that by some latent operation of it, the slaves who are so now, will be manumitted. At the same moment it is opposed for being promotive and destructive of slavery! He contended that it was advantageous to Virginia, that it should be in the power of Congress to prevent the importation of slaves after twenty years, as it would then put a period to the evil complained of.

As the Southern States would not confederate without this clause, he asked, if the Gentlemen would rather dissolve the Confederacy than to suffer this temporary inconvenience, admitting it to be such.

ONE FINAL WORD FROM MR. MADISON

Article VII of the Constitution provided that when nine state conventions ratified the Constitution it was to be "established" among those nine states and any others that followed. On June 21, 1788, New Hampshire's convention became the ninth to ratify, by a vote of 57–47. The Constitution was in effect. The conventions of New York and Virginia were meeting at this time. Virginia ratified on June 25, by a vote of 89–79, before news of New Hampshire's action arrived. On July 26 New York ratified, 30–27. But on August 2, North Carolina's Convention refused to ratify until a bill of rights and other amendments were adopted. North Carolina was not to join the other states until November 1789, and Rhode Island not until May 1790.

Congress under the Articles of Confederation adopted an election ordinance on September 13 that provided for the election of presidential electors and that called for the new government under the Constitution to begin operating on March 4, 1789. In January electors were chosen and on February 4, George Washington was elected President by the unanimous vote of the electors. The First Federal Congress began operating in April 1789 and Washington was inaugurated on April 30. On June 8 congressman James Madison proposed to the House of Representatives a bill of rights in response to the calls by the state conventions. On September 25 Congress proposed twelve amendments and sent them to the states for ratification. When Virginia became the eleventh state to ratify ten of these amendments on December 15, 1791, the Bill of Rights became a part of the Constitution.

The Constitution as it came from the Convention was superbly molded for this nation and this people, but it was imperfect. Free and open debate improved the Constitution because it resulted in the Bill of Rights. Though the Antifederalists were fearful of giving power to this new government before a bill of rights was adopted, they had faith enough to allow the system to work. The result was the Bill of Rights and a legacy of peaceful, democratic government.

It is fitting that James Madison have the last word. His genius was the basis of the Virginia Plan, which shaped the debates in the Constitutional Convention. In the debate over ratification, his contributions to The Federalist essays were brilliant and innovative. In the Virginia Convention he led the Federalist forces to victory. Despite his reservations about the value of a bill of rights, it was Madison who introduced amendments and shepherded *them through a reluctant Congress. His service to his country in 1786–1789 has earned him our eternal gratitude.*

VIRGINIA CONVENTION DEBATES, 24 JUNE 1788

James Madison: Mr. Chairman.—Nothing has excited more admiration in the world, than the manner in which free Governments have been established in America. For it was the first instance from the creation of the World to the American revolution, that free inhabitants have been seen deliberating on a form of Government, and selecting such of their citizens as possessed their confidence, to determine upon, and give effect to it. But why has this excited so much wonder and applause? Because it is of so much magnitude, and because it is liable to be frustrated by so many accidents. If it has excited so much wonder, that the United States have in the middle of war and confusion, formed free systems of Government, how much more astonishment and admiration will be excited, should they be able, peaceably, freely and satisfactorily, to establish one General Government, when there is such a diversity of opinions, and interests, when not cemented or stimulated by any common danger? How vast must be the difficulty of concentrating in one Government, the interests, and conciliating the opinions of so many different heterogeneous bodies? . . . When we consider this Government, we ought to make great allowances. We must calculate the impossibility that every State should be gratified in its wishes, and much less that every individual should receive this gratification. It has never been denied by the friends of the paper on the table, that it has defects. But they do not think that it contains any real danger. They conceive that they will in all probability be removed when experience will shew it to be necessary. I beg that Gentlemen in deliberating on this subject, would consider the alternative. . . . It is a most awful thing that depends on our decision—no less than whether the thirteen States shall Unite freely, peaceably, and unanimously, for the security of their common happiness and liberty, or whether every thing is to be put in confusion and disorder. Are we to embark in this dangerous enterprise, uniting various opinions to contrary interests, with the vain hopes of coming to an amicable concurrence?

It is worthy of our consideration, that those who prepared the paper on the table [the Constitutional Convention], found difficulties not to be described, in its formation—Mutual deference and concession were absolutely necessary. Had they been inflexibly tenacious of their individual opinions, they would never have concurred. Under what circumstances was it formed? When no party was formed, or particular proposition made, and men's minds were calm and dispassionate. Yet under these circumstances, it was difficult, extremely difficult to agree on any general system....

I have revolved this question in my mind, with as much serious attention, and called to my aid as much information as I could, yet I can see no reason for the apprehensions of Gentlemen; but I think that the most happy effects for this Country would result from adoption, and if Virginia will agree to ratify this system, I shall look upon it as one of the most fortunate events that ever happened, for human nature. I cannot, therefore, without the most excruciating apprehensions, see a possibility of losing its blessings—It gives me infinite pain to reflect, that all the earnest endeavours of the warmest friends of their Country, to introduce a system promotive of our happiness, may be blasted by a rejection....

... As to a solemn declaration of our essential rights, he thought it unecessary and dangerous—Unnecessary, because it was evident that the General Government had no power but what was given it, and the delegation alone warranted the exercise of power—Dangerous, because an enumeration which is not complete, is not safe.... He declared that such amendments as seemed in his judgment, to be without danger, he would readily admit, and that he would be the last to oppose any such amendment as would give satisfaction to any Gentleman, unless it were dangerous.

Index

Adams, John, 28; *Defence of the Constitutions*, 28–30, 125; identified, 28; letter from, 157
Adams, Samuel, 164, 177
Agrarian Unrest, 11
Amendments to Constitution: called for by New York and Virginia conventions, 174; efforts to prevent in state conventions, 154, 156; favored, 123, 182–183; Jefferson's proposals for, 158; opposed by Boston tradesmen's meeting, 166; prohibited in case of slave trade, 241–42; proposed by Massachusetts Convention, 173, 188, 190, 192; proposed in Confederation Congress, 121, 123; provision for in Constitution praised, 157, 185, 236–37; Sam Adams said to favor, 164; should be adopted before Constitution is ratified, ix, 110, 222–24, 229, 239; should be proposed by state conventions, 110; will be provided after ratification, ix, 180, 189, 238–40, 245. *See also* Bill of Rights
American Herald (Boston), 206
American Revolution: fear that war will have been in vain, 74–75, 76; endangered by Constitution, xi, 118, 149, 176, 212; principles of motivate Antifederalists, 229–30; requires republican government, 167–68; role of common people in, 93; slavery and slave trade inconsistent with principles of, 98, 170–71; support for Constitution equated with, 118–19, 167
Ames, Fisher, 175

Anarchy: danger if Constitution is rejected, ix, 139, 175, 176–78, 185; danger of under Articles of Confederation, 10, 44, 48; denial of danger if Constitution is rejected, 140–41
"An Old Man," 160–62
Antifederalists: agree on need to revise Articles of Confederation, vii–viii; agree to support Constitution, xii, 179, 181, 188, 189, 227, 238, 239; attacked as unpatriotic, 225; attacked by mob in Philadelphia, 136, 155; called upon to support Constitution, 225–27; compared with Loyalists during Revolution, 96; compared with Shaysites, 185, 187, 227; concern that their newspapers are stopped by post office, 206, 206–7, 207–8; control few newspapers, 116, 118, 206; criticize House of Representatives, 142; in New York, 228, 229, 230; in Pennsylvania, 117, 151, 154, 185, 187, 225, 227, 238; interstate cooperation among, 228, 229–30; object to judicial review as restraint on democracy, 200; riot in Carlisle, Pa., 160, 160–62, 185, 185–87; seek amendments to Constitution in Confederation Congress, 116; speeches in Pennsylvania Convention not reported, 151; Washington criticizes, 219, 219–20. *See also* Bill of Rights
"A Patriotic Citizen," 225–27
"A Plebeian," 216, 217–18
Aristocracy, 124–26; Constitution will create, 110, 138, 162–63, 191;

247

charge that many members of Constitutional Convention support, 139–40, 174; defended in Constitutional Convention, 92–93; defined, 151; denial that Constitution creates, 151, 151–53, 183; representation of in government, 28; represented in Senate, 214; seeks power for itself, 149; should have check on democracy, 56–57; will control Congress, 84–85, 176; will control House of Representatives, 142, 143–44

Armstrong, John, 219

Army, Standing: danger of, 111, 125–26, 137–38, 157–59, 211

Articles of Confederation: abandoned by Constitutional Convention, 31, 48, 49–50; amendment of insufficient, 14–15; amendments to supported, vii, 18, 20–21, 228–230; defects of, vii–viii, 43, 46–48, 70, 236–37; no power to ban slave trade under, 242–43; political and economic conditions under, 1, 2–4, 5–7, 11, 12–13, 26, 27, 42, 44, 74–76, 95–96, 124, 126, 127, 130–131, 141, 188–89, 192, 221, 235–36, 236–37; provide for amendment by legislatures of states, 25, 105; should be abandoned, 22–24; violated by Constitution, 107, 122

Assembly, Right of, 224

Attainder, Bills of, 231

Baldwin, Abraham, 102

Bartgis, Matthias, 206, 208

Bedford, Gunning, 80

Bicameralism, 241, 22–23, 28, 29–30

Bill of Rights (1689), 233

Bill of Rights: called for by New York, 174; called for by Virginia, 174; considered in Constitutional Convention, 109–10; Constitution itself as, 234; North Carolina demands, 244; omission from Constitution criticized, ix, xi, 32, 109–10, 124, 137, 148–49, 158–59, 209, 217–18, 232; omission from Constitution defended, ix–xi, 110, 216–17, 232, 232–34, 245–46; proposed by U.S. Congress, xi, 244; proposed in Confederation Congress, 116, 121, 122–23; ratified by the states, 244

Boston: tradesmen of support Constitution, 164, 164–66

Bowdoin, James, 164

Broom, Jacob, 82

"Brutus," 116, 130, 200; responded to by *The Federalist*, 145; texts of, 130–32, 142–44, 200–202, 213–15

"Brutus, Junior," 139–141

Bryan, Samuel: as author of "Centinel" essays, 116, 124; "Centinel" essays satirized, 185, 185–86; text of "Centinel" essay, 124–26

Burr, Aaron, 194

Butler, Pierce, 51–52, 55, 79, 92

Cabinet, 168

Caligula, 162

Campbell, James, 74, 76

Capital, Federal, 214

Carlisle, Pa.: riot in, 117, 160, 160–162, 185, 186

Carroll, Daniel, 90, 106

"Centinel" (Samuel Bryan), 116, 124; essays satirized, 185, 185–86; text of, vii, 124–26

Checks and Balances: 85–87, 210

Cincinnati, Society of the, 18, 8–9

"Citizen of New York, A" (John Jay), 173, 216; response to, 217–218; text of, 216–217

Civil War: Antifederalists fear, 122–23, 160, 238, 239; if Constitutional Convention fails, ix, 79–80; if Constitution is rejected, 139, 139–40, 141; denial of danger if Constitution is rejected, 140

"Civis," 68–70

Clergy, 163

Clinton, George, 231

Clymer, George, 76, 155

Coercive Power, 189

"Columbian Patriot, A" (Mercy Otis Warren), 191, 192

Columbus, 74–76

Commerce: Congress given power to regulate in New Jersey Plan, 31–32; declining under Articles of Confederation, viii, 236–37; hurt by money shortage, 221; opposition to power to regulate, 110, 111; regulation of by federal government supported, 22, 27, 48, 128, 140, 165

Committee of Detail, 91, 91–93, 170, 170–71

Common Law: and freedom of the press, 217–218

Common Sense (Thomas Paine), 30

Congress, Confederation: adopts election ordinance for first elections under Constitution, 244; amendments to Constitution proposed in, 121, 123; calls Constitutional Convention, 1, 3; debates Constitution, 116, 121–23; states could recall delegates to, 215; transmits Constitution to states, 121–22, 123

Congress, U.S.: begins operation, 244; compensation of, 110–111; denial that it is too powerful, 182–83; judicial review as check on, 200–202; powers of too great, 136–37; president as check on, 85–87; property as qualification for membership, 88–90; representation in, 21. *See also* House of Representatives, U.S.; Senate, U.S.

Connecticut, x, 11, 16, 42, 117; Antifederalists in support Constitution, 226; debates sending delegates to Constitutional Convention, 42–44; delegates to Constitutional Convention described, 35–36; divided on direct election of House of Representatives in Constitutional Convention, 55–56; divided over motion to create national government in Constitutional Convention, 51–52; refuses to pay requisition, 26, 42; suffers from import duties in New York and Massachusetts, 44

Consolidated Government: argument that Constitution creates, 131–32

Constitutional Convention, 81–84; adopts Constitution, 32; advice to delegates, 14–15; argument that it exceeded its power, 49–50; bill of rights, 109, 110; called by Confederation Congress, 3; caucus of large states, 82–84; Committee of Detail report, 91, 91–93, 170, 170–171; debates importance of public opinion to, 79–80; debates power of to abolish Articles of Confederation, 61–63; debates representation of states in Congress, 213; debates representation in House of Representatives, 71; delegates appointed to, 1, 31; delegates criticized, vii, 19, 33, 139–40, 175, 176, 218; delegates to described, 33–41; delegates praised, vii, 11, 19, 33, 68–69,

69–70, 75–76, 96–97, 118, 139, 216–17, 226–27; dispute between large and small states in, 78–80, 78, 81–84; Franklin proposes language for adoption of Constitution, 112, 115; freedom of press provision defeated in, 110; hopes and concerns for, 5–7, 14–15, 18, 19, 20, 25, 27, 45–46, 68, 68–70, 75, 76–77, 94–95; need for compromise in, 246; New Jersey Plan considered by, 61–63; newspapers report on events in, 94–97; opposition to idea of second convention, 110, 183–84; praised, 68, 68–70, 76–77, 182; praised by newspapers, 118; proposals for second convention, 107, 110, 111, 124, 126, 158–59, 175; purpose of, 151, 236–37; rule of secrecy in, vii, 82, 94, 94–95, 95–96, 110, 113–14, 154; rules adopted, 45–46; signing of Constitution in, 114–15; slavery and slave trade debated, 98–104, 170–72, 241, 241–43; unanimity sought in, 114–115; votes for Virginia Plan over New Jersey Plan, 32, 61; Washington's hesitancy to attend, 219, 219–21

Contracts, Obligation of, 172

Conventions, State: proposal to ratify Constitution by, x, 21, 23–24, 31, 105–8

Cooley, Daniel, 181

Corruption, 159

Counsel, ix, 224

Creditors: as political faction, 65; in foreign nations will have confidence in federal courts, 198–99; protected by Constitution, 172; unjustly treated by states, 89–90; will benefit if Constitution is adopted, 128–29. *See also* Debt, private; Debt, public

"D," 30

Dagget, David, 74, 74–75

Dane, Nathan: and calling of Constitutional Convention, 18; identified, 4, 18; letter from, 18; moves in Confederation Congress to criticize Constitutional Convention, 121

Davenport, James, 44

Dawson, John, 25, 26

Debt, Private: as cause of evils in legislatures, 88–90; debtors as political faction, 65–66; efforts to abolish less likely to be enacted under Constitution, 146–47; relief sought from, 26, 27; under Articles of Confederation, 236. *See also* Creditors

Debt, Public, vii, 1, 25, 26–27, 140–41, 236

Declaration of Independence, 76, 77

Declaration of Rights (1688), 232

Defence of the Constitutions (John Adams), 29–30, 123, 124–25

Delaware: as part of separate confederacy, 16 delegates to Constitutional Convention described, 38–39; divided on direct election of House of Representstives, 55; impeachment in, 169; president of, 168–69; ratifies Constitution, x, 117; support for Constitution in, 118; supports New Jersey Plan in Constitutional Convention, 61; votes for national government in Constitutional Convention, 51

Delegated Power: Constitution limits government to, ix, 246; should be limited, 210

Democracy: argument that Constitution creates, 151, 151–52; as critical element in republican government, 167–68; Constitution endangers, 191; dangers of, 5, 7, 8, 26, 48, 54, 56, 66, 194–95, 198–99; debate over in Constitutional Convention, 53–56, 92; and House of Representatives, 142, 143; importance of educating common people, 159; judicial review as restraint on, 200–202; newspaper report that Constitutional Convention will abandon, 95; representation of in government, 29; restraints upon necessary, 19–20, 30, 66–67

Depression, Economic: argument that Constitution will restore prosperity, 127, 127–28; as evidence of failure of Articles of Confederation, 1; as reason for calling Constitutional Convention, 2–3, 11; effects of in Boston, 182. *See also* Articles of Confederation, political and economic conditions under

Dickinson, John, 38–39, 89, 92, 103

"Dissent of the Minority of the Pennsylvania Convention," 117, 154, 154–56, 226

Duties, 175–76. *See also* Commerce

Elections, U.S.: allow people to control government, 183–84; congressional power to regulate opposed, 110–111; qualifications for electors for House of Representatives, 91–93; ordinance for first elections under Constitution, 244; should be frequent, 70, 138, 224

Electors, Presidential, 86–87, 194–96, 244

Ellsworth, Oliver: identified, 35–36; in Constitutional Convention, 57, 87, 91–92, 94, 96, 99, 100

Europe: immigration from if Constitution is adopted, 128–29, 153; no danger to America from, 125; views events in America, 74–76, 119; will respect America if Constitution is adopted, 157. *See also* Foreign nations

Expenses of Government, 150

Ex Post Facto Laws, 198

Faction: defined, 145–46

Farmers: called upon to support Constitution, 176–78; will benefit from Constitution, 127–28, 176–78; will not be properly represented in House of Representatives, 143. *See also* Shays' Rebellion

"Federal Farmer," 116, 194, 222, 222–24, 229

Federalism: new concept in Constitution, 167

Federalist, The (Alexander Hamilton, James Madison, John Jay): advertisement for, 204–5; book version, 202–3, 230; copies sent by Hamilton to Virginia, 231; described, 116, 194, 222, 222–24, 229; possibly response to "Brutus," 130; praised, 219–20, 220–21; preface to first volume, 205; texts of, 133–35, 145–46, 167–69, 194–96, 232–34

Federalists: argue that economic conditions are bad, 127–28; attacked in Carlisle, Pa., 160, 160–62; control most newspapers, 116, 118, 206; effort to enlist their support for amendments, 239–40; in Pennsylvania, 117; interstate cooperation among, 228, 230–31; seek approval of Constitution by Confederation Congress, 116; seek quick ratification of Constitution, 154

Findley, William, 151

Florida, 128

Foreign Invasion, 47

Foreign Nations: danger from, 13, 68–69, 79–80, 195; defense against as object of Constitution, 189; defense against as object of government, 190; foreign creditors will have confidence in federal courts, 199; no danger from, 125. *See also* Europe; France; Great Britain; Spain

France, 158

Franklin, Benjamin: as possible president of Convention, 27; calls for unanimous support for Constitution in Convention, 112; identified, 37; motion in Constitutional Convention, 115; old age of, 124; optimism for America, 112, 114; praised as delegate to Constitutional Convention, 69–70, 76; proposes prayer in Constitutional Convention, 71–72; and speeches in Constitutional Convention, 71–72, 72, 93, 113–15; use of name to support Constitution criticized, 124

Franklin, State of, 15–16

Freeman's Journal (Philadelphia), 206

General Welfare Clause, 124

"Genuine Information" (Luther Martin), 117, 170–72

Georgia, x, 16, 41, 117; favors slave trade in Constitutional Convention, 98, 103, 170–71, 242–43

Gerry, Elbridge: identified, 34; incorrectly thought to be author of "Columbian Patriot" essay, 191; motions in Constitutional Convention, 107, 110; opposes direct election of House of Representatives, 53; praised as delegate to Constitutional Convention, 76; refuses to sign Constitution, 32, 109, 112, 115; speeches in Constitutional Convention, 50–51, 53–54, 55, 58, 83, 87, 107, 110, 111

Gilman, Nicholas, 33–34

Gladstone, William, vii

God: proposal to begin sessions of Constitutional Convention with prayer, 71–73; slave trade as insult to, 170–71; will punish America for slavery, 99

Gore, Christopher, 164

Gorham, Nathaniel, 48, 94, 96, 106

Granger, Abraham, 43

Grayson, William, 25, 26–27

Great Britain, viii; constitution of, 55, 65, 233; freedom of press in, 217; insurrections in, 159; judiciary in, 200–202; monarchy of praised, 67; prevented abolition of slave trade, 99. *See also* Foreign nations

Great Names, 124; invocation to support Constitution criticized, 124–25, 136–37, 192, 218; invoked to support Constitution, 216, 217; motivated by desire for power not patriotism, 149–150

Habeas Corpus, 158, 224, 231

Hamilton, Alexander: as author of *The Federalist*, 116, 133–35, 173, 194–96, 203, 205, 232–34; as note taker in Constitutional Convention, 46; calls for unanimous support for Constitution in Convention, 112; identified, 36; letter from, 230–31; proposes plan of government to Constitutional Convention, 64–67; seeks cooperation with Virginia Federalists, 228; sends *The Federalist* to Virginia, 228; speech in Constitutional Convention, 65–67, 72–73

Hancock, John: advocates reconciliation, 179; proposes compromise in Massachusetts Convention, 173, 188; role in Massachusetts ratification criticized, 191, 192; speech in Massachusetts Convention, 179–81; speech to Massachusetts state legislature, 188–190

Happiness: as object of Constitution, 189; as object of government, 142, 189–90, 219, 222; best secured by adopting Constitution, 134, 245; Constitutional Convention intended to secure, 151

Henry, Patrick: resigns as delegate to Constitutional Convention, 19; said to favor separate confederacies, 14; in Virginia Convention, 235, 235–36, 243

Higginson, Stephen, 5, 5–7

History, 134–35, 210

House of Representatives, U.S.: as democratic branch, 142, 143, 152; bill of rights proposed in, xi, 244; election of, 23, 53, 53–56, 157–59, 168–69; qualification of electors of, 91, 91–93; representation in, viii, 71, 78–80, 80, 136, 142, 142–44, 157–59

Human Nature, 212

Humphry, Hosea, 43–44

Huntington, Jedidiah, 42–43

Immigration: will increase under Constitution, 129–153

Impeachment, 169

Impost: rejected by New York, 26. *See also* Duties

Independent Gazetteer (Philadelphia), 206

Insurrection, Domestic: danger of exaggerated, 126, 159; no power to suppress under Articles of Confederation, 47–48; not prevented by strong government, 159; slavery creates danger of, 172. *See also* Agrarian unrest; Carlisle, Pa.; Shays' Rebellion

Jackson, William, 116, 121

Jay, John: as author of "A Citizen of New York," 173, 216, 216–17; as author of *The Federalist*, 116, 133, 203; identified, 216; proposed treaty with Spain, 14

Jefferson, Thomas, xi; does not fear rebellions, 11, 13; letters from, 11, 13, 157–59; praises delegates to Constitutional Convention, vii, 18, 33; and presidential election of 1800, 194

Jenifer, Daniel of St. Thomas, 57–58

Johnson, William Samuel, 35, 54

Judicial Review, 200–202

Judiciary, U.S.: appellate jurisdiction from state courts supported, 22–23; appointment of, 168; criticism of, viii, 200–202; jurisdiction of praised, ix, 198–99; salaries of, 201–202; tenure of, 119, 168, 201

Jury, Trial by: absence of protection for criticized, 112, 137, 151, 157–59, 190, 210, 216, 217; absence of protection for defended, 216–17; as natural right, 224; protected in Constitution in criminal cases, 232–33

Kentucky, 16

King, Rufus: as note taker in Constitutional Convention, 46; identified, 34; in Constitutional Convention, 83, 86, 88, 103, 106, 107

Knox, Henry, 8–9, 9–10

Lafayette, Marquis de, 182
Lamb, John, 228, 228–30
Langdon, John, 33–34, 103
Lansing, John, Jr., 61–62
Lawyers, 128, 175, 176
Lee, Henry, 11
Lee, Ludwell, 123
Lee, Richard Henry, ix, 116, 121, 122–23, 228
Liberty: best secured by distrust of power, 211; best secured by a strong government, 70, 133–35; defined, 224; democratic forces cannot protect, 92–93; depends on good sense of common people, 159; endangered by Constitution, viii–ix, 127, 136–37, 138, 156, 162–63, 181, 197, 228–29, 235–37; government should protect, 150; is equally shared in America, 221; is protected under Articles of Confederation, 140; love of as motive of Antifederalists, 230; permits existence of faction, 146; protected by Constitution, 119, 135, 151, 157, 165, 197, 197–99, 218, 244; will spread through world if Constitution is adopted, 153
Lucas, John, 164
"Lycurgus," 15–16

McHenry, James, 46, 106
McKean, Thomas, 151, 160, 162
Madison, James: and Virginia Plan, 1, 21–24, 31, 45, 244; argues that Constitution protects slavery, 241; argues that republican government can exist in large country, 140; as author of *The Federalist*, 116, 133, 145–47, 167–69, 173, 203, 244; as Federalist leader in Virginia Convention, 235, 244; as note taker in Constitutional Convention, 46; condemns protection for slave trade, 101; defines republican government, 166; favors direct election of House of Representatives, 53; favors radical changes in Confederation government, 18, 21; identified, 39–40; letters from, 3–4, 22–24; letter from quoted, 45–46; praises delegates to Constitutional Convention, 33; proposes bill of rights in House of Representatives, 244; speeches in Constitutional Convention, 55, 58, 59, 78, 86–87, 88, 93, 106; speeches in Virginia Convention, 242–43, 245–46; supports ratification of Constitution by the people, 105; urges Washington to attend Constitutional Convention, 1
Magna Carta, 232–33
Manufactures, 89
Marbury v. *Madison*, 200
"Marcus," 128–29
Marshall, John, 14, 235
Marshall, Thurgood, vii
Martin, Luther, 225; "Address," 210–12; as author of "Genuine Information," 117, 170, 170–72; identified, 39, 210; in Constitutional Convention, 85, 87, 98, 107; proposes allowing Congress to ban slave trade, 98; ridiculed, 226–27
Maryland, 16; agrarian unrest in, 11, 18; Antifederalists in ridiculed, 226–27; constitution of, 168; delegates to Constitutional Convention described, 39; divided over Virginia Plan, 61; legislature calls upon delegates to report on Constitutional Convention, 169; paper money in, 26–27; prohibited slave trade, 99–100; ratifies Constitution, 173, 225; state Convention

does not propose amendments, 173; terms of senate of, 57

Mason, George, 45; condemns slavery and slave trade in Constitutional Convention, 98, 170–71, 241; favors direct election of House of Representatives, 53; identified, 39; in Virginia Convention, 235; refuses to sign Constitution, 32, 109, 115; speeches in Constitutional Convention, 54, 88, 92, 93, 99–100, 108, 109; speech in Virginia Convention, 241–42

Massachusetts: Antifederalists in state Convention agree to support Constitution, 179, 226–27; as part of separate confederacy, 16; delegates to Constitutional Convention described, 34–35; democracy in criticized, 53–54; political conditions in, 12–13; public support for Constitution in, 164, 164–66; ratifies Constitution with proposed amendmerits, x, xi, 173, 179, 181, 188, 240; Shays' Rebellion exaggerated, 159; state Convention criticized, 188–90; state Convention debates Constitution, 175, 175–78; state Convention praised, 189; supports direct election of House of Representatives in Constitutional Convention, 55; votes for national government in Constitutional Convention, 52. *See also* Shays' Rebellion

Mercer, John Francis, 93

Merchants, 127–28, 143. *See also* Commerce

Methodists, 104

Military, 224

Militia, 138, 210, 224

Miller, Robert, Jr., 160–62

M'Lean, John and Archibald, 203–4

Monarchy: charge that members of Constitutional Convention support, 139–40; Constitution will create, 110, 138; danger of, 14; no danger of under Constitution, 183

Money, viii, 26, 221. *See also* Paper money

Money Bills, 78–80. *See also* Taxation

Monopolies, 112, 157–59

Monroe, James, 14, 235

Montesquieu, Charles, Baron de, 124, 130. *See also* Republican government

Morris, Gouverneur: drafts Franklin's proposed language for adoption of Constitution, 113, 115; identified, 37–38; motions in Constitutional Convention, 87, 91, 103, 106, 107; speeches in Constitutional Convention, 51, 51–52, 79–80, 85–86, 88, 90, 92–93, 103, 106, 107

Morris, Robert, 37–38, 76

Moustier, Comte de, 33

Natural Rights, 224

Necessary and Proper Clause, 111

Necker, Jacques, 65

Nero, 162

"Nestor," 18

New England, 2–3, 100

New Hampshire, 11, 16; Antifederalist cooperation with New York and Virginia, 228, 229–30; delegates to Constitutional Convention described, 33–34; ratifies Constitution, x, 173, 244

New Jersey, x, 16, 26; delegates to Constitutional Convention described, 36–37; opposes direct election of House of Representatives in Constitutional Convention, 55; ratifies Constitution, 117; support for Constitution in, 118; supports New Jersey Plan in Constitutional Convention, 61–62

New Jersey Plan, 31–33, 61–63, 66–67

Newspapers: Antifederalist writers in, 173; charge that Antifederalist papers are being intercepted, 206, 206-7, 207–8; criticized for intimidating Antifederalists, 154; denial that Antifederalist papers are intercepted, 207–8; in 18th century, 118, 206; in debate over ratification of the Constitution, 116, 118, 206; independence of asserted by Bartgis, 208–9; report on events in Constitutional Convention, 94–97. *See also* Press, freedom of

New York, 16, 26; Antifederalist cooperation with New Hampshire and Virginia suggested, 173–74, 228, 229–31; Antifederalists in are uncompromising, 230; Antifederalists seek reconciliation, 238; constitution of compared with U.S. Constitution, 168–69, 216–17, 217–18, 234; delegates to Constitutional Convention described, 36; election for delegates to the state Convention, 216, 230–31; George Clinton as Antifederalist leader, 230; prospects for ratification in, 225, 230–31; ratifies Constitution, x, xi, 174, 244; rejects federal impost, 25, 26; supports direct election of House of Representatives in Constitutional Convention, 55; supports New Jersey Plan in Constitutional Convention, 61–62

New York City, 118

New York Journal, 206

Nicholas, George, 197–99, 244

Nobility, Titles of, 169, 224

North Carolina, 16, 27; delegates to Constitutional Convention described, 40; favors slave trade in Constitutional Convention, 98; and importation of slaves, 99–100, 103; refuses to ratify Constitution without amendments, x, 173, 174, 244; supports direct election of House of Representatives in Constitutional Convention, 55; votes for national government in Constitutional Convention, 52; will follow Virginia's lead on Constitution, 225

Northern States: will support representation by population, 23–24

Officeholders, State: denial that they oppose Constitution to hold offices, 142; oppose giving additional power to federal government, 54; will not benefit from Constitution, 128–29; will oppose Constitution, 68

Officeholders, U.S.: absence of rotation criticized, 136, 157–59; open qualifications for, 152. *See also* Rotation in office

"Officer of the Late Continental Army, An," 136–38

Oligarchy, 183

"One of the People," 208

Oswald, Eleazer, 185

Paine, Thomas, 30

Paper Money, 12–13, 22, 26; emission prohibited by Constitution, 147, 172. *See also* Money

Paterson, William: as note taker in Constitutional Convention, 46; identified, 36; proposal for adjournment of Constitutional Convention, 82; proposes New Jersey Plan, 61; speeches in Constitutional Convention, 62, 82, 86

Pendleton, Edmund, 123, 235, 236–37
Pendleton, Henry, 122–23
Pennsylvania, 16–17, 26; agrarian unrest in, 11, 19; Antifederalism, in, 117, 238; Antifederalists in criticized, 185, 186–87, 226–27; calling of state Convention in, 154, 154–55, 155–56; delegates to Constitutional Convention described, 37–38; elections for state Convention, 136, 155; precipitate ratification of Constitution by criticized, 164; ratifies Constitution, x, 117, 154, 160; state ratifying Convention described, 151; supports direct election of House of Representatives in Constitutional Convention, 55; threat of second ratifying Convention in, 225; violence in, 155, 160, 160–62; votes for national government in Constitutional Convention, 52. *See also* Carlisle, Pa.; Philadelphia
Pennsylvania Gazette, 118–19
Perkins, Daniel, 53
Petition, Right to, ix, 224
Petition of Right (1628), 231–32
Pettit, Charles, 238, 238–39
Philadelphia: mob attacks Antifederalists in, 136, 155; petitions calling for state Convention in, 118–19, 154–55
"Philadelphiensis" (Benjamin Workman), 148–50
Pierce, William, 33, 41, 46, 59
Pinckney, Charles: identified, 41; motions in Constitutional Convention, 88, 107, 110; speeches in Constitutional Convention, 99, 101, 106, 110

Pinckney, Charles Cotesworth: identified, 41; in Constitutional Convention, 50, 63, 82, 101, 103
Poetry, 14, 17
Post Office, 206–8
Preamble to Constitution, 233
President, U.S.: debated in the Constitutional Convention, 85–87; election of, 55, 85–87, 168, 194, 194–96; has no special privileges, 152; impeachment of, 169; praised, 152–53; reeligibility of criticized, 157–59; veto power of praised, 68–70; Washington will be first, 111, 218, 218–19; will be king, viii, 137
Press, Freedom of: absence of protection for criticized, ix, 126, 137, 151, 157–59, 191, 211, 216, 217–18; absence of protection for defended, x, 211, 233–34; as natural right, 224; cannot be defined, 233–34; danger to from government interference with newspaper circulation, 208; provision for defeated in Constitutional Convention, 110. *See also* Newspapers
Property, Private: as cause of faction, 145; as qualification for being member of Congress, 88–90; as qualification for voting for House of Representatives, 91–93; dangers to, 5–7; distribution of in future, 92–93; efforts to redistribute less likely to be enacted under Constitution, 147; endangered by power of Congress, 136, 150; government should protect, 150; is protected under Articles of Confederation, 140–41; protected by Constitution, 111, 128–29, 135, 165, 197, 197–99; security for needed, 20; security of as natural right, 224

Public Opinion: debate over importance of in work of Constitutional Convention, 58, 62–63, 79–80; evenly divided on Constitution, 225; Federalists claim overwhelming public support for Constitution, 225–26; is against Constitution, 192; probably closest to New Jersey Plan, 67; uneasy about Constitution, 235–37; will favor Constitution initially, 107

Quakers, 104, 119
Quartering of Troops, 224

Randolph, Edmund, 228; as delegate to Constitutional Convention, 10; as member of Committee of Detail, 94, 96; calls for reform of Articles of Confederation, 20; identified, 40; in Virginia Convention, 235; motion for temporary adjournment of Constitutional Convention, 81, 81–82; moves first resolution of Virginia Plan, 49; praised, 191; refuses to sign Constitution, 32, 110, 112, 114; speeches in Constitutional Convention, 45, 46–48, 56, 59, 63, 73, 81–82, 104, 110

Ratification, Procedure for: by state conventions, x, 20, 23, 31; Constitutional Convention debates, 105–8; Federalists seek rapid ratification, 154; in Pennsylvania criticized, 154–55; Jefferson's proposal for, 158; nine states sufficient to establish Constitution, x, 244; should not be done precipitately, 141

Read, George, 76
"Reason," 14–15
Recall, 214–15

Religion, 129, 145, 147. *See also* God
Religion, Freedom of: absence of protection for criticized, 151, 158–59, 191, 211; as natural right, 224
Representation: by population will be supported by North and South, 23–24; dispute between large and small states over, 78–80; diversity of population should be represented in Congress, 90, 137, 142–44; of slaves unfair, 111; of states in Senate, 81–84; slaves counted as three-fifths of person, 241
Republican Government: and size of country, 14, 15–17, 85–86, 124, 126, 130, 132, 145, 146; bicameralism as contrary to, 30; Constitution creates, 135, 147, 167, 168–69; Constitution important to American experiment in, 118; danger of popular ferment in, 194–95; defined, 146, 167, 167–68; endangered by Constitution, 235–36; flaws in, 146; guaranteed to states, 169; importance of to Union, 23–24; incompatible with slavery, 171; principles of led to American Revolution, 228–29; principles of motivate Antifederalists, 229; property should not be qualification for officeholding in, 88; requires support of democratic element, 55; supported by Hamilton, 65–66; will of majority should prevail, 159, 180, 192–93
Requisitions, 3–4, 25, 26–27
Revere, Paul, 164
Revolution, Right of, 107
Rhode Island: Antifederalism of held in contempt, 227–28; as part of separate confederacy, 16; certain not to ratify Constitution, 224;

does not elect delegates to Constitutional Convention, 31, 42–43; paper money in, 26–27; policies of criticized, 19; proposal to redistribute property, 2–3; ratifies Constitution in 1790, x, 173, 174, 244–45; terms of lower house, 57

Rotation in Office, 71, 137, 158–59, 213–15

Rush, Benjamin, 14

Russell, Benjamin, 164

Rutledge, John: as member of Committee of Detail, 94, 96; identified, 40–41; motion in Constitutional Convention, 57; quoted, 71; speeches in Constitutional Convention, 83, 93, 98–99, 103

Saratoga, Battle of, 75

Search and Seizure, 224

Sectionalism, 14, 16–17

Self–incrimination, ix, 224

Senate, U.S.: as restraint on democracy, viii, 55–56; classes in praised, 152–53; election of, 23, 53, 55, 56, 168; reeligibility of, 111, 213–15; representation in, 78–80, 81–84, 158–59, 213, 214; size of, 55–56, 137; states should be able to recall Senators, 214–15; term of, 59–60, 111, 213, 213–15. *See also* Aristocracy

"Senex," 30

Separate Confederacies: advocated, 14–17; danger of, 3–4, 14, 23–24, 133–35

Separation of Powers: as natural right, 224; insufficient under Constitution, 137, 191; proposed in Constitutional Convention, 50; supported, 29, 86–87, 158–59, 182, 183–84

Shays' Rebellion: danger of in other states, 19, 26; debt as cause of, 26–27; demonstrates need for Constitution, 175, 176–78; importance exaggerated, 158–59, 191; Jefferson on, 13; weakens Confederation government, 2–3, 3–4, 5–7, 11, 12–13

Sherman, Roger: identified, 35–36; motions in Constitutional Convention, 57, 72; opposes direct election of House of Representatives, 53; praised as delegate to Constitutional Convention, 77; speeches in Constitutional Convention, 53, 59, 72, 86, 99, 103–4, 109

Short, William, 25

"Sidney," 29–30

Singletary, Amos, 175, 175–76

Slavery: abolition of will occur naturally, 99, 100; abolition of supported in Constitutional Convention, 171; and voting in South, 87; as matter for states to regulate, 99; criticized in Constitutional Convention, 98, 99–100; debated in Virginia Convention, 241–42; federal government has no power to regulate, 242–43; fugitive-slave clause, 241, 241–43, 243; inconsistent with American Revolution, 98; may expand under Constitution, 138; opposition to declines after Revolution, 172; opposition to in Virginia, 240; slaves counted as three-fifths of person for taxation and representation, 111, 241; slaves should not be considered property, 103–4

Slave Trade: considered barbaric, 241; criticism that it is protected for 20 years, 138; debated in Constitutional Convention, 98–104,

170–72, 241–43; debated in Virginia Convention, 241–43; power to prohibit after 1808 praised, 243; tax on limited, 241–43; will be checked by Constitution, 119–20

Smilie, John, 151

Smith, Jonathan, 175, 176–78

Social Compact, 142

Song, 14

South America, 128

South Carolina, x, 10, 16, 26–27; delegates to Constitutional Convention described, 40–41; delegates favor slave trade in Constitutional Convention, 98, 99–100, 101, 103, 170, 241–43; governor of, 168–69; state convention proposes amendments, 239–40; prospect for ratifying Constitution, 224, 228; senate of, 168–69; supports direct election of House of Representatives in Constitutional Convention, 54; terms of lower house, 57; votes for national government in Constitutional Convention, 52

Southern States: demanded protection for slave trade, 98–104, 170–72, 241–43; will support representation by population, 25

Sovereignty: dual sovereignty denied, 50, 50–51; of states destroyed by Constitution, 136; people are source of all power, 107, 223, 224

Spaight, Richard Dobbs, 54, 59

Spain, 14

Stamp Tax, 137

States: appoint delegates to Constitutional Convention, 1, 31; argument that Constitution endangers, viii, 125–26, 131–32, 191, 235–37; caucus of large states in Constitutional Convention, 81, 83; commercial disagreements among, 2–3; Constitution guarantees republican government, 169; constitutions of, 109, 167, 168–69; courts to be subordinate to federal government, 22–23; democratic representation exists in assemblies of, 143–44; endangered property rights under Confederation, 197, 197–99; formation of free governments during Revolution praised, 245–46; governments of criticized, 55–56, 59–60, 66, 128–29; judiciaries of endangered by Constitution, 125–26; laws of U.S. supreme over state constitutions, 109–10; legislation to prohibit slave trade, 172; must compromise to achieve federal government, 244; no power to resolve disputes among under Articles of Confederation, 47; no power to suppress insurrections in under Articles of Confederation, 47; not complying with requisitions, vii, 26–27; officeholders to swear obedience to federal government, 31; power of reduced by Constitution as individual rights enlarged, 119; proposal for ratification of Constitution by conventions in, 105–8; protection for from domestic insurrection or invasion, 21, 23–24; ratifying conventions should propose amendments, 110; representation in Senate, 79, 80–84, 158–59, 213; should be able to recall Senators, 215; should call upon U.S. Congress to propose amendments, 240; should mold constitutions to conform to U.S. Constitution, 119–20; slavery as matter for states to regulate, 99; slave trade as matter for states to regulate, 101–2; sovereignty of as obstacle to reform, 14, 16; sovereignty of criticized, 50, 95–96; sovereignty of destroyed by Constitution, 137; sovereignty of must be reduced, 14–15, 22–23; sovereignty of not sufficiently protected, 109; to be annihilated under Virginia Plan, 49; unicameral governments of criticized, 28–29; veto power over state laws, 21, 22, 27, 31

Stiles, Ezra, 11

Stone, Thomas, 123

Suffrage, 87, 91–93

Supremacy, 22; of federal government proposed, 50, 51

Supremacy Clause, 109; advocated, 21, 51; criticism of, 124, 125–26; in New Jersey Plan, 31–32, 61–62

Taxation: and representation, 157–59; as cause of American Revolution, 175–76; as cause of discontent in states, 26–27; power of in Constitution criticized, 111, 125–26, 150, 175–76, 217–18; power of in Constitution defended, 157–59, 198; slaves counted as three-fifths of person for, 241; under Articles of Confederation, 2–3, 12–13, 25, 26–27, 140–41; use of to abolish slavery, 241–43

Taylor, John, 182

Tennessee, 16

"The State Soldier," 197–99

Tiebout, John, 205

Traders, 127

Treaties, 214

Turkey, 159

Tyranny: danger of if Constitution is rejected, 175, 176–78; no danger of under Constitution, 183; will result from Constitution, 122–23, 149–50

Union: danger to, 2–3, 4, 13, 14, 14–15, 65, 137, 236–37, 242–43, 243, 245; George Clinton said to oppose, 230; importance of, 17, 95–96, 135, 145–47, 157, 188–89, 190; must be based on republican principles, 23–24

Vermont, 16

Veto: of acts of Congress, 21, 31, 157–59; over state laws, 21, 22, 27, 31

Vice President, 111

Virginia, 11, 16, 26; Antifederalist cooperation with New York and New Hampshire, 173–74, 228–31; Antifederalists seek reconciliation, 238; debates in state Convention, 235–37, 241–43, 245–46; debtors in, 26; delegates to Constitutional Convention described, 39–40; delegation to Constitutional Convention caucuses, 45; delegation to Constitutional Convention praised, 10; impeachment in, 169; opposition to Constitution sought in, 122–23; prohibited slave trade, 99–100; ratifies Bill of Rights, xi, 244; ratifies Constitution, x, xi, 174, 244; senate of, 169; supports direct election of House or Representatives in Constitutional Convention, 56; uncertain prospect for ratifying Constitution, 225; votes for national government in Constitutional Convention, 52

Virginia Plan: annihilates Articles of Confederation, 49; debated in Constitutional Convention, 61–63; described, 31, 45–46; introduced in Constitutional Convention, 45, 46–48, 49; origins of, 21;

Virtue, 159, 182

Wadsworth, Jeremiah, 44
War Power, 47
Warren, Mercy Otis, 173, 190, 192–93
Washington, George: approves subterfuge in Confederation Congress, 121; as first President of U.S., 219, 244; considers Antifederalist objections unjustified, 173; described, 39; elected President of United States, 244; favors strengthening government, 8, 18, 20; hesitant about attending Constitutional Convention, 1, 8, 8–10, 18–19, 219; importance of to Constitutional Convention, 10; in debate over ratification of Constitution, 182; letters from, 8–9, 20, 45, 182–84, 219–21; praised as delegate to Constitutional Convention, 69, 69–70, 76; report that he will attend Convention, 10; reverence for in America, 8; said to be duped into supporting Constitution, 124; use of name to support Constitution criticized, 124; will be first president, 119–20; will be president of Constitutional Convention, 27
Webster, Noah, 203

Western Country, 18
Western Lands, 99
West Indies, 128
White, Abraham, 181
Whitehill, Robert, 151, 238
Widgery, William, 181
Williamson, Hugh, 40, 73, 103
Wilson, James, 140; burned in effigy, 160, 162; identified, 37, 151; in Pennsylvania Convention, 151–53; praised as delegate to Constitutional Convention, 76; speeches in Constitutional Convention, 53, 54, 62–63, 86, 90, 91, 94, 96, 102, 151
Wilson, James A., 160–62
Winthrop, John, 164
Workers: will benefit from Constitution, 127, 128; will not be properly represented in House of Representatives, 143–44; will suffer if Constitution is defeated, 165
Workman, Benjamin, 148–50
Wythe, George, 76

Yates, Robert, 46
Yorktown, Battle of, 75